# MEGA YUMMY CROCHET

Mega Yummy Crochet
Published in 2025 by Zakka Workshop,
a division of World Book Media LLC

www.zakkaworkshop.com
134 Federal Street
Salem, MA 01970
info@zakkaworkshop.com



Original Japanese edition published by NIHONBUNGEISHA Co., Ltd.
English translation rights arranged with NIHONBUNGEISHA Co., Ltd. through
Japan UNI Agency, Inc., Tokyo. English language rights, translation & production
by World Book Media, LLC.

Publisher: Hibiki Takemura
Editor: Mie Takechi
Design: Chiyomi Ito
Photography: Takashi Sakamoto & Norihito Amano
Proofread: Midorinokuma
Hair & Makeup: Eri Fukurome
Models: Ranju Chan & Nana Chan
Translation: Kyoko Matthews
English Editor: Lindsay Fair
Technical Editor: Lynne Rowe



ISBN: 978-1940552-98-9
Printed in China

## About the Author

Miya first started making amigurumi in 2001 after becoming a mother. Her work aims to tell a story through crochet. As a practicing clinical psychologist, Miya recognizes the positive impact that creating things with your hands can have on mental health. She is the author of multiple books published in Japan and she regularly holds classes to teach others how to crochet. Follow her on Instagram @miya_amigurumi and visit her website at http://ouvrir.jp.

# MEGA YUMMY CROCHET

## 26 Larger Than Life Amigurumi Treats

MIYA

# Contents

# Introduction

As a child, I was captivated by Hansel and Gretel's candy house. In the fairytale, it turns out that the edible house was actually a trap set by a scary witch. Inspired by the feelings of excitement and wonder generated by the idea of a candy house, I set out to create an amigurumi book filled with super-sized sweets and treats.

Don't be afraid of the large scale of these projects—they are made with thick yarn and large crochet hooks, so even beginners will be able to finish projects quickly. In addition to oversized cushions and stuffies for cuddling, you'll also find some smaller items perfect for imaginative play.

Have fun using colorful yarn to crochet these fun treats, then use them to decorate your home or inspire endless hours of playtime.

# French Crullers

This easy-to-make treat is constructed by crocheting a flat parallelogram and then sewing it together to form a three-dimensional shape. Experiment with different color combinations to create different flavors!

Instructions **54**

01

03

02

03.04.05

## Donuts

These cute and colorful donuts are crocheted and then decorated with embroidery stitches and pompoms to create frosting and sprinkles. A few different flavors are shown here, but the possibilities are endless. In addition to making a cool statement in your room, these donuts serve as a comfortable spot to relax—see them in action on the next page!

**Instructions 56**

Donut forget about me!

06.07.08

## Macarons

These macarons are composed of two cookies made with half double crochet, plus a cream section sandwiched in between. Use a different color of yarn for each layer to create a fun ombré effect when you stack multiple.

**Instructions 60**

Blueberry
06
Mint
Mix and match to create your favorite flavors!
07
Strawberry
Cherry
08
Lime
Lemon

09.10

## Ice Cream Cones

I scream, you scream, we all scream for ice cream! Try a single scoop of strawberry (09) or a double scoop of lime and orange (10). Ruffled edges capture the way ice cream melts where the scoop meets the cone.

Instructions 63

## 11 Lollipop

This colorful candy features six different shades of yarn and is constructed by rolling a crocheted tube into a spiral. Wooden skewers inside the stick provide structure and allow the lollipop to be displayed standing up.

Instructions 68

## 12 Polka Dot Candy

This classic candy design makes a fun and eye-catching pillow. First crochet a polka dot cylinder, and then add the ruffles to the ends.

Instructions 70

## 13 Striped Candy

This colorful candy has a round shape and frills on both ends. Use different color combinations to change the overall impression.

Instructions 73

# Can I take your order?

Hamburger bun

Cheese

Hamburger patty

Tomato

Lettuce

Hamburger bun

## 14 Burger

These realistic-looking hamburger buns, tomato slices, and patties are all made with single crochet. Just add lettuce and cheese, and stack everything to create a supersize burger!

Instructions 76

Bread
Fried egg
Lettuce
16 Egg on Toast
Stack a fried egg and a piece of lettuce on top of a classic slice of white bread for an open-faced sandwich. Add polyester stuffing to the egg yolk to create a three-dimensional shape.
Instructions 87
15 Hot Dog
Layer a hot dog and piece of lettuce on a bun for a classic cookout treat. The swirls of ketchup and mustard are created using a felting needle to tack long strands of yarn in place.
Instructions 83
Hot dog
Lettuce
Hot dog bun

Who you calling hot dog!?
Play with your food!

It looks just like a real hamburger!?

17

## Naked Cake

This two tiered cake is bursting with colorful berries. Since it's a naked cake, which means that there is no frosting on the sides, you can clearly see all the pretty layers.

Instructions 92

18 Strawberry Cupcake
19 Chocolate Roll Cake

SUGAR
TEA
COFFEE
SUGAR
TEA
COFFEE
20 Strawberry Shortcake
21 Fruit Tarte
22 Mousse au Citron
23 Charlotte Cake

22
Mousse au Citron
This citrus mousse features a gradated yellow to orange color scheme that creates a refreshing impression.
Instructions 109
23
Charlotte Cake
To create this fancy cake, biscuits are arranged vertically and the center is filled with a creamy custard. Pink roses add an artful touch to the top.
Instructions 112
21
Fruit Tarte
Stack a variety of grapes and blueberries in a tower on top of a baked tarte shell to create this vibrant fruit dessert.
Instructions 106

19

## Chocolate Roll Cake

Use three different colors of yarn to create a mesmerizing swirl of cake and frosting. Pearlescent beads add a special touch.

Instructions 100

18

## Strawberry Cupcake

This colorful treat combines a pink cupcake with a swirl of vanilla and chocolate cream, and a striped cupcake liner that is actually removable!

Instructions 97

20

## Strawberry Shortcake

This slice of cake showcases the classic combination of sponge cake, juicy strawberries, and whipped cream.

Instructions 102

26
24
25
27

24

## Custard

Create a useful storage box inspired by a classic dessert beloved around the world. Whether you know it as custard, flan, or purin, this dessert features a creamy pudding topped with caramel, whipped cream, and a cherry.

**Instructions 115**

25

## Pancakes

This fun storage box is composed of a stack of fluffy pancakes. One pancake serves as the lid, while the other creates a nice round base perfect for storing both everyday essentials and special treasures.

**Instructions 119**

26

## Cream Soda

This uniquely-shaped box is inspired by a popular Japanese treat, cream soda, which consists of melon flavored soda topped with vanilla ice cream—it's like an ice cream float. This box is ideal for storing long items.

**Instructions 122**

27

## Dessert Plate

This dessert plate is useful for displaying your amigurumi treats. Simply change the number of crochet rounds to adjust the size of the finished plate. Have fun creating different color combinations and patterns!

**Instructions 126**

26
Cream Soda
27
Dessert Plate
What's your favorite food?

24
Custard
My favorite food is custard!
25
Pancakes

28

29

28.29

## Nerikiri/Chrysanthemum & Clematis

These Japanese sweets are inspired by two popular flowers: chrysanthemums (28) and clematis (29). Special crochet stitches and stunning color combinations capture the delicacy of these treats, which are often served at Japanese tea ceremonies.

Instructions 127 & 128

30

## Sakura Mochi

This cherry blossom-inspired dessert is enjoyed throughout the season of spring in Japan. It features an oval-shaped mochi, or rice cake, wrapped in a beautiful leaf.

Instructions 130

31

## Taiyaki

A popular street food in Japan, taiyaki is a fish-shaped cake made of a waffle batter and stuffed with a sweet filling. Use three double crochet stitches to create the fish scale pattern, then embroider the eyes and mouth.

Instructions 132

Cute to use! Fun to play!

# Tools & Materials

All of the amigurumi designs in this book can be made with these basic crochet tools and craft supplies.

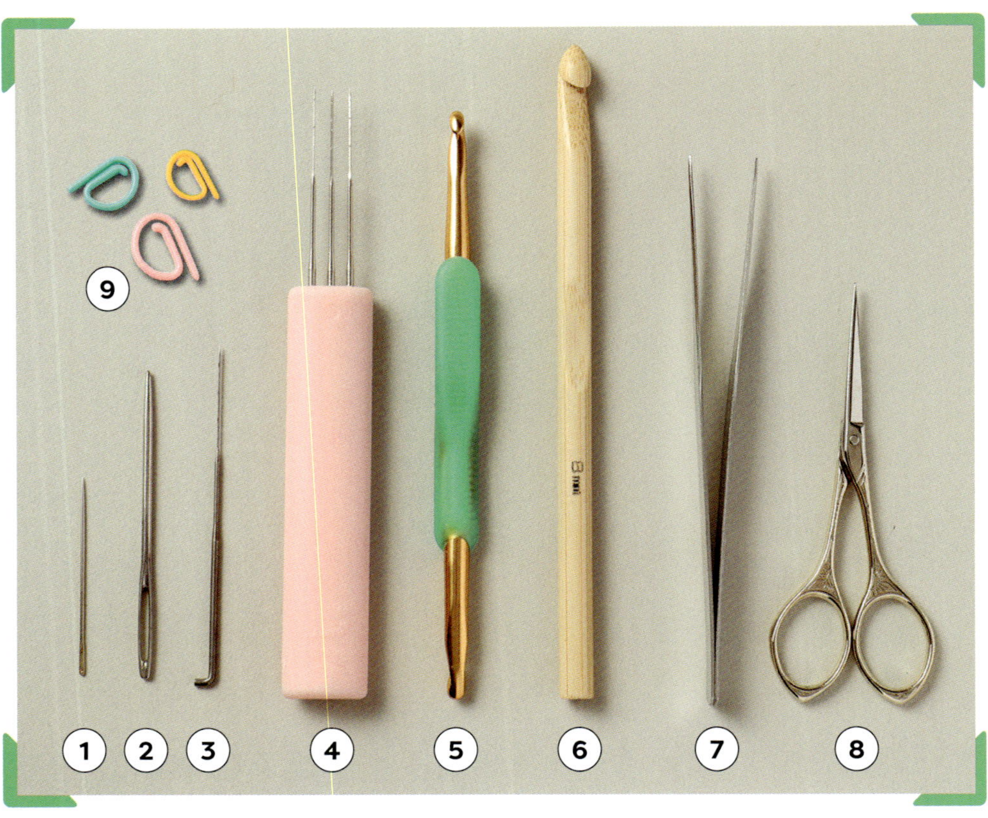


1. **Sewing needle:** Use to sew small parts, such as beads, pompoms, and other embellishments.
2. **Yarn needle:** Use to weave in the yarn ends and to sew pieces of crocheted fabric together.
3. 
4. **Felting needles:** Use wool felting needles to attach pieces of yarn to the crocheted fabric to create an embroidered look, such as when adding mustard to a hot dog or frosting to a donut. Felting needles can be sold individually (3) or as a tool that contains multiple needles (4).
5. **Metal crochet hook:** Look for crochet hooks that are comfortable to hold with an ergonomic grip. The one pictured here is dual-ended and includes two different size hooks. Refer to the individual project instructions for crochet hook size.
6. **Bamboo crochet hook:** In addition to metal and plastic, crochet hooks are also available in wood. The hook pictured here is large and used for projects that call for extra bulky yarn or are crocheted with multiple strands of yarn.
7. **Tweezers:** Use to insert polyester stuffing into narrow areas or to arrange embellishments, such as beads or pompoms.
8. **Thread scissors:** Use to cut excess yarn.
9. **Stitch markers:** Use to mark the number of stitches and rounds.

1 **Bamboo skewers:** Adds structural support inside select projects, such as the lollipop.

2 **Craft glue:** Use to attach small parts, such as beads and pompoms.

3 **Sewing thread:** Use polyester thread to sew embellishments, such as beads, to the crocheted fabric.

4 **Polyester stuffing:** Use stuffing designed for filling toys.

5 6 7 **Assorted ribbons and lace:** Use to decorate some crochet projects, such as cakes and candy.

8 **Pompoms:** Use to decorate some crochet projects, such as donuts and ice cream.

9 10 **Assorted beads:** Use to decorate some crochet projects, such as the cupcake and the chocolate roll cake.

11 **Acrylic bulky-weight yarn:** The majority of projects in this book are made with 100% acrylic bulky-weight yarn, such as Hamanaka Bonny. Look for a yarn that is available in a wide variety of colors.

12 **Acrylic super bulky-weight yarn:** Select projects, such as the French crullers, are made with even thicker yarn, such as Hamanaka Jumbonny.

# Basic Techniques

The following guide highlights a few basic crochet techniques that are used in this book. Please note that this book uses US crochet terms, which differ than crochet terms used in the UK.

### HOW TO CROCHET WITH TWO STRANDS OF YARN

The individual projects will note how many strands of yarn to use. When a project notes to crochet with two strands of yarn, simply hold two strands together. If you have two separate skeins of yarn, you can simply pull the yarn from each skein. However, if you're working from one single skein of yarn, try the following trick: Locate both the beginning and end of the skein and use these as your two strands.

## Technique Spotlight: Polka Dot Candy

The following guide spotlights techniques used to crochet the Polka Dot Candy on page 70.

### GETTING STARTED: MAKE A LOOP WITH CHAINS

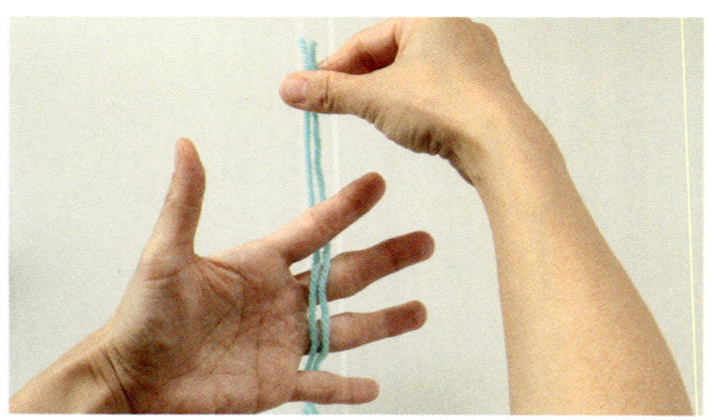

01 Bring 2 strands of yarn between pinky and ring finger of left hand. Take yarn to back over middle finger, under index finger, then forward again over index finger.

02 Hold the yarn end with your thumb and middle finger.

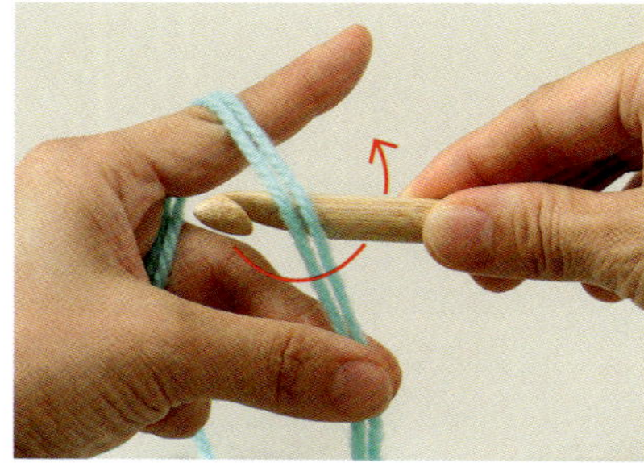

03 Hold the crochet hook with your right hand. Wrap the yarn around the hook as shown by the arrow.

04 The yarn is wrapped, making a loop.

05 Hold the crossed section of the loop with your thumb and middle finger. Yarn over the hook and pull through the loop.

06 The first stitch is complete (does not count as a stitch).

07 Yarn over the hook and pull through the loop in the direction of the arrow.

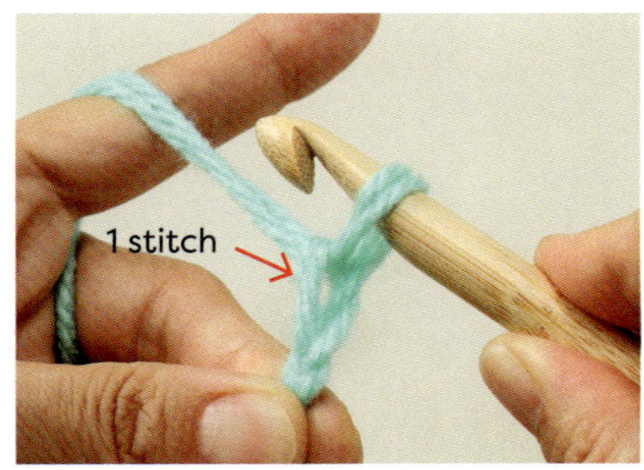


08 One chain stitch is complete.

09 Repeat steps 7 and 8 to make a total of 12 chain stitches.

10 Insert the hook through the first chain stitch.

11 Yarn over the hook and pull through all loops. The chain loop is complete.

### FIRST ROUND (SINGLE CROCHET) TO SECOND ROUND (CENTER SINGLE CROCHET INCREASE)

12 Make one chain stitch as the beginning stitch (does not count as a stitch).

13 Insert the hook at the same stitch as step 12. Yarn over the hook and pull through the loop. Then yarn over the hook and pull through two loops in the direction of the arrow.

14 One single crochet is complete.

15 Insert the hook in the stitch next to the one from step 12 and repeat steps 13 and 14. Continue to make one single crochet in each chain stitch, making 12 single crochets in total.

16 Insert the hook through the top loops of the first stitch on the first round and yarn over. Pull through in the direction of the arrow.

17 The slip stitch on the first round is complete.

18 From the second round, make center single crochet. For center single crochet, insert the hook between the vertical base from the previous round to make single crochet.

19 Pull the hook out from the right side of the vertical part of single crochet. The above photo shows the view from the back.

20 Completed view of one center single crochet. Insert the hook in the same spot as step 18 and make another center single crochet.

21 As noted in the pattern, make two single crochet for each stitch on the previous round between the vertical base.

22 Work until the third stitch on the 9th round.

23 For the fourth stitch, make center single crochet halfway.

24 Prepare to change to white yarn (Yarn B) as noted in the pattern. Yarn over.

25 Pull Yarn B through.

26 Leave the teal yarn (Yarn A) behind the crocheted fabric and make center single crochet using Yarn B. Continue crocheting and changing yarn color as noted in the pattern.

27 Once you resume crocheting with Yarn A for a while, bring Yarn B to the front after crocheting 4-5 stitches. Insert the hook into the next stitch under Yarn B, yarn over with Yarn A, and pull in the direction of the arrow.

28 Further yarn over, then pull through in the direction of the arrow and crochet over Yarn B.

29 Make center single crochet using Yarn A and Yarn B as noted in the pattern. When crocheting with Yarn A for a while, crochet over Yarn B every 4-5 stitches so that Yarn B will not become too loose.

***View from Right Side***

Two stitches with Yarn B are crocheted every 8 stitches.

***View from Wrong Side***

Crochet over Yarn B every 4-5 stitches. When you find it too loose, you can crochet over at every stitch.

## ROUND 49 (2 CENTER SINGLE CROCHET TOGETHER [DECREASE] TO MAKE FRILLS)

30 Continue center single crochet from rounds 10–48 as noted in the pattern. At 9th stitch on round 49, make center single crochet halfway.

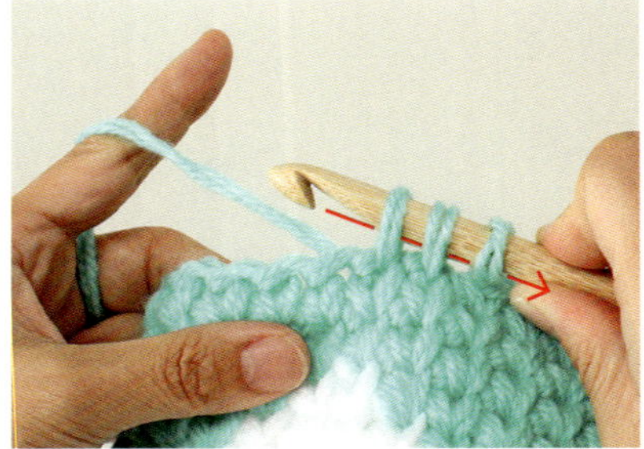

31 Continue to insert the hook in the next stitch, yarn over, and pull through and make two halfway single crochet. Yarn over and pull through 3 loops at once as shown by the arrow.

32 Decrease with 2 single crochet together.

33 Continue to round 52 as you decrease stitches as noted in the pattern. Fill with polyester stuffing, then continue to round 53.

34 Insert the hook at top of round 53, yarn over with purple yarn. Next, make the frills.

35 Pull the purple yarn through.

36 Make one chain stitch at the beginning, and insert the hook into the same stitch as step 34. Make one single crochet.

37 Continue to make three chain stitches.

38 Make single crochet in the next stitch.

39 Repeat chain stitch and single crochet as noted in the pattern.

40 At the last stitch, make one chain, yarn over, then insert the hook at the top of the first single crochet.

41 Make half double crochet, and continue crocheting round 2.

42 Work five rounds of frills with purple yarn as noted in the pattern.

43 Change yarn color for round 6 to crochet with white yarn.

44 Thread two 28" (70 cm) long strands of purple yarn onto a needle. Sew running stitch through round 1 of the frill. (pink yarn is used for visual clarity).

45 After sewing running stitch, pull the yarn tails to gather the frill. Begin to tie a knot.

46 Complete the knot and cut the remaining yarn. Insert the yarn tails into the body. For the opposite side, scoop the half loop of the chain on the body, and repeat steps 34–46. The Polka Dot Candy is now complete!

## Technique Spotlight: Chocolate Roll Cake

The next guide focuses on techniques used to crochet the Chocolate Roll Cake on page 100.

### GETTING STARTED: MAGIC RING TO ROUND 1

01 Using 2 strands, wrap the yarn around your left index finger twice to make a double ring.

02 Remove the ring from your finger. Bring the working yarn (the one attached to the skein) over your left index finger.

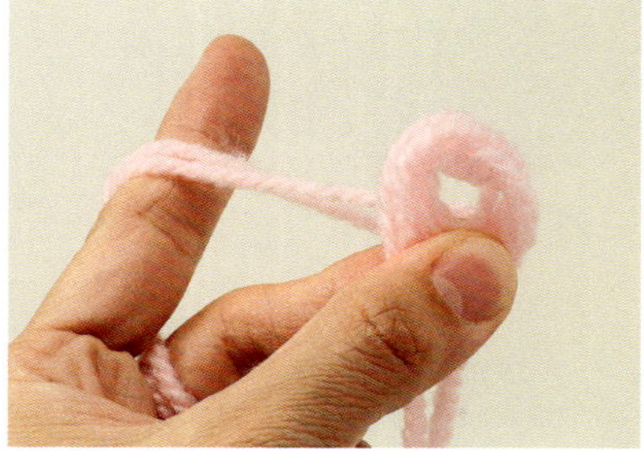

03 Hold the crossed section of the ring with your left thumb and middle finger to keep the shape of the loop.

04 Insert the hook into the ring, and yarn over. Pull the yarn through the loop in the direction of the arrow.

05 View once the yarn has been pulled through the ring.

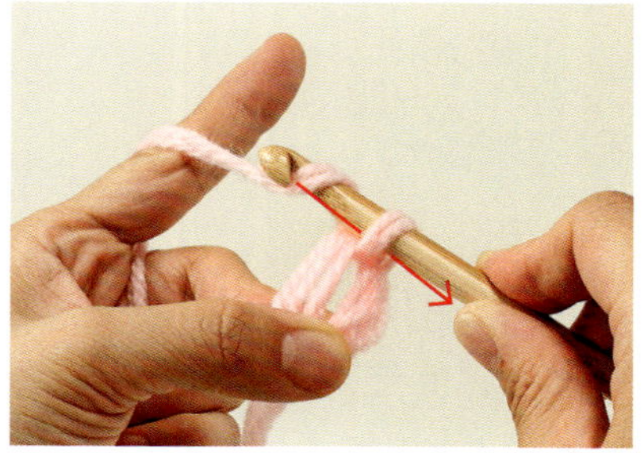

06 Continue to yarn over the hook, and pull in the direction of the arrow.

07 The first chain stitch is complete (does not count as a stitch).

08 Insert the hook into the ring, yarn over, and pull through in the direction of the arrow.

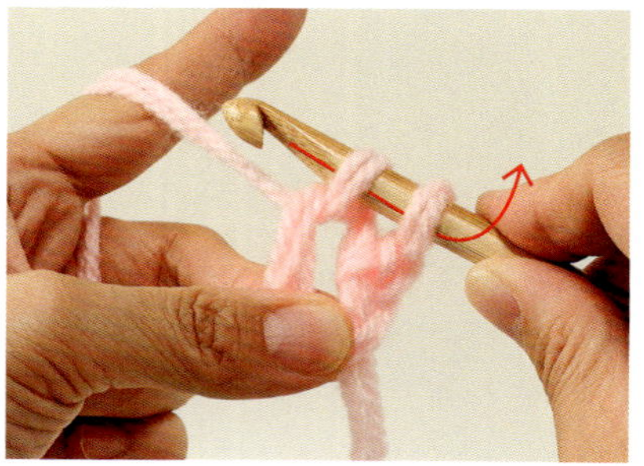

09 Further yarn over, and pull through two loops at once.

10 One single crochet is complete.

11 Attach a stitch marker in the first stitch of the round.

12 Continue to make a total of 9 single crochet stitches.

13 Pull the starting end of yarn to close the magic ring.

14 Without making a chain stitch, make single crochet stitch in the top of the first stitch of round 1. Move the stitch marker.

15 Make another single crochet stitch at the same position as step 14 to increase.

16 Continue to make two single crochet stitches in the top of the second stitch.

**17** For round 2, leave the pink yarn (Yarn A), insert the hook in the top of the third stitch of round 1, and pull brown yarn (Yarn B) through.

**18** Make one chain stitch, then make two single crochet stitches in the same stitch.

**19** Crochet round 2 to Yarn B section as noted in the pattern.

**20** Leave Yarn B for round 3, and insert the hook through Yarn A again.

**21** Make one beginning chain stitch, and make one single crochet stitch in the top of the first stitch of round 2.

**22** Crochet Yarn A section of round 3 as noted in the pattern.

**23** Cut Yarn A, leaving a 4" (10 cm) long yarn tail and pull out.

**24** For round 4, insert the hook through Yarn B.

**25** Crochet until round 4 as noted in the pattern, then cut Yarn B and pull out. Insert the hook into the next stitch and yarn over with dark brown yarn (Yarn C).

26 Pull yarn through and make one chain stitch.

27 Crochet round 5 with Yarn C as noted in the pattern.

## ROUND 6 TO END

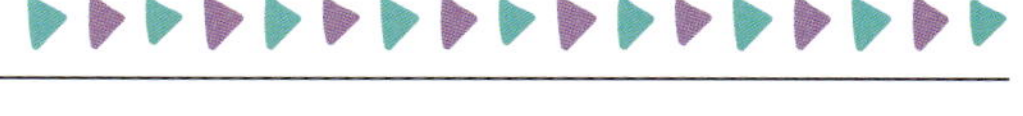

28 Make one chain stitch.

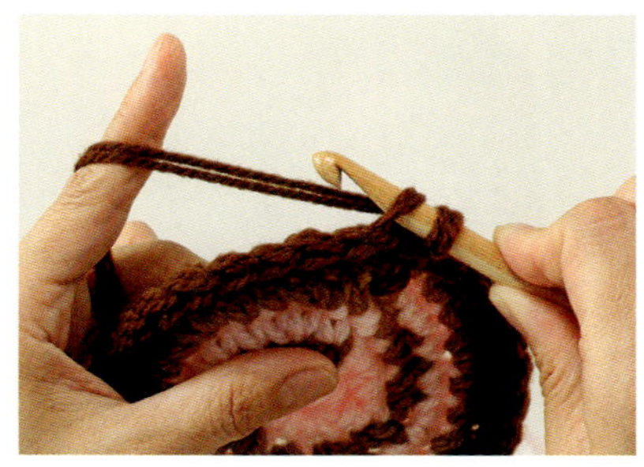

29 Insert the hook through back loop of the previous round, yarn over, and pull the yarn through.

30 Further yarn over and pull through two loops at once. Complete one single crochet in back loop only.

31 Continue to single crochet in back loop only on round 6 without increasing or decreasing.

32 Continue to single crochet rounds 7–9 without increasing or decreasing. Cut the yarn, leaving a 1 yard (1 m) long tail. Body A is now complete.

33 Follow rounds 1–5 as noted in the pattern to make Body B. Tie the ends of Yarn A and B together at round 4 and 5 to secure.

34 Finish the yarn ends in the same way for Body A.

35 Thread the remaining yarn tail for Body A onto a needle. Align Body B on top of Body A. Sew together, scooping the top loops of the last round of Body A and B.

36 Continue whipstitching until you are ⅔ of the way around the cake.

37 Fill firmly with polyester stuffing, using tweezers to help insert the stuffing.

38 Continue whipstitching around the rest of the cake.

## CLUSTER WITH 5 DOUBLE CROCHET

39 To crochet the whipped cream, start by making four chain stitches.

40 Yarn over and insert the hook through the first chain stitch.

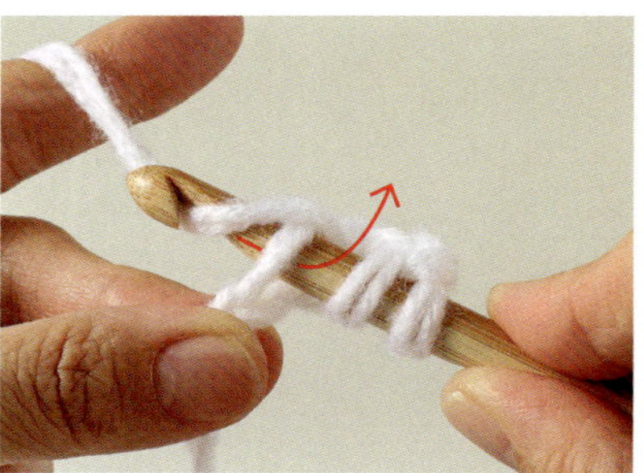

41 Yarn over the hook, and pull through as shown by the arrow.

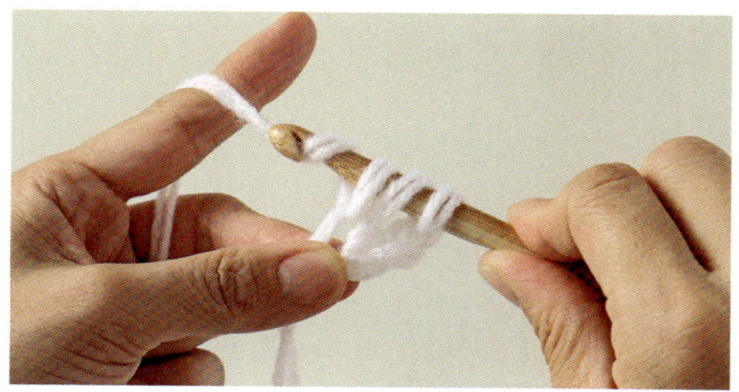

42 Yarn over the hook again, and pull through the front two loops (incomplete double crochet).

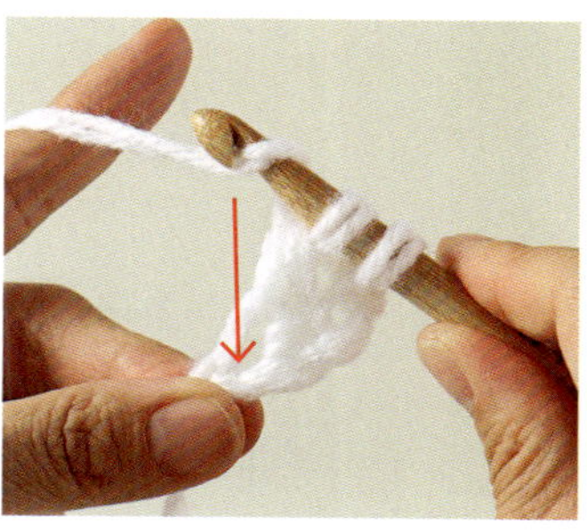

43 Yarn over and insert the hook into the same stitch.

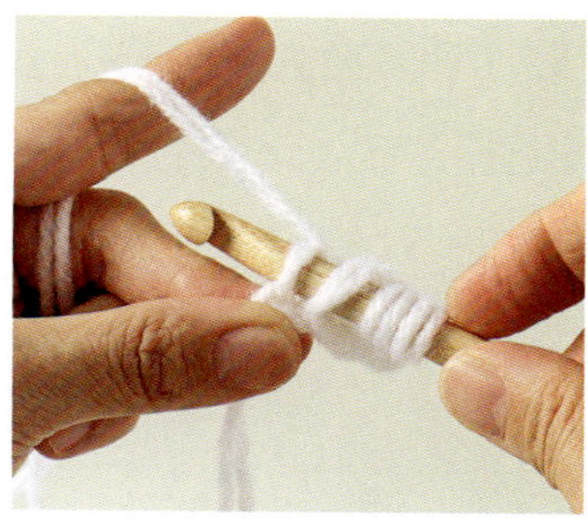

44 View once the hook has been inserted.

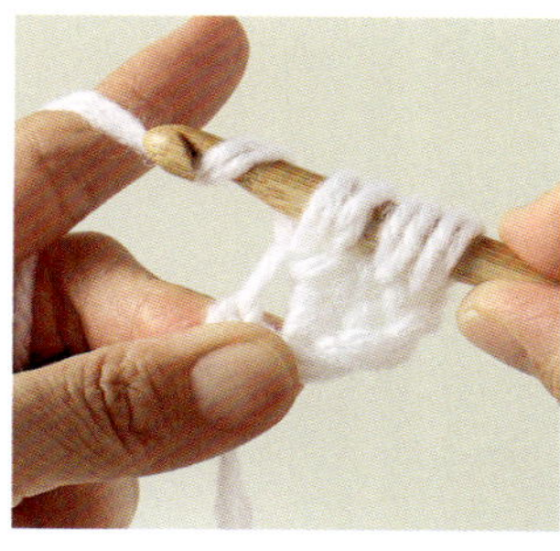

45 Yarn over and pull through the front loop.

46 Repeat steps 43–45 three more times.

47 Crochet 5 incomplete double crochet and yarn over the hook. Pull the hook through 6 loops at once as shown by the arrow.

48 The cluster with 5 double crochet is now complete.

49 Continue to make four chain stitches.

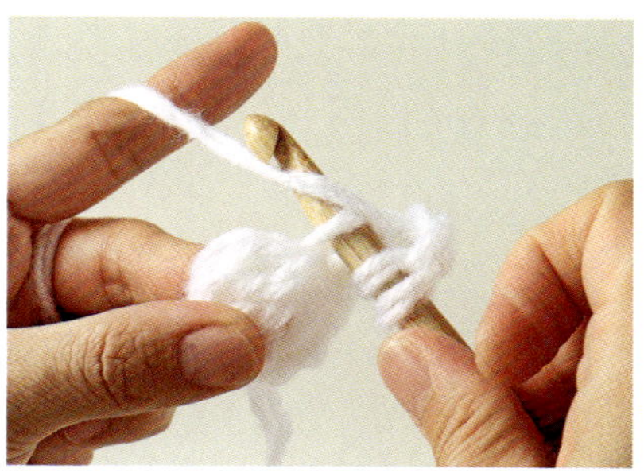

50 Repeat steps 40–48.

48 Crochet six clusters with 5 double crochet in total. The whipped cream is now complete.

49 Crochet the strawberry as noted in the pattern. Attach the strawberry and whipped cream to the top center of the cake, then sew the beads in place to complete the chocolate roll cake.

01.02

# French Crullers

SHOWN ON PAGE 8

01

02

Finished Size:
15¾" (40 cm) diameter x 6" (15 cm) tall

## TOOLS & MATERIALS

### Yarn

**For 01**

- 100% acrylic super bulky-weight yarn
  - 263 yds (240 m) in dark beige
  - 184 yds (168 m) in off-white

**For 02**

- 100% acrylic super bulky-weight yarn
  - 263 yds (240 m) in light pink
  - 184 yds (168 m) in dark brown

### Other Materials

- 670 g of polyester stuffing each

### Tools

- US P/Q (15 mm) crochet hook
- Yarn needle

## CONSTRUCTION STEPS

Note: Use 2 strands of yarn throughout.

**1.** Crochet the body: Make 36 foundation chains, then work flat in rows, until row 31. Cut the yarn, leaving a 1 yard (1 m) long tail.

**2.** Align the stitches at the beginning and end of the crocheted body. Join together with whipstitch to make a tube (see **Figure A**).

**3.** Fold the tube in half with wrong sides together. Whipstitch the edges together, skipping every other stitch and stuffing as you sew (see **Figure B**).

**4.** Bring the seam from step 3 toward the inside of the ring and adjust the shape (see **Figure C**).

*Figure A*

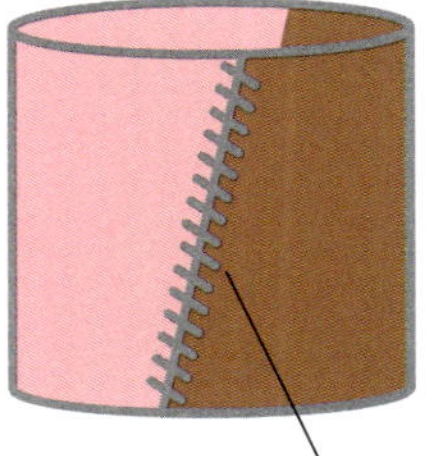



*Figure B*

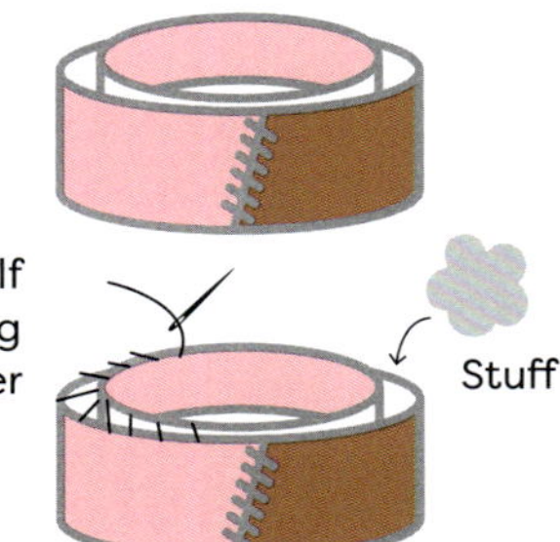



*Figure C*

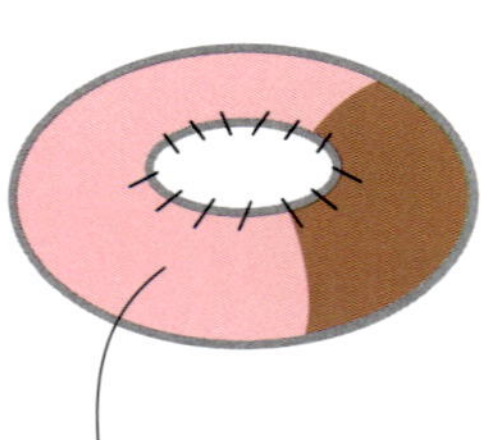

## CROCHET INSTRUCTIONS

### For 01: Body

With dark beige and US P/Q (15 mm) hook, ch36.

**Row 1: hdc1 in fourth ch from hook (counts as 2hdc), hdc1 in each ch to the end, turn [34]**

**Row 2: ch1 and hdc in BLO of next st (counts as hdc2tog), hdc31 BLO, hdc2 in BLO of last st, turn [34]**

**Row 3: ch2 and hdc in BLO of first st (counts as 2 hdc), hdc31, hdc2tog BLO, turn [34]**

**Rows 4–19:** rep rows 2 and 3 eight more times.

Change to off-white

**Rows 20–31:** with dark brown, rep rows 2 and 3 six times.

Cut yarn and fasten off, leaving a 1 yard (1 m) long tail. Make up following steps 2–4 on page 54.

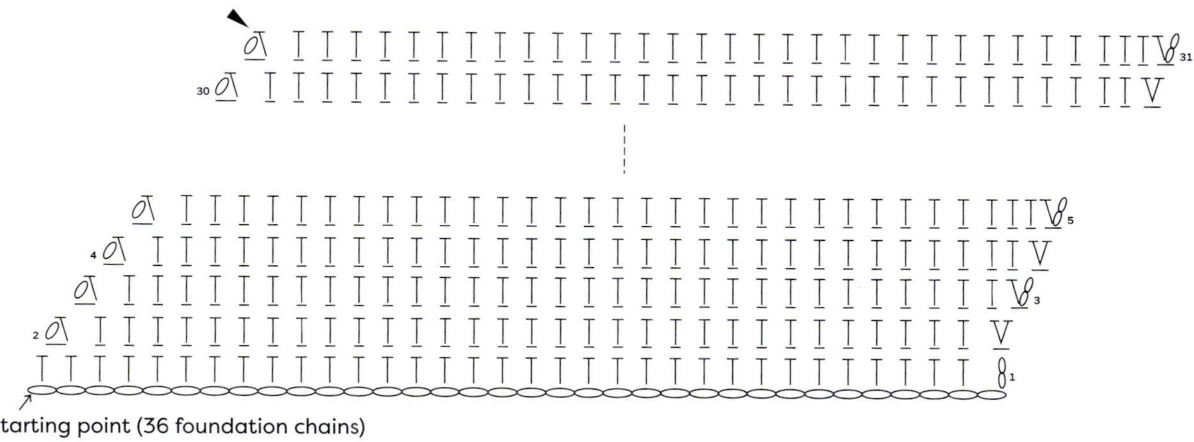


### For 02: Body

With light pink and US P/Q (15 mm) hook, ch36.

**Row 1:** hdc1 in fourth ch from hook (counts as 2hdc), hdc1 in each ch to the end, turn [34]

**Row 2:** ch1 and hdc in BLO of next st (counts as hdc2tog), hdc31 BLO, hdc2 in BLO of last st, turn [34]

**Row 3:** ch2 and hdc in BLO of first st (counts as 2 hdc), hdc31, hdc2tog BLO, turn [34]

**Rows 4–19:** rep rows 2 and 3 eight more times.

Change to dark brown

**Rows 20–31:** with dark brown, rep rows 2 and 3 six times.

Cut yarn and fasten off, leaving a 1 yard (1 m) long tail. Make up following steps 2–4 on page 54.

03.04.05

# Donuts

**SHOWN ON PAGE 9**

03

04

05

Finished Size:
16½" (42 cm) diameter x 4¾" (12 cm) tall

## TOOLS & MATERIALS

### Yarn

#### For 03

***For crochet***

- 100% acrylic bulky-weight yarn
  - 302 yds (276 m) in golden brown
  - 289 yds (264 m) in light pink

***For embroidery***

- 100% acrylic bulky-weight yarn
  - 10 yds (9 m) in white, dark pink, lime green, and aqua blue
- 100% acrylic super bulky-weight yarn
  - 7 yds (6 m) in off-white

#### For 04

***For crochet***

- 100% acrylic bulky-weight yarn
  - 302 yds (276 m) in light brown
  - 289 yds (264 m) in aqua blue

***For embroidery***

- 100% acrylic super bulky-weight yarn
  - 7 yds (6 m) in off-white and dark brown

#### For 05

***For crochet***

- 100% acrylic bulky-weight yarn
  - 302 yds (276 m) in golden brown
  - 86 yds (78 m) in lemon and dark brown

***For embroidery***

- 100% acrylic bulky-weight yarn
  - 20 yds (18 m) in dark beige
  - 14 yds (12 m) in golden brown and brown
- 100% acrylic super bulky-weight yarn
  - 7 yds (6 m) in dark brown

### Other Materials

- 400 g of polyester stuffing each
- 18 pompoms (for 05 only): ¾" (2 cm) diameter in six colors (three of each color)

### Tools

- US L-11 (8 mm) crochet hook
- Yarn needle
- Felting needle

## CONSTRUCTION STEPS

Note: Use 2 strands of yarn throughout.

**1.** Crochet the body: Make 42 foundation chains, slip stitch in first chain to form a loop, then single crochet in each chain. Continue to single crochet as you increase, until round 16. The wrong side is used as the outside, so when you change colors for 05, leave the yarn at front, and yarn over every 5 to 6 stitches (see below). Crochet as instructed until you reach round 36, then cut the yarn, leaving a 1 yard (1 m) long tail.

**2.** Turn the crocheted fabric inside out, sew the other half of foundation chains and the top stitch on round 36 together with whipstitch as you fill with polyester stuffing.

**3.** Working through the spare front loops of stitches on round 16, crochet the frosting.

**4.** Add toppings to each donut (see page 59).

#### How to Change Yarn Colors for 05

Make foundation chains using golden brown. Continue with dark brown until the 6th stitch on round 1. Use lemon for stitches 7–27 and then dark brown for stitches 28- 42. When you change color, bring the finished yarn toward the front.

Continue crocheting as you yarn over every 5 to 6 stitches so that the yarn will not become too loose.

## CROCHET INSTRUCTIONS

### For 05: Body

With golden brown and US L-11 hook, ch42. Slip stitch into first of these chains to form a large loop. Change to dark brown. Now work into the chains, joining each round with a slip stitch. Join in lemon when needed and carry yarns not in use along front of work, making a yarn over every 5 or 6 stitches to trap the yarn into the stitches.

**Rnd 1:** ch1 (does not count as a st throughout), sc6, change to lemon, ch21, change to dark brown, sc15, slst in beg ch1 [42]

**Rnd 2:** in dark brown, ch1, sc6, in lemon sc21, in dark brown sc15, slst in beg ch1

**Rnd 3:** in dark brown, ch1, sc2 in first st, sc5, in lemon sc1, (sc2 in next st, sc6) twice, sc2 in next st, sc5, in dark brown sc1, (sc2 in next st, sc6) twice, slst in beg ch1 [48]

**Rnd 4:** in dark brown, ch1, sc5, sc2 in next st, sc1, in lemon sc6, (sc2 in next st, sc7) twice, sc2 in next st, sc1, in dark brown sc6, sc2 in next st, sc7, sc2 in next st, sc2, slst in beg ch1 [54]

**Rnd 5:** in dark brown, ch1, sc8, sc2 in next st working first st in dark brown and second st in lemon, in lemon sc8, (sc2 in next st, sc8) twice, sc2 in next st working first st in lemon and second st in dark brown, in dark brown (sc8, sc2 in next st) twice, slst in beg ch1 [60]

**Rnd 6:** in dark brown, ch1, sc2, sc2 in next st, sc6, in lemon sc3, sc2 in next st, (sc9, sc2 in next st) twice, sc6, in dark brown sc3, sc2 in next st, sc9, sc2 in next st, sc7, slst in beg ch1 [66]

**Rnd 7:** in dark brown, ch1, sc5, sc2 in next st, sc4, in lemon sc6, (sc2 in next st, sc10) twice, sc2 in next st, sc4, in dark brown sc6, sc2 in next st, sc10, sc2 in next st, sc5, slst in beg ch1 [72]

**Rnd 8:** in dark brown, ch1, sc9, sc2 in next st, sc1, in lemon sc10, (sc2 in next st, sc11) twice, sc2 in next st, sc1, in dark brown sc10, sc2 in next st, sc11, sc2 in next st, sc2, slst in beg ch1 [78]

**Rnd 9:** in dark brown, ch1, sc2 in first st, sc11, in lemon sc1, (sc2 in next st, sc12) twice, sc2 in next st, sc11, in dark brown sc1, (sc2 in next st, sc12) twice, slst in beg ch1 [84]

**Rnd 10:** in dark brown, ch1, sc4, sc2 in next st, sc8, in lemon sc5, (sc2 in next st, sc13) twice, sc2 in next st, sc8, in dark brown sc5, sc2 in next st, sc13, sc2 in next st, sc9, slst in beg ch1 [90]

**Rnd 11:** in dark brown, ch1, sc13, sc2 in next st, in lemon (sc14, sc2 in next st) 3 times, in dark brown (sc14, sc2 in next st) twice, sc1, slst in beg ch1 [96]

**Rnd 12:** in dark brown, ch1, sc10, sc2 in next st, sc4, in lemon sc11, (sc2 in next st, sc15) twice, sc2 in next st, sc4, in dark brown sc11, sc2 in next st, sc15, sc2 in next st, sc5, slst in beg ch1 [102]

**Rnd 13:** in dark brown, ch1, sc3, sc2 in next st, sc12, in lemon sc4, (sc2 in next st, sc16) twice, sc2 in next st, sc12, in dark brown sc4, sc2 in next st, sc16, sc2 in next st, sc13, slst in beg ch1 [108]

**Rnd 14:** in dark brown, ch1, sc9, sc2 in next st, sc7, in lemon sc10, (sc2 in next st, sc17) twice, sc2 in next st, sc7, in dark brown sc10, sc2 in next st, sc17, sc2 in next st, sc8, slst in beg ch1 [114]

**Rnd 15:** in dark brown, ch1, sc18, sc2 in next st working first st in dark brown and second st in lemon, in lemon sc18, (sc2 in next st, sc18) twice, sc2 in next st working first st in lemon and second st in dark brown, in dark brown (sc18, sc2 in next st) twice, slst in beg ch1 [120]

**Rnd 16:** in dark brown, ch1, sc19, in lemon sc60, in dark brown sc41, slst in beg ch1 [120]

Cut lemon. Change to golden brown.

**Rnd 17:** ch1, sc120 in BLO, slst in beg ch1

**Rnds 18–20:** ch1, sc120, slst in beg ch1 (3 rnds)

**Rnd 21:** ch1, (sc18, sc2tog) 6 times, slst in beg ch1 [114]

**Rnd 22:** ch1, (sc9, sc2tog, sc8) 6 times, slst in beg ch1 [108]

**Rnd 23:** ch1, (sc3, sc2tog, sc13) 6 times, slst in beg ch1 [102]

**Rnd 24:** ch1, (sc10, sc2tog, sc5) 6 times, slst in beg ch1 [96]

**Rnd 25:** ch1, (sc13, sc2tog, sc1) 6 times, slst in beg ch1 [90]

**Rnd 26:** ch1, (sc4, sc2tog, sc9) 6 times, slst in beg ch1 [84]

**Rnd 27:** ch1, (sc2tog, sc12) 6 times, slst in beg ch1 [78]

**Rnd 28:** ch1, (sc9, sc2tog, sc2) 6 times, slst in beg ch1 [72]

**Rnd 29:** ch1, (sc5, sc2tog, sc5) 6 times, slst in beg ch1 [66]

**Rnd 30:** ch1, (sc2, sc2tog, sc7) 6 times, slst in beg ch1 [60]

**Rnd 31:** ch1, (sc8, sc2tog) 6 times, slst in beg ch1 [54]

**Rnd 32:** ch1, (sc5, sc2tog, sc2) 6 times, slst in beg ch1 [48]

**Rnd 33:** ch1, (sc2tog, sc6) 6 times, slst in beg ch1 [42]

**Rnds 34–36:** ch1, sc42, slst in beg ch1 (3 rnds)

Cut yarn and fasten off. Make up following step 2 instructions on page 56.

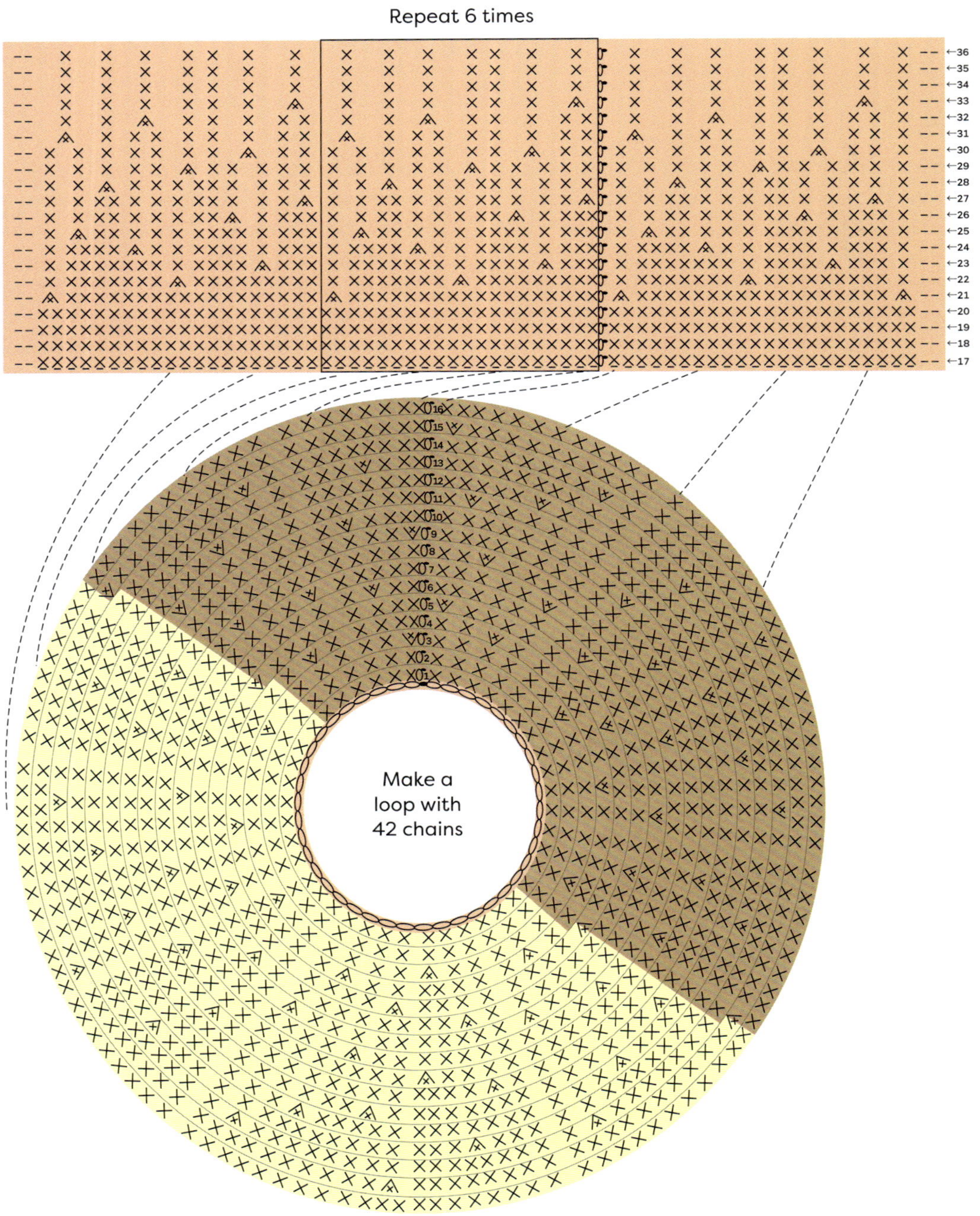

## For 05: Frosting

With dark brown and US L-11 hook, work into the spare loops from rnd 16 of the body.
Join into beg ch1 with a slst.
Change to lemon when needed, then back to dark brown, to match body colors.
**Rnd 1:** ch1 (does not count as a st), (1sc, 2hdc, 1sc, 2slst, 1sc, 1hdc, 2dc, 1hdc, 1sc, 1slst, 1sc, 3dc, 2hdc, 1sc) 6 times, slst in beg ch1 [120]
Cut yarn and fasten off.
Add toppings following instructions on page 59.

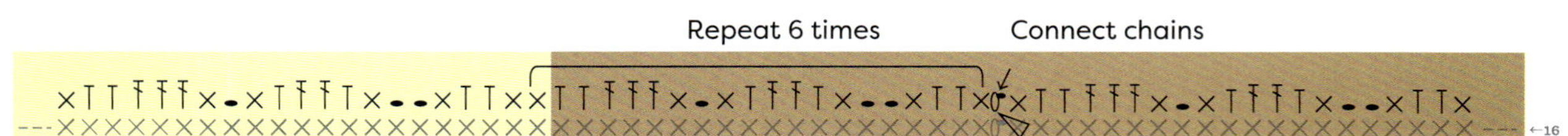

For 03

Follow the instructions for 05 on pages 57-58, omitting color changes in Body. Make Body in light pink to rnd 16, then change to golden brown for rnds 17 to end. Make Frosting in light pink.

For 04

Follow the instructions for 05 on pages 57-58, omitting color changes in Body. Make Body in aqua blue to rnd 16, then change to light brown for rnds 17 to end. Make Frosting in aqua blue.

## FINISHING TECHNIQUES

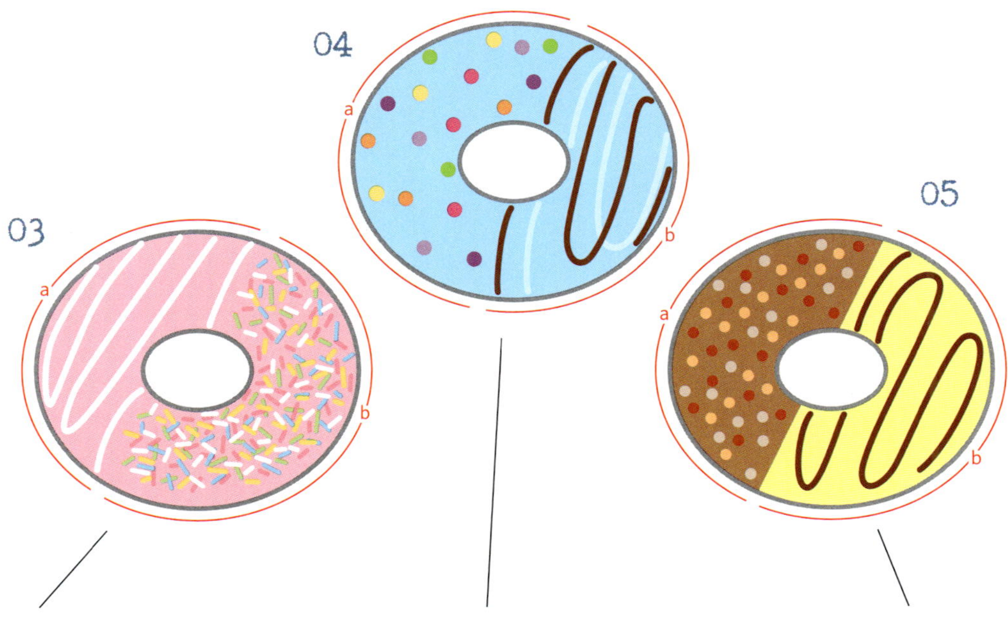


On half a, arrange two strands of off-white yarn in a squiggly shape for the vanilla drizzle, then secure in place using a felting needle. On half b, embroider ¾" (2 cm) long straight stitches in assorted colors using two strands of yarn.

Sew the pompoms in place on half a. On half b, arrange two strands of off-white yarn in a squiggly shape for the vanilla drizzle, then secure in place using a felting needle. Follow the same process to attach two strands of dark brown for the chocolate drizzle, overlapping the vanilla as necessary.

On half a, make French knots to embroider the nuts (refer to chart below).

| Yarn Color | Number of Wraps |
|---|---|
| Dark beige | 8 |
| Golden brown | 5 |
| Brown | 6 |

On half b, arrange two strands of dark brown yarn in a squiggly shape for the chocolate drizzle, then secure in place using a felting needle.

06.07.08

# Macarons

SHOWN ON PAGE 12

Finished Size:
16½" (42 cm) diameter x
6" (15 cm) tall

## TOOLS & MATERIALS

### Yarn

**For All**

- 100% acrylic bulky-weight yarn
  - 66 yds (60 m) in off-white

**For 06**

- 100% acrylic bulky-weight yarn
  - 329 yds (300 m) in light blue
  - 329 yds (300 m) in lavender

**For 07**

- 100% acrylic bulky-weight yarn
  - 329 yds (300 m) in light pink
  - 329 yds (300 m) in rose pink

**For 08**

- 100% acrylic bulky-weight yarn
  - 329 yds (300 m) in cream
  - 329 yds (300 m) in peppermint green

### Other Materials

- 370 g of polyester stuffing each

### Tools

- US L-11 (8 mm) crochet hook
- Yarn needle

## CONSTRUCTION STEPS

Note: Use 2 strands of yarn throughout.

**1.** Crochet one cookie: Make 9 half double crochet into the magic ring, and crochet as instructed. For round 16, single crochet in front loops only. For round 17, make reverse single crochet in the single crochet stitches of round 16. Cut yarn and fasten off.

**2.** Crochet the cream section: Join the off-white yarn into the unworked BLO on round 15 of the cookie and crochet as instructed. Cut yarn and fasten off, leaving a 3 yard (2.6 m) long tail.

**3.** Crochet the second cookie.

**4.** Align the second cookie with the free edge of the cream section. Sew the second cookie to the top of half double crochet from step 2 using whipstitch. After sewing around ⅔ of the cookie, fill with polyester stuffing, and the continue sewing and stuffing to the end.

## CROCHET INSTRUCTIONS

### For 06: Cookie (make 2)

With light blue and US L-11 hook, make a magic ring.

**Rnd 1:** ch2 (counts as first hdc throughout), hdc8 in magic ring, slst in top of beg ch2 [9]

Place stitch marker in first st of rnd 1 and move it up after each round

**Rnd 2:** ch2, hdc1 in same st at base of ch2, (hdc2 in next st) 8 times, slst in top of beg ch2 [18]

**Rnd 3:** ch2, hdc2 in next st, (hdc1, hdc2 in next st) 8 times, slst in top of beg ch2 [27]

**Rnd 4:** ch2, hdc1 in same st at base of ch2, hdc2, (hdc2 in next st, hdc2) 8 times, slst in top of beg ch2 [36]

**Rnd 5:** ch2, hdc1, (hdc2 in next st, hdc3) 8 times, hdc2 in next st, hdc1, slst in top of beg ch2 [45]

**Rnd 6:** ch2, hdc3 (hdc2 in next st, hdc4) 8 times, hdc2 in next st, slst in top of beg ch2 [54]

**Rnd 7:** ch2, (hdc2 in next st, hdc5) 8 times, hdc2 in next st, hdc4, slst in top of beg ch2 [63]

**Rnd 8:** ch2, hdc3, (hdc2 in next st, hdc6) 8 times, hdc2 in next st, hdc2, slst in top of beg ch2 [72]

**Rnd 9:** ch2, hdc1 in same st at base of ch2, (hdc7, hdc2 in next st) 8 times, hdc7, slst in top of beg ch2 [81]

**Rnd 10:** ch2, hdc3, (hdc2 in next st, hdc8) 8 times, hdc2 in next st, hdc4, slst in top of beg ch2 [90]

**Rnd 11:** ch2, hdc8, (hdc2 in next st, hdc9) 8 times, hdc2 in next st, slst in top of beg ch2 [99]

**Rnd 12:** ch2, hdc2, (hdc2 in next st, hdc10) 8 times, hdc2 in next st, hdc7, slst in top of beg ch2 [108]

**Rnd 13–15:** ch2, hdc1 in each st, slst in top of beg ch2 (3 rnds)

**Rnd 16:** ch1 (does not count as a st throughout), 1sc in each st FLO, slst in beg ch1

**Rnd 17:** ch1, 1rsc in each st, slst in beg ch1 (see step 1 on page 60)

Cut yarn and fasten off.

Refer to instructions on page 62 to crochet the cream section.

Repeat rounds 1–17 to make another cookie using lavender yarn. Make up following step 4 instructions on page 60.

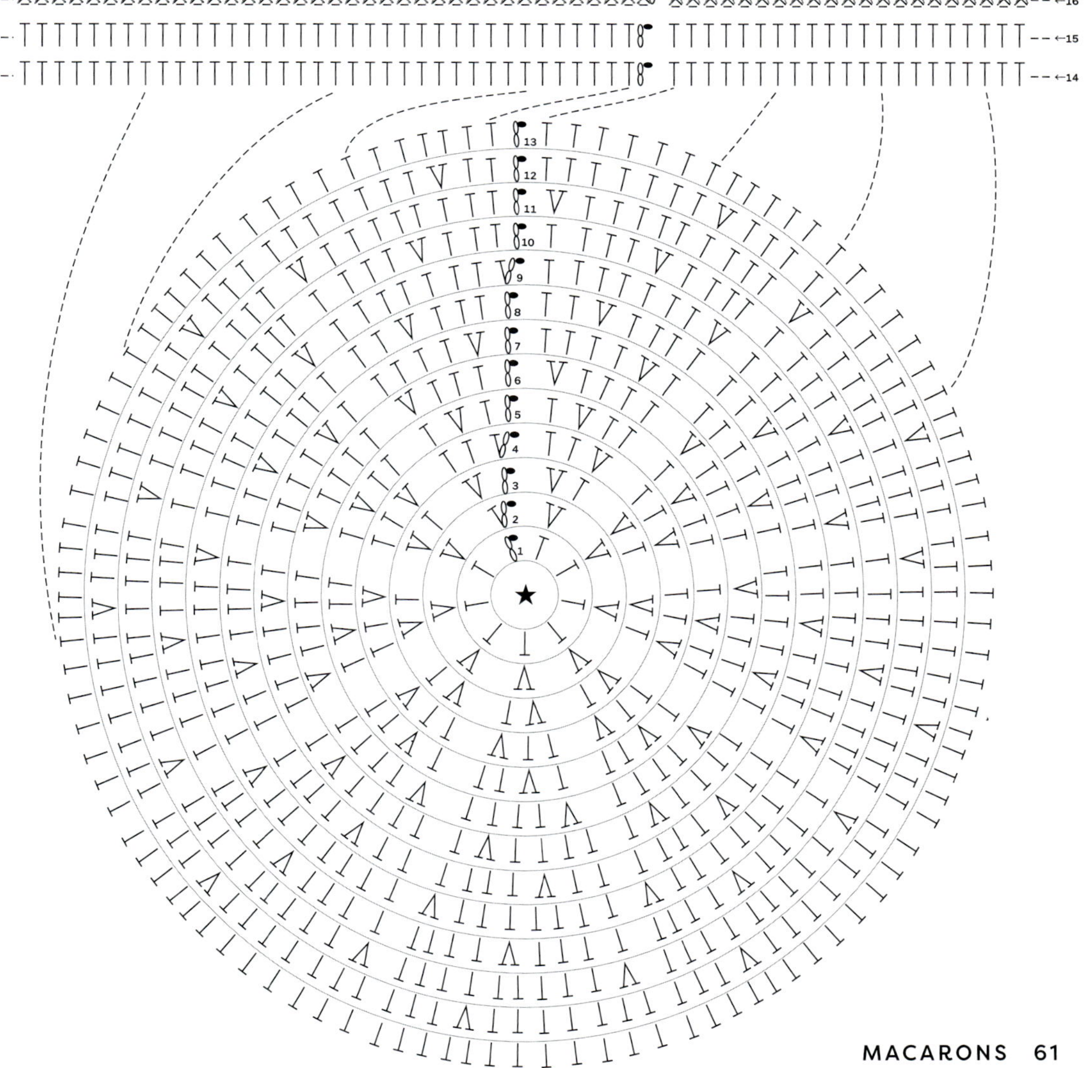

### For 07

Follow the instructions for 06 on page 61, making one cookie in light pink and one in rose pink.

### For 08

Follow the instructions for 06 on page 61, making one cookie in cream and one in peppermint green.

### For 06–08: Cream

Join off-white in unworked BLO of rnd 15.
**Rnd 1:** ch2, hdc7, hdc2 in next st, (hdc8, hdc2 in next st) 11 times [120]
Cut yarn and fasten off, leaving a 3 yard (2.6 m) long tail.

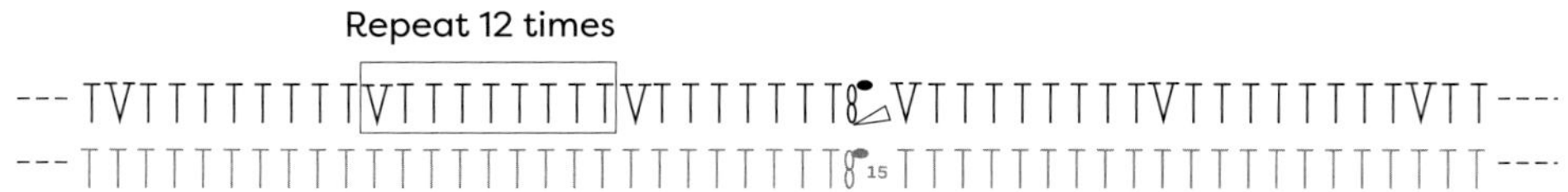

09.10

# Ice Cream Cones

SHOWN ON PAGE 14

Finished Size:
For 9: 8¼" (21 cm) diameter x 17¾" (45 cm) tall
For 10: 7¼" (18.5 cm) diameter x 23½" (60 cm) tall

## TOOLS & MATERIALS

### Yarn

#### For 09

- 100% acrylic bulky-weight yarn
  - 145 yds (132 m) in white
  - 66 yds (60 m) in dark beige
  - 14 yds (12 m) in bright pink
  - 14 yds (12 m) in aqua blue
  - 79 yds (72 m) in light pink
  - 79 yds (72 m) in pink
  - 79 yds (72 m) in dark pink
  - 27 yds (24 m) in off-white

#### For 10

- 100% acrylic bulky-weight yarn
  - 145 yds (132 m) in white
  - 66 yds (60 m) in dark beige
  - 14 yds (12 m) in bright pink
  - 14 yds (12 m) in aqua blue
  - 210 yds (192 m) in lime green
  - 92 yds (84 m) in light orange
  - 92 yds (84 m) in orange

### Other Materials

- 280 g of polyester stuffing for 9 and 360 g for 10
- 15 pompoms (for 10 only): ½" (1.2 cm) diameter in three colors (five of each color)

### Tools

- US L-11 (8 mm) crochet hook
- Yarn needle

## CONSTRUCTION STEPS

#### For 09–10

Note: Use 2 strands of yarn throughout.

**1.** Crochet the cone: Make 6 single crochet in magic ring and continue as instructed in diagram or written instructions.

**2.** Crochet the first scoop: Make 8 half double crochet in magic ring and continue as instructed in diagram or written instructions. For 09, change color as shown. Cut yarn, leaving a 1½ yard (1.3 m) long tail.

**3.** Fill the cone and first scoop with polyester stuffing. Whipstitch the first scoop to the cone using the yarn tail from step 2. When stitching, scoop inside half loop only on the ice cream and scoop top half loop of the slip stitch on the cone.

**4.** Work into the remaining half loop from step 3 and crochet the frilled edge.

#### For 10 Only

**5.** Crochet the second scoop as instructed in diagram or written instructions. Cut yarn, leaving a 1¼ yard (1.2 m) long tail. Stuff and sew on top of the first scoop, scooping inside half stitch of the second scoop.

**6.** As in step 4, scoop the remaining half loop of step 5 and crochet the frilled edge.

**7.** Sew on pompoms.

## CROCHET INSTRUCTIONS

### Cone

With white and US L-11 hook, make a magic ring.
**Rnd 1:** ch1 (does not count as a st throughout), sc6 in magic ring, slst in beg ch1 [6]
Place stitch marker in first st of rnd 1 and move it up after each round
**Rnd 2:** ch1, (sc1, sc2 in next st) 3 times, slst in beg ch1 [9]
**Rnd 3:** ch1, (sc2 in next st, sc2) 3 times, slst in beg ch1 [12]
**Rnd 4:** ch1, sc2, (sc2 in next st, sc3) twice, sc2 in next st, sc1, slst in beg ch1 [15]
**Rnd 5:** ch1, (sc4, sc2 in next st) 3 times, slst in beg ch1 [18]
**Rnd 6:** ch1, sc1 in each st, slst in beg ch1
**Rnd 7:** ch1, sc1, (sc2 in next st, sc5) twice, sc2 in next st, sc4, slst in beg ch1 [21]
**Rnd 8:** As rnd 6
**Rnd 9:** ch1, sc3, (sc2 in next st, sc6) twice, sc2 in next st, sc3, slst in beg ch1 [24]
**Rnd 10:** As rnd 6
**Rnd 11:** ch1, sc6, (sc2 in next st, sc7) twice, sc2 in next st, sc1, slst in beg ch1 [27]
**Rnd 12:** As rnd 6
**Rnd 13:** ch1, (sc2 in next st, sc8) 3 times, slst in beg ch1 [30]
**Rnd 14:** As rnd 6
**Rnd 15:** ch1, sc6, (sc2 in next st, sc9) twice, sc2 in next st, sc3, slst in beg ch1 [33]
**Rnd 16:** As rnd 6
**Rnd 17:** ch1, (sc10, sc2 in next st) 3 times, slst in beg ch1 [36]
**Rnd 18:** As rnd 6
**Rnd 19:** ch1, sc2, (sc2 in next st, sc11) twice, sc2 in next st, sc9, slst in beg ch1 [39]
**Rnd 20:** As rnd 6
**Rnd 21:** ch1, sc6, (sc2 in next st, sc12) twice, sc2 in next st, sc6, slst in beg ch1 [42]
**Rnd 22:** As rnd 6
**Rnd 23:** ch1, sc10, (sc2 in next st, sc13) twice, sc2 in next st, sc3, slst in beg ch1 [45]
Change to aqua blue
**Rnd 24:** As rnd 6
Change to white
**Rnd 25:** ch1, sc4 BLO, (sc2 BLO in next st, sc14 BLO) twice, sc2 BLO in next st, sc10 BLO, slst in beg ch1 [48]
Change to bright pink
**Rnd 24:** ch1, sc1 BLO in each st, slst in beg ch1
Change to white
**Rnd 27:** ch1, sc9 BLO, (sc2 BLO in next st, sc15 BLO) twice, sc2 BLO in next st, sc6 BLO, slst in beg ch1 [51]
**Rnd 28:** as rnd 6
Change to dark beige
**Rnd 29:** ch1, sc25 BLO, sc2 BLO in next st, sc25 BLO, slst in beg ch1 [52]
**Rnd 30:** ch1, sc2 BLO, (FPdc 2 sts to right on 1 rnd below leaving last 2 loops on hook, FPdc 2 sts to left on 1 rnd below leaving last 2 loops on hook, yrh and pull through all 4 loops, sc3 BLO) 12 times, FPdc 2 sts to right on 1 rnd below leaving last 2 loops on hook, FPdc 2 sts to left on 1 rnd below leaving last 2 loops on hook, yrh and pull through all 4 loops, sc1 BLO, slst in beg ch1
**Rnd 31:** ch1, (sc2 in next st, sc12) 4 times, slst in beg ch1 [56]
**Rnd 32:** ch1, *(FPdc 2 sts to right on 1 rnd below leaving last 2 loops on hook, FPdc 2 sts to left on 1 rnd below leaving last 2 loops on hook, yrh and pull through all 4 loops, sc3 BLO) twice**, FPdc 2 sts to right on 1 rnd below leaving last 2 loops on hook, FPdc 2 sts to left on 1 rnd below leaving last 2 loops on hook, yrh and pull through all 4 loops, sc4 BLO*, rep from * to * twice more, then rep instructions in bracket from * to ** three times instead of twice, FPdc 2 sts to right on 1 rnd below leaving last 2 loops on hook, FPdc 2 sts to left on 1 rnd below leaving last 2 loops on hook, yrh and pull through all 4 loops, sc4 BLO, slst in beg ch1
**Rnd 33:** slst in each st, slst in first slst
Cut yarn and fasten off.

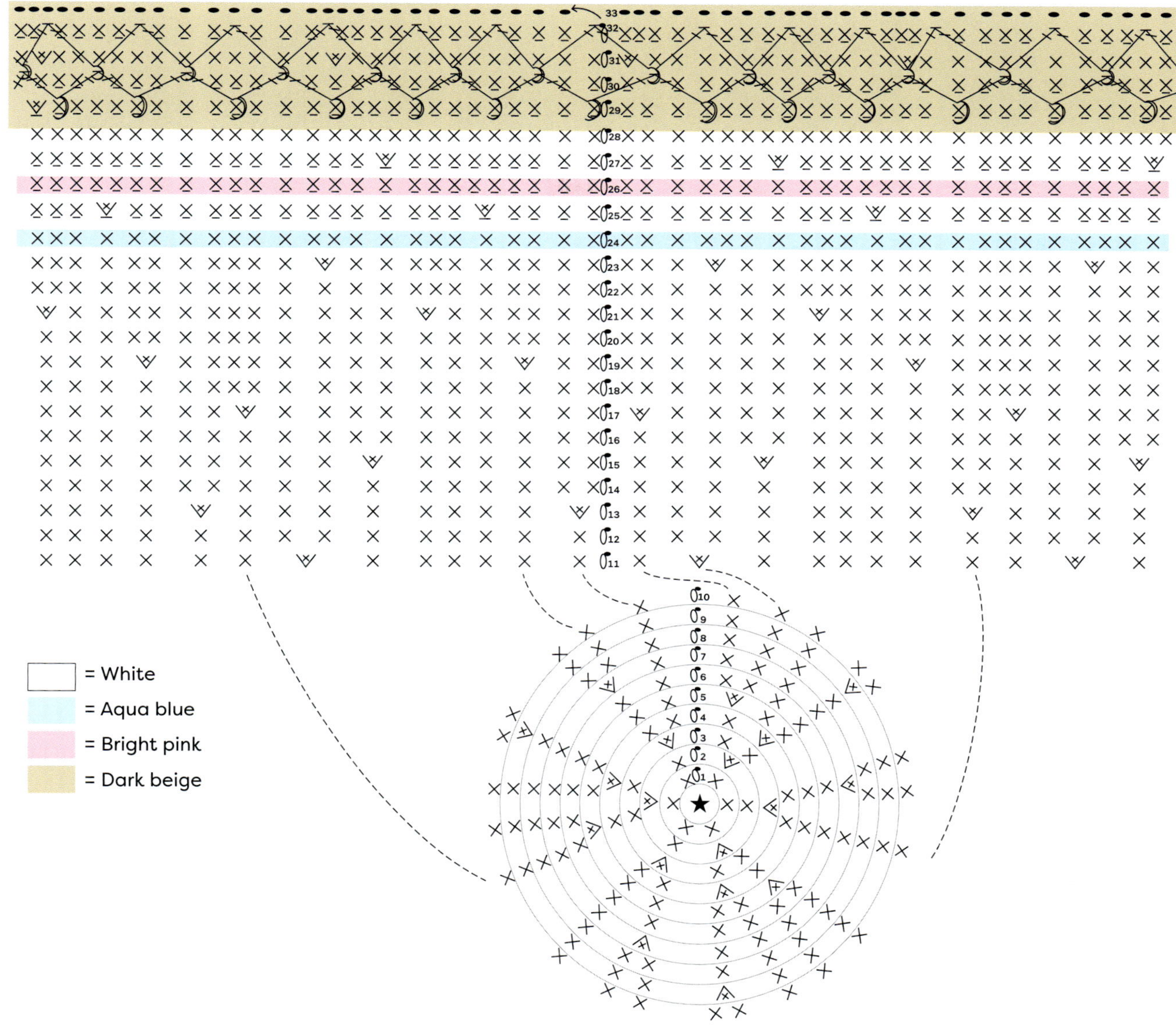


## For 09: First Scoop

With dark pink and US L-11 hook, make a magic ring.

**Rnd 1:** ch2 (counts as first hdc throughout), hdc7 in magic ring, slst in top of beg ch2 [8]

Place stitch marker in first st of rnd 1 and move it up after each round

**Rnd 2:** ch2, hdc1 in same st at base of ch2, (hdc2 in next st) 7 times, slst in top of beg ch2 [16]

**Rnd 3:** ch2, hdc2 in next st, hdc1, hdc2 in next st, change to dark pink + pink, (hdc1, hdc2 in next st) 6 times, slst in top of beg ch2 [24]

**Rnd 4:** ch2, hdc1 in same st at base of ch2, hdc2, (hdc2 in next st, hdc2) twice, change to pink, (hdc2 in next st, hdc2) 5 times, slst in top of beg ch2 [32]

**Rnd 5:** ch2, hdc1, hdc2 in next st, hdc3, hdc2 in next st, hdc1, change to pink + light pink, hdc2, (hdc2 in next st, hdc3,) 5 times, hdc2 in next st, hdc1, slst in top of beg ch2 [40]

Change to light pink.

**Rnd 6:** ch2, hdc3, (hdc2 in next st, hdc4) 4 times, hdc2 in next st, change to light pink + off-white, (hdc4, hdc2 in next st) 3 times, slst in top of beg ch2 [48]

**Rnd 7:** ch2, hdc2 in next st, hdc5, hdc2 in next st, hdc2, change to dark pink, hdc3, (hdc2 in next st, hdc5) twice, hdc2 in next st, hdc1, change to dark pink +pink, hdc4, (hdc2 in next st, hdc5) twice, hdc2 in next st, change to pink, hdc4, slst in top of beg ch2 [56]

**Rnd 8:** ch2, hdc2, hdc2 in next st, hdc6, hdc2 in next st, hdc3, change to pink + light pink, hdc3, (hdc2 in next st, hdc6) twice, hdc2 in next st, changing to light pink on second of these sts, (hdc6, hdc2 in next st) twice, hdc3, change to light pink + off-white, hdc3, hdc2 in next st, hdc3, slst in top of beg ch2 [64]

**Rnd 9:** ch2, hdc11, change to dark pink, hdc20, change to dark pink + pink, hdc 20. Change to pink, hdc12, slst in top of beg ch2

**Rnd 10:** ch2, hdc7, change to pink + light pink, hdc20, change to light pink, hdc20, change to light pink + off-white, hdc16, slst in top of beg ch2

**Rnd 11:** ch2, hdc3, change to dark pink, hdc20, change to dark pink + pink, hdc20, change to pink, hdc20, change to pink + light pink, slst in top of beg ch2

**Rnd 12:** ch2, hdc2, hdc2tog, (hdc6, hdc2tog) twice, hdc2, change to light pink, hdc4, (hdc2tog, hdc6) twice, hdc2tog, hdc1, change to light pink + off-white, hdc5, hdc2tog, hdc6, hdc2tog, hdc3, slst in top of beg ch2 [56]

**Rnd 13:** ch2, hdc3, change to dark pink, hdc20, change to dark pink + pink, hdc20, change to pink, hdc12, slst in top of beg ch2

**Rnd 14:** ch2, hdc7, change to pink + light pink, hdc20, change to light pink, hdc20, change to light pink + off-white, hdc8, slst in top of beg ch2

Cut yarn and fasten off, leaving a 1½ yard (1.3 m) long tail. Make up following steps 3–4 on page 63. The frill will be added after the first scoop is attached to the cone.

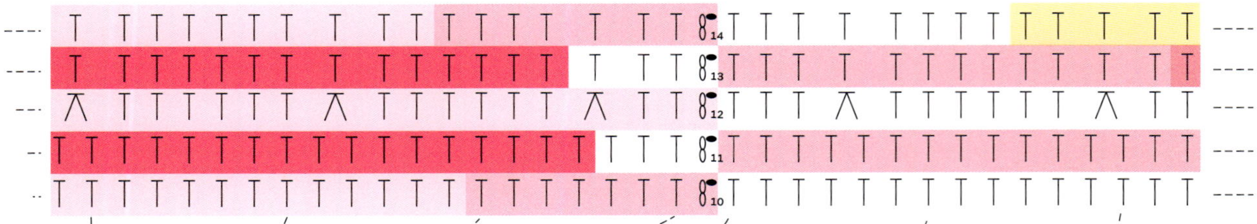

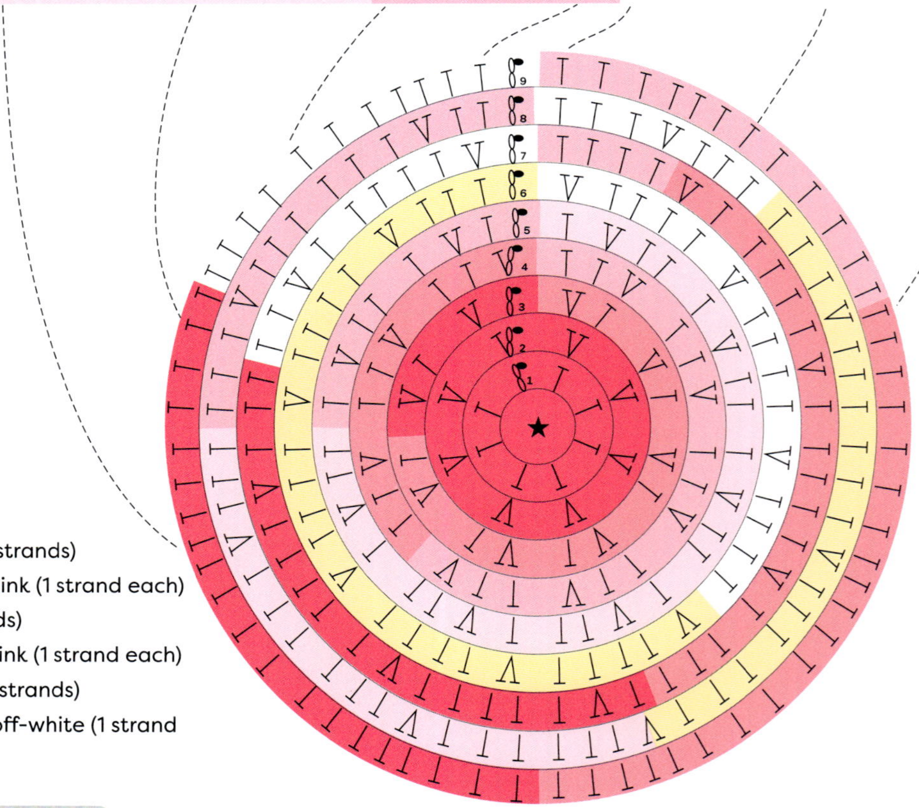

Note: Alternate yarn color every 30 stitches until midway through round 7, then alternate color every 20 stitches for the remaining rounds.

= Dark pink (2 strands)

= Dark pink + pink (1 strand each)

= Pink (2 strands)

= Pink + light pink (1 strand each)

= Light pink (2 strands)

= Light pink + off-white (1 strand each)

## For 09: Frilled Edge

Join off-white to first st, and ch1, (sc3 in next st) 4 times, change to dark pink, (sc3 in next st) 10 times, change to dark pink + pink, (sc3 in next st) 10 times, change to pink, (sc3 in next st) 10 times, change to pink + light pink, (sc3 in next st) 10 times, change to light pink, (sc3 in next st) to end, slst in beg ch1. Cut yarn and fasten off.

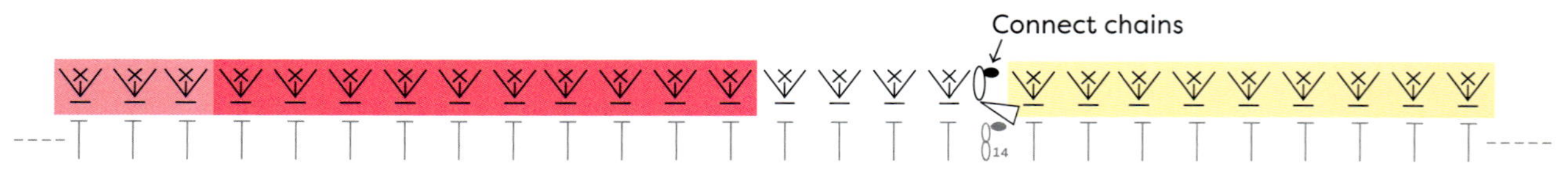

After making the first 13 stitches, change yarn color every 30 stitches

## For 10: First Scoop and Frilled Edge

Follow instructions for 09 on pages 65-66, working in lime throughout.

## For 10: Second Scoop

Using light orange + orange held together, work as given for first scoop to end of rnd 7, ignoring any color change instruction.

**Rnds 8–10:** ch2, hdc1 in each st, slst in top of beg ch2 (3 rnds)

**Rnd 11:** ch2, hdc2tog, (hdc5, hdc2tog) 7 times, hdc4, slst in top of beg ch2 [48]

**Rnds 12–13:** ch2, hdc1 in each st, slst in top of beg ch2 (2 rnds)

Cut yarn and fasten off, leaving a 1¼ yard (1.2 m) long tail. Make up following steps 5–7 on page 63. The frill will be added after the second scoop is attached to the first one.

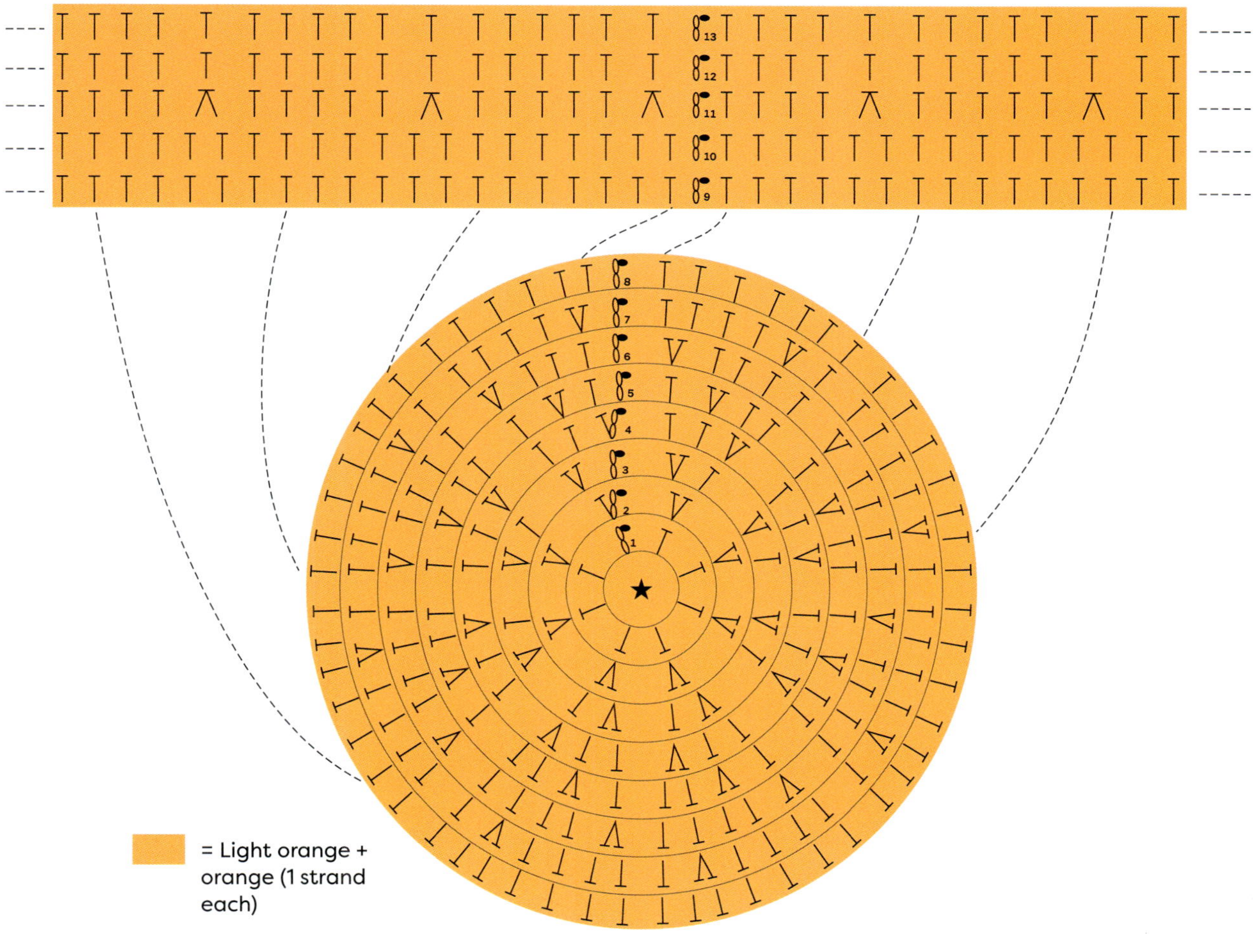

= Light orange + orange (1 strand each)

## For 10: Frilled Edge

Join light orange + orange to first st, and ch1, (sc3 in next st) to end, slst in beg ch1. Cut yarn and fasten off.

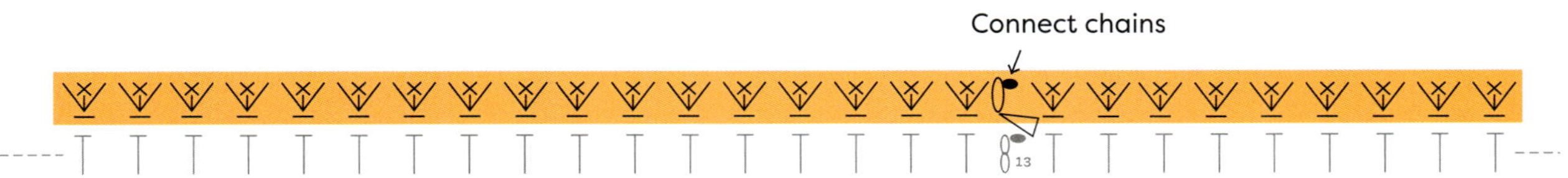

11

# Lollipop

**SHOWN ON PAGE 16**

Finished Size:
Candy: 13½" (34 cm) diameter x 2¼" (5.5 cm) tall
Stick: 2¼" (5.5 cm) diameter x 12¾" (32 cm) tall

## TOOLS & MATERIALS

### Yarn

- 100% acrylic bulky-weight yarn
  - 171 yds (156 m) in white
  - 92 yds (84 m) in beige
  - 66 yds (60 m) in lemon
  - 66 yds (60 m) in orange
  - 66 yds (60 m) in light blue
  - 66 yds (60 m) in dark pink
  - 66 yds (60 m) in lime green

### Other Materials

- 220 g of polyester stuffing
- Two 14¼" (36 cm) long x ⅛" (3 mm) diameter bamboo skewers
- 1 yard (1 m) of 2½" (6 cm) wide ribbon (optional)

### Tools

- US L-11 (8 mm) crochet hook
- Yarn needle

## CONSTRUCTION STEPS

Note: Use 2 strands of yarn throughout.

**1.** Crochet the candy: Make 7 half double crochet in magic ring and continue until round 120, adding polyester stuffing as you work. Cut the yarn, leaving a 16" (40 cm) long tail. Use whipstitch to sew the tube closed at the end of round 120. Wrap the tube in a spiral, starting at the center and working outward. As you wrap, sew adjacent white sections together to hold the spiral in place (see **Figure A**).

**2.** Crochet the stick: Make 8 single crochet in magic ring and continue until round 31. Cut the yarn, leaving a 16" (40 cm) long tail.

**3.** Insert the bamboo skewers and polyester stuffing into the crocheted stick. The bamboo skewers should extend about 6¼" (16 cm) beyond the crocheted stick. (see **Figure B**).

**4.** Insert the ends of the bamboo skewers into the candy. Sew the candy to the crocheted stick (see **Figure C**).

**5.** Tie the ribbon around the stick and make a bow (optional).

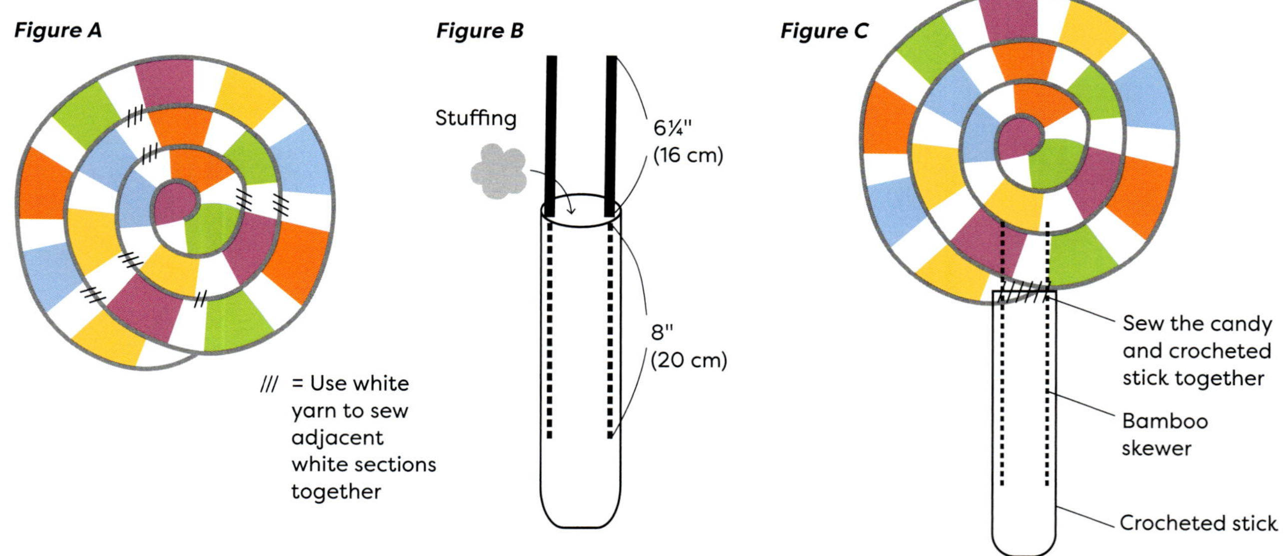

## CROCHET INSTRUCTIONS

### Candy

With dark pink and US L-11 hook, make a magic ring.
**Rnd 1:** ch2 (counts as first hdc throughout), hdc6 in magic ring, slst in top of beg ch2 [7]
Place stitch marker in first st of rnd 1 and move it up after each round
**Rnd 2:** ch2, hdc1 in same st as ch2, (hdc2 in next st) 6 times, slst in top of beg ch2 [14]
**Rnds 3–4:** ch2, hdc13, slst in top of beg ch2 (2 rnds)
Change to white
**Rnds 5–6:** ch2, hdc13, slst in in top of beg ch2 (2 rnds)
Change to lime green
**Rnds 7–10:** ch2, hdc13, slst in in top of beg ch2 (4 rnds)
Change to white
**Rnds 11–12:** as rnds 5–6 (2 rnds)
Begin to stuff, adding more stuffing as you go.
Change to orange
**Rnds 13–16:** as rnds 7–10 (4 rnds)
Change to white
**Rnds 17–18:** as rnds 5–6 (2 rnds)
Change to light blue
**Rnds 19–22:** as rnds 7–10 (4 rnds)
Change to white
**Rnds 23–24:** as rnds 5–6 (2 rnds)
Change to lemon
**Rnds 25–28:** as rnds 7–10 (4 rnds)
Change to white
**Rnds 29–30:** as rnds 5–6 (2 rnds)
*Change to dark pink
**Rnds 31–34:** as rnds 7–10 (4 rnds)
Change to white
**Rnds 35–36:** as rnds 5–6 (2 rnds)
Change to lime green
**Rnds 37–40:** as rnds 7–10 (4 rnds)
Change to white
**Rnds 41–42:** as rnds 5–6 (2 rnds)
Change to orange
**Rnds 43–46:** as rnds 7–10 (4 rnds)
Change to white
**Rnds 47–48:** as rnds 5–6 (2 rnds)
Change to light blue
**Rnds 49–52:** as rnds 7–10 (4 rnds)
Change to white
**Rnds 53–54:** as rnds 5–6 (2 rnds)
Change to lemon
**Rnds 55–58:** as rnds 7–10 (4 rnds)
Change to white
**Rnds 59–60:** as rnds 5–6 (2 rnds)*
**Rnds 61–120:** rep from * to * twice more (60 rnds)
Cut yarn and fasten off, leaving a 16" (40 cm) long tail. Make up following step 1 instructions on page 68.

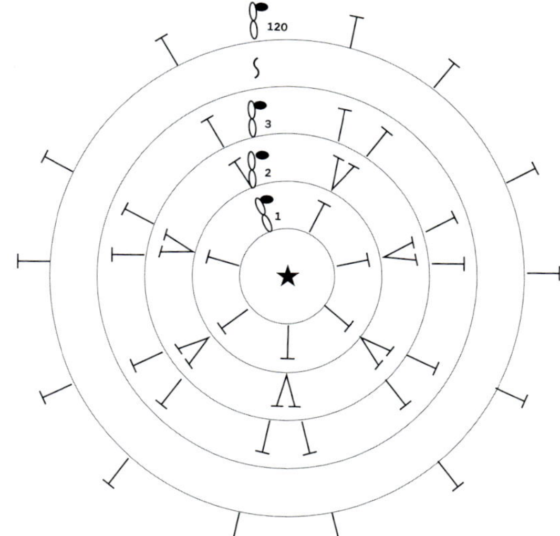


### Stick

With beige and US L-11 hook, make a magic ring.
**Rnd 1:** ch1 (does not count as a st throughout), sc8 in magic ring, slst in beg ch1 [8]
Place stitch marker in first st of rnd 1 and move it up after each round
**Rnd 2:** ch1, (sc2 in next st) 8 times, slst in beg ch1 [16]
**Rnd 3:** ch1, sc16, slst in beg ch1
**Rnds 4–31:** as rnd 3 (28 rnds)
Cut yarn and fasten off, leaving a 16" (40 cm) long tail. Make up following steps 3–5 on page 68.

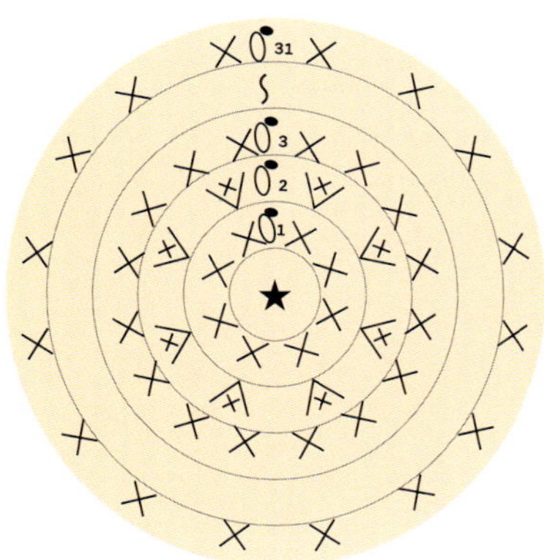

12

# Polka Dot Candy

**SHOWN ON PAGE 17**

Finished Size:
27½" (70 cm) long x
6¼" (16 cm) tall

## TOOLS & MATERIALS

### Yarn

- 100% acrylic bulky-weight yarn
  - 329 yds (300 m) in aqua blue
  - 184 yds (168 m) in white
  - 105 yds (96 m) in light purple

### Other Materials

- 370 g of polyester stuffing

### Tools

- US N-15 (10 mm) crochet hook
- Yarn needle

Refer to page 42 for crochet technique photos for this project.

## CONSTRUCTION STEPS

Note: Use 2 strands of yarn throughout.

**1.** Crochet the body: Make 12 foundation chains, join into a loop work in single crochet, following the diagram or written instructions. Work in center single crochet from round 2 until round 53. From round 52, start to fill with polyester stuffing as you crochet.

**2.** Crochet one frill: Join the light purple yarn to round 53 of the body and crochet as instructed.

**3.** Crochet another frill: At the opposite end, work into the spare loop from the foundation chain of the body and crochet another frill as instructed.

**4.** Thread matching yarn through round 1 of the frills, one stitch at a time, and sew running stitches around, then gather. Fasten off (refer to page 47).

## CROCHET INSTRUCTIONS

### Body

With aqua blue and US N-15 hook, ch12, slst in first chain to form a ring.

**Rnd 1:** ch1 (does not count as a st throughout), sc12 into ring, slst in beg ch1 [12]

Place stitch marker in first st of rnd 1 and move it up after each round. Work in center single crochet for rnds 2–53.

**Rnd 2:** ch1, (sc1, sc2 in next st) 6 times, slst in beg ch1 [18]

**Rnd 3:** ch1, (sc2 in next st, sc2) 6 times, slst in beg ch1 [24]

**Rnd 4:** ch1, sc2, (sc2 in next st, sc3) 5 times, sc2 in next st, sc1, slst in beg ch1 [30]

**Rnd 5:** ch1, (sc4, sc2 in next st) 6 times, slst in beg ch1 [36]

**Rnd 6:** ch1, (sc8, sc2 in next st) 4 times, slst in beg ch1 [40]

**Rnds 7–8:** ch1, sc1 in each st, slst in beg ch1 (2 rounds)

Join white.

**Rnd 9:** in aqua blue ch1, sc4, in white sc2, (in aqua blue sc8, in white sc2) 3 times, in aqua blue sc4, slst in beg ch1

**Rnd 10:** in aqua blue ch1, sc3, in white sc4, (in aqua blue sc6, in white sc4) 3 times, in aqua blue sc3, slst in beg ch1

**Rnds 11–14:** in aqua blue ch1, sc2, in white sc6, (in aqua blue sc4, in white sc6) 3 times, in aqua blue sc2, slst in beg ch1 (4 rounds)

**Rnd 15:** as rnd 10

**Rnd 16:** as rnd 9

**Rnds 17–18:** in aqua blue, work as rnds 7–8 (2 rounds)

**Rnd 19:** in white ch1, sc1, in aqua blue sc8, (in white sc2, in aqua blue sc8) 3 times, in white sc1, slst in beg ch1

**Rnd 20:** in white ch1, sc2, in aqua blue sc6, (in white sc4, in aqua blue sc6) 3 times, in white sc2, slst in beg ch1

**Rnds 21–24:** in white ch1, sc3, in aqua blue sc4, (in white sc6, in aqua blue sc4) 3 times, in white sc3, slst in beg ch1 (3 rounds)

**Rnd 25:** As rnd 20

**Rnd 26:** As rnd 19

**Rnds 27–28:** in aqua blue, work as rnds 7–8 (2 rounds)

**Rnds 29–48:** As rnds 9–28 (20 rnds)

Continue in aqua blue only.

**Rnd 49:** ch1, (sc8, sc2tog) 4 times, slst in beg ch1 [36]

Add polyester stuffing, then continue crocheting.

**Rnd 50:** ch1, (sc4, sc2tog) 6 times, slst in beg ch1 [30]

**Rnd 51:** ch1, sc2, (sc2tog, sc3) 5 times, sc2tog, sc1, slst in beg ch1 [24]

**Rnd 52:** ch1, (sc2tog, sc2) 6 times, slst in beg ch1 [18]

**Rnd 53:** ch1, (sc1, sc2tog) 6 times, slst in beg ch1 [12]

Add more stuffing if needed, then cut yarn and fasten off.

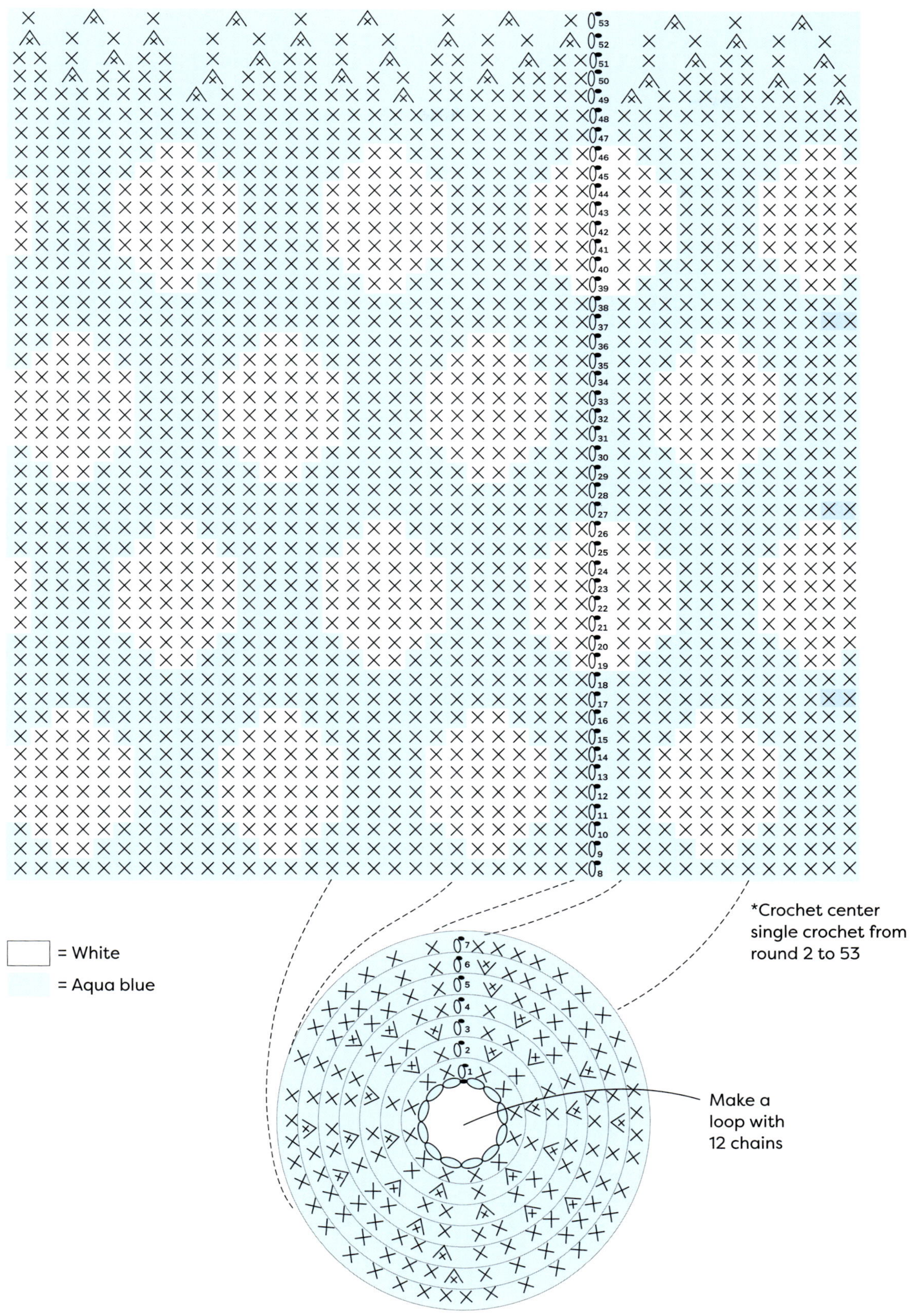

= White
= Aqua blue
*Crochet center single crochet from round 2 to 53
Make a loop with 12 chains

## Frills (make 2)

With light purple and US N-15 hook, start at rnd 53 of body and join yarn with slst in any st.

**Rnd 1:** ch1 (does not count as a st throughout), sc1 in same st, (ch3, sc1 in next st) 11 times, ch1, hdc in first sc (counts as last ch3-sp) [12 ch3-sps, 12 sc]

**Rnd 2:** ch1, sc1 in same sp, (ch4, sc1 in next ch-sp) 11 times, ch2, hdc in first sc (counts as last ch4-sp) [12 ch4-sps, 12 sc]

**Rnd 3:** ch1, sc1 in same sp, ch4, sc1 in next ch-sp, *(ch4, sc1, ch4, sc1) all in next ch-sp, (ch4, sc1 in next ch-sp) 3 times*; rep from * to * once more, (ch4, sc1, ch4, sc1) all in next ch-sp, (ch4, sc1 in next ch-sp) once, ch2, hdc in first sc (counts as last ch4-sp) [15 ch4-sps, 15 sc]

**Rnd 4:** ch1, sc1 in same sp, (ch5, sc1 in next ch-sp) 14 times, ch2, dc in first sc (counts as last ch5-sp) [15 ch5-sps, 15 sc]

**Rnd 5:** ch1, sc1 in same sp, (ch5, sc1 in next ch-sp) twice *(ch5, sc1, ch5, sc1) all in next ch-sp, (ch5, sc1 in next ch-sp) 4 times*; rep from * to * once more, (ch5, sc1, ch5, sc1) all in next ch-sp, (ch5, sc1) in next ch-sp, ch2, dc in first sc (counts as last ch5-sp) [18 ch5-sps, 18 sc]
Change to white.

**Rnd 6:** ch1, sc1 in same ch-sp, (ch5, sc1 in next ch-sp) 17 times, ch5, slst in beg ch1, fasten off.

At opposite end, join light purple with slst in any st (working into spare loops of foundation ch). Repeat Frill instructions from Rnd 1 to end.

Finish off following step 4 instructions on page 70.

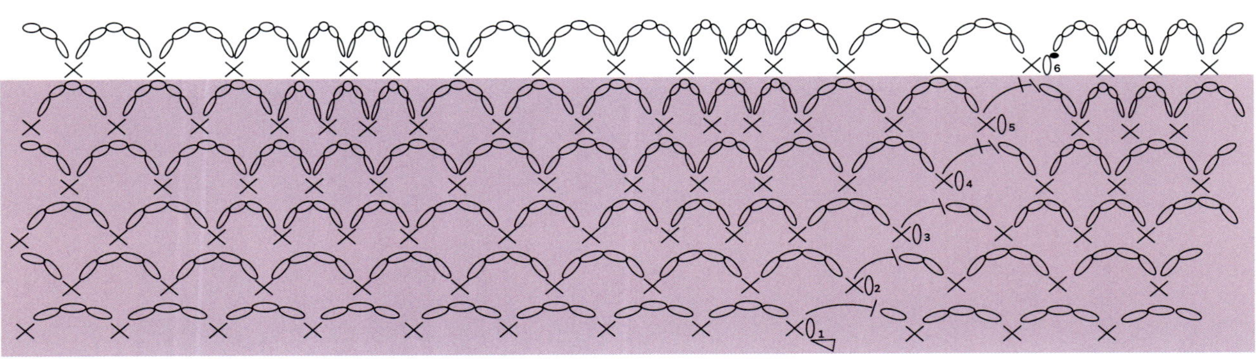


= White

= Light purple

13

# Striped Candy

**SHOWN ON PAGE 17**

Finished Size:
19¾" (50 cm) long x
8¾" (22 cm) tall

## TOOLS & MATERIALS

### Yarn

- 100% acrylic bulky-weight yarn
  - 184 yds (168 m) in lemon
  - 171 yds (156 m) in rose pink
  - 132 yds (120 m) in ice green
  - 119 yds (108 m) in white

### Other Materials

- 300 g of polyester stuffing

### Tools

- US L-11 (8 mm) crochet hook
- Yarn needle

## CONSTRUCTION STEPS

Note: Use 2 strands of yarn throughout.

**1.** Crochet the body: Make 8 half double crochet in magic ring and continue through round 25, changing color as instructed. Fill with polyester stuffing. Continue crocheting as instructed until completing round 27, then fill a bit more. Cut the yarn, leaving a 12" (30 cm) long tail. Use a yarn needle and the tail to gather up the stitches from round 27 and close the hole.

**2.** Make the frills by crocheting into the unworked FLO on rounds 2 and 25 of the body.

**3.** Thread matching yarn through round 1 of the frills, one stitch at a time, and sew running stitches around, then gather. Fasten off (refer to page 47).

## CROCHET INSTRUCTIONS

### Body

With rose pink and US L-11 hook, make a magic ring.
**Rnd 1:** ch2 (counts as first hdc throughout), hdc7 in magic ring, slst in top of beg ch2 [8]
Place stitch marker in first st of rnd 1 and move it up after each round
**Rnd 2:** ch2, hdc1 in same st at base of ch2, (hdc2 in next st) 7 times, slst in top of beg ch2 [16]
**Rnd 3:** ch2, (hdc2 BLO in next st, hdc1 BLO) 7 times, hdc2 BLO in next st, slst in top of beg ch2 [24]
**Rnd 4:** ch2, hdc1 in same st at base of ch2, (hdc2, hdc2 in next st) 7 times, hdc2, slst in top of beg ch2 [32]
**Rnd 5:** ch2, hdc1, (hdc2 in next st, hdc3) 7 times, hdc2 in next st, hdc1, slst in top of beg ch2 [40]
**Rnd 6:** ch2, hdc3, (hdc2 in next st, hdc4) 7 times, hdc2 in next st, slst in top of beg ch2 [48]
**Rnd 7:** ch2, (hdc2 in next st, hdc5) 7 times, hdc2 in next st, hdc4, slst in top of beg ch2 [56]
**Rnd 8:** ch2, hdc1 in each st, slst in top of beg ch2
**Rnd 9:** ch2, hdc6, (hdc2 in next st, hdc7) 6 times, hdc2 in next st, slst in top of beg ch2 [63]
Change to white.
**Rnd 10:** as rnd 8
Change to lemon.
**Rnd 11:** ch2, hdc3, (hdc2 in next st, hdc8) 6 times, hdc2 in next st, hdc4, slst in top of beg ch2 [70]
Change to ice green.
**Rnd 12:** as rnd 8
Change to white.
**Rnd 13:** ch1 (does not count as a st), sc1 in each st, slst in beg ch1
Change to ice green.
**Rnd 14:** as rnd 8
Change to white.
**Rnd 15:** as rnd 13
Change to ice green.
**Rnd 16:** as rnd 8, working every st in BLO
Change to lemon.
**Rnd 17:** ch2, hdc3, (hdc2tog, hdc8) 6 times, hdc2tog, hdc4, slst in top of beg ch2 [63]
Change to white.
**Rnd 18:** as rnd 8
Change to rose pink.
**Rnd 19:** ch2, hdc6, (hdc2tog, hdc7) 6 times, hdc2tog, slst in top of beg ch2 [56]
**Rnd 20:** as rnd 8
**Rnd 21:** ch2, (hdc2tog, hdc5) 7 times, hdc2tog, hdc4, slst in top of beg ch2 [48]
**Rnd 22:** ch2, hdc3, (hdc2tog, hdc4) 7 times, hdc2tog, slst in top of beg ch2 [40]
**Rnd 23:** ch2, hdc1, (hdc2tog, hdc3) 7 times, hdc2tog, hdc1, slst in top of beg ch2 [32]

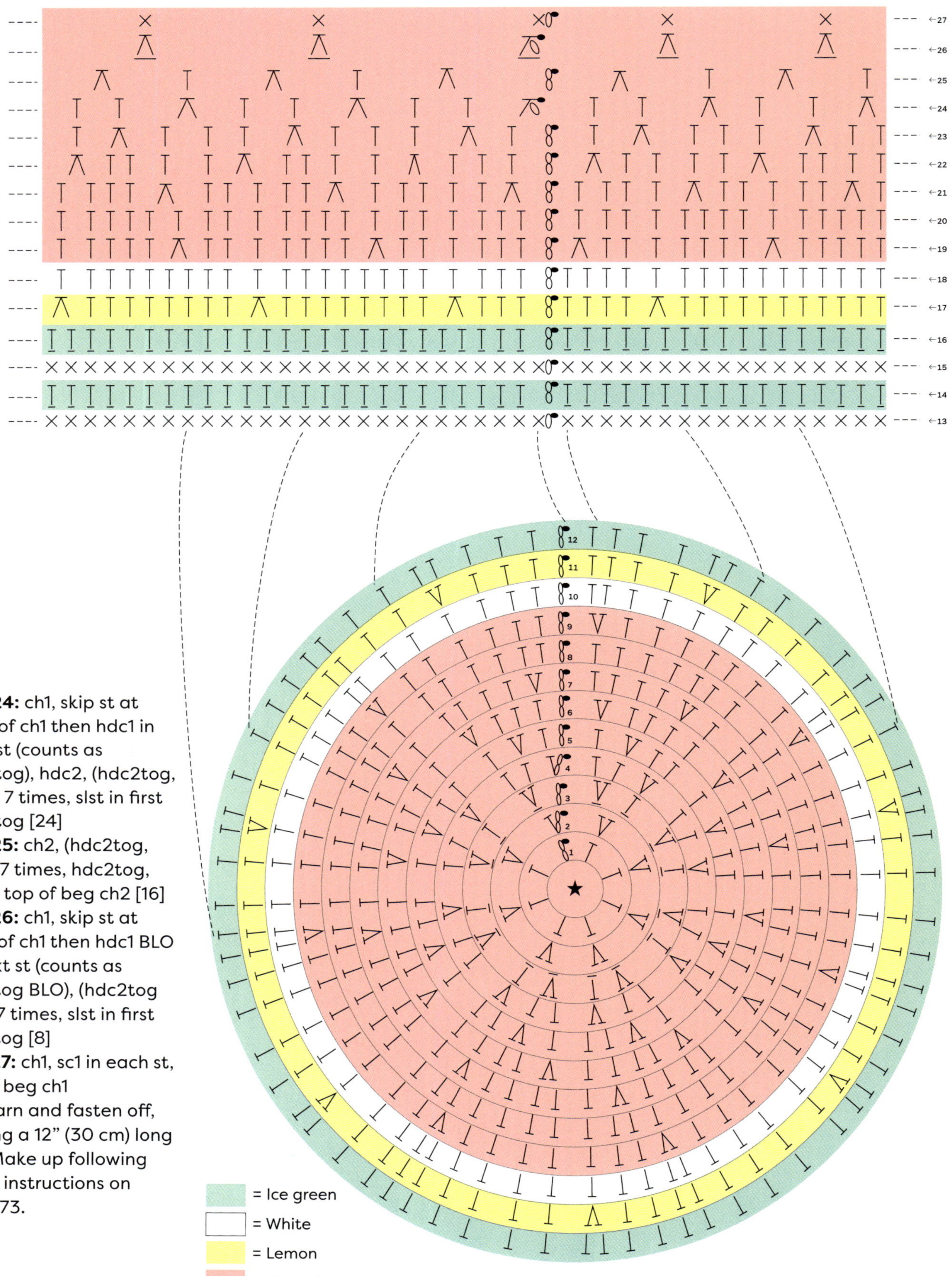


**Rnd 24:** ch1, skip st at base of ch1 then hdc1 in next st (counts as hdc2tog), hdc2, (hdc2tog, hdc2) 7 times, slst in first hdc2tog [24]

**Rnd 25:** ch2, (hdc2tog, hdc1) 7 times, hdc2tog, slst in top of beg ch2 [16]

**Rnd 26:** ch1, skip st at base of ch1 then hdc1 BLO in next st (counts as hdc2tog BLO), (hdc2tog BLO) 7 times, slst in first hdc2tog [8]

**Rnd 27:** ch1, sc1 in each st, slst in beg ch1

Cut yarn and fasten off, leaving a 12" (30 cm) long tail. Make up following step 1 instructions on page 73.

## Frills (make 2)

With lemon and US L-11 hook, work into the spare front loops from rnd 2.
Join into beg ch2 with a slst.
**Rnd 1:** ch3 (counts as first dc), dc1 in same st at base of ch3, (dc2 in next st) 15 times, slst in beg ch3 [32]
**Rnd 2:** ch3, (dc2 in next st, dc1) 15 times, dc2 in next st, slst in top of beg ch3 [48]
**Rnd 3:** ch3, dc1 in same st at base of ch3, (dc2, dc2 in next st) 15 times, dc2, slst in top of beg ch3 [64]
**Rnd 4:** ch3, dc1, (dc2 in next st, dc3) 15 times, dc2 in next st, dc1, slst in top of beg ch3 [80]
Change to white
**Rnd 5:** ch3, dc3, (dc2 in next st, dc4) 15 times, dc2 in next st, slst in top of beg ch3 [96]
Change to ice green
**Rnd 6:** ch3, (dc2 in next st, dc5) 15 times, dc2 in next st, dc4, slst in top of beg ch3 [112]
Cut yarn and fasten off.
Repeat rnds 1–6 for second frill, working into the spare front loops from rnd 25.

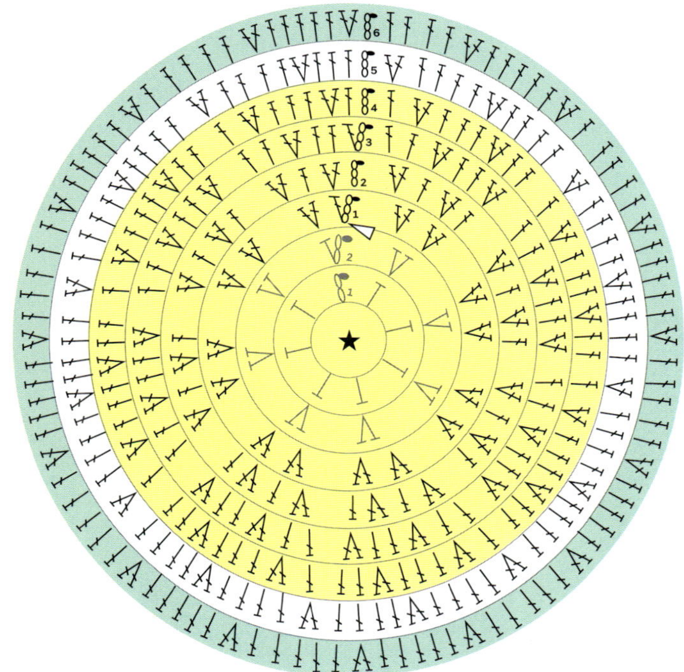


= Ice green
= White
= Lemon

14

# Burger

SHOWN ON PAGE 20

*See page 82 for the finished sizes of the components.*

## TOOLS & MATERIALS

### Yarn

***For the Buns***

- 100% acrylic bulky-weight yarn
  - 722 yds (660 m) in golden brown
  - 394 yds (360 m) in off-white
  - 14 yds (20 m) in beige

***For the Hamburger Patty***

- 100% acrylic bulky-weight yarn
  - 525 yds (480 m) in dark brown

***For the Tomato***

- 100% acrylic bulky-weight yarn
  - 197 yds (180 m) in cherry pink
  - 158 yds (144 m) in red
  - 145 yds (132 m) in red orange
  - 53 yds (48 m) in rose pink
  - 22 yds (20 m) in light orange

***For the Lettuce***

- 100% acrylic bulky-weight yarn
  - 197 yds (180 m) in lime green
  - 40 yds (36 m) in pistachio

***For the Cheese***

- 100% acrylic bulky-weight yarn
  - 302 yds (276 m) in lemon

### Other Materials

- 830 g of polyester stuffing (500 g for the buns, 230 g for the hamburger patty, and 100 g for the tomato)

### Tools

- US L-11 (8 mm) crochet hook
- Yarn needle

## CONSTRUCTION STEPS

Note: Use 2 strands of yarn throughout.

**1.** Crochet the bun components: Start with magic rings and crochet the top outside bun, two inside buns, and the bottom outside bun. For the inside buns, cut the yarn, leaving a 3 yard (2.6 m) long tail.

**2.** Assemble the buns: Align the top outside bun and one of the inside buns with right sides together. Use the yarn tail from the inside bun to whipstitch the two pieces together, scooping the inner half loop on the final round of the outside bun and two loops on the final round of the inside bun. After sewing around ⅔ of the bun, fill with polyester stuffing, and the continue sewing and stuffing to the end. Follow the same process to assemble the bottom bun.

**3.** Embroider the sesame seeds on the top bun (see **Figure A**).

**4.** Crochet the hamburger patty: Start with a magic ring and crochet through round 20. Make two pieces. Cut yarn, leaving a 3 yard (2.6 m) long tail for one piece.

**5.** Assemble the hamburger patty: Align the two pieces with right sides together. Use the yarn tail to whipstitch the two pieces together. After sewing around ⅔ of the patty, fill with polyester stuffing, and the continue sewing and stuffing to the end.

**6.** Crochet the tomato: Start with a magic ring and crochet one piece through round 20 and another piece through round 18, following the diagram or written instructions. Cut yarn, leaving a 3 yard (2.6 m) long tail for one piece.

**7.** Assemble the tomato: Align the two pieces with wrong sides together. Use the yarn tail to whipstitch the two pieces together. After sewing around ⅔ of the tomato, fill with polyester stuffing, and the continue sewing and stuffing to the end.

**8.** Embroider the seeds with straight stitch using 2 strands of light orange yarn (refer to diagram on page 80 for placement). Each stitch should be the length of three rounds of crochet.

**9.** Crochet the lettuce: Make 14 foundation chains and continue as you change the color of yarn as shown in the diagram and written instructions.

**10.** Crochet the cheese: Make 37 foundation chains and crochet through row 40. Continue to crochet the edge.

For the sesame seeds, embroider 40 straight stitches in a random pattern using 2 strands of off-white yarn. Each stitch should be the length of one round of crochet.

***Figure A***

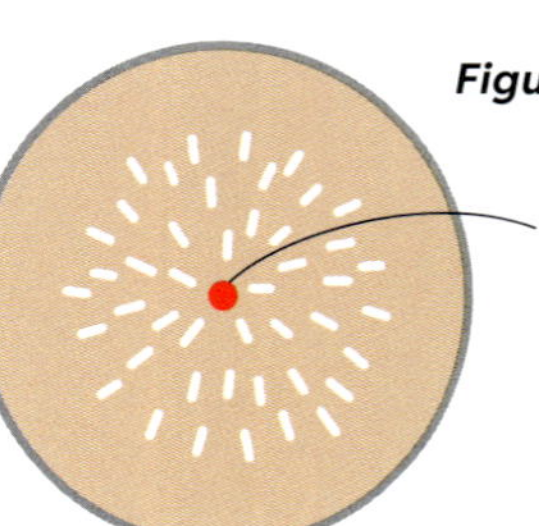

Embroider in a radial pattern, starting at the center and working outward

## CROCHET INSTRUCTIONS

### Top Outside Bun

With golden brown and US L-11 hook, make a magic ring.

**Rnd 1:** ch1 (does not count as a st throughout), sc6 in magic ring, slst in beg ch1 [6]

Place stitch marker in first st of rnd 1 and move it up after each round

**Rnd 2:** ch1, (sc2 in next st) 6 times, slst in beg ch1 [12]

**Rnd 3:** ch1, (sc1, sc2 in next st) 6 times, slst in beg ch1 [18]

**Rnd 4:** ch1, (sc2 in next st, sc2) 6 times, slst in beg ch1 [24]

**Rnd 5:** ch1, sc2, (sc2 in next st, sc3) 5 times, sc2 in next st, sc1, slst in beg ch1 [30]

**Rnd 6:** ch1, (sc4, sc2 in next st) 6 times, slst in beg ch1 [36]

**Rnd 7:** ch1, sc1, (sc2 in next st, sc5) 5 times, sc2 in next st, sc4, slst in beg ch1 [42]

**Rnd 8:** ch1, sc3, (sc2 in next st, sc6) 5 times, sc2 in next st, sc3, slst in beg ch1 [48]

**Rnd 9:** ch1, sc6, (sc2 in next st, sc7) 5 times, sc2 in next st, sc1, slst in beg ch1 [54]

**Rnd 10:** ch1, (sc2 in next st, sc8) 6 times, slst in beg ch1 [60]

**Rnd 11:** ch1, sc4, (sc2 in next st, sc9) 5 times, sc2 in next st, sc5, slst in beg ch1 [66]

**Rnd 12:** ch1, sc7, (sc2 in next st, sc10) 5 times, sc2 in next st, sc3, slst in beg ch1 [72]

**Rnd 13:** ch1, (sc11, sc2 in next st) 6 times, slst in beg ch1 [78]

**Rnd 14:** ch1, sc2, (sc2 in next st, sc12) 5 times, sc2 in next st, sc10, slst in beg ch1 [84]

**Rnd 15:** ch1, sc6, (sc2 in next st, sc13) 5 times, sc2 in next st, sc7, slst in beg ch1 [90]

**Rnd 16:** ch1, sc10, (sc2 in next st, sc14) 5 times, sc2 in next st, sc4, slst in beg ch1 [96]

**Rnd 17:** ch1, sc14, (sc2 in next st, sc15) 5 times, sc2 in next st, sc1, slst in beg ch1 [102]

**Rnd 18:** ch1, sc1, (sc2 in next st, sc16) 5 times, sc2 in next st, sc15, slst in beg ch1 [108]

**Rnd 19:** ch1, sc5, (sc2 in next st, sc17) 5 times, sc2 in next st, sc12, slst in beg ch1 [114]

**Rnd 20:** ch1, sc9, (sc2 in next st, sc18) 5 times, sc2 in next st, sc9, slst in beg ch1 [120]

**Rnds 21-26:** ch1, sc1 in each st, slst in beg ch1 (6 rnds)

Cut yarn and fasten off.

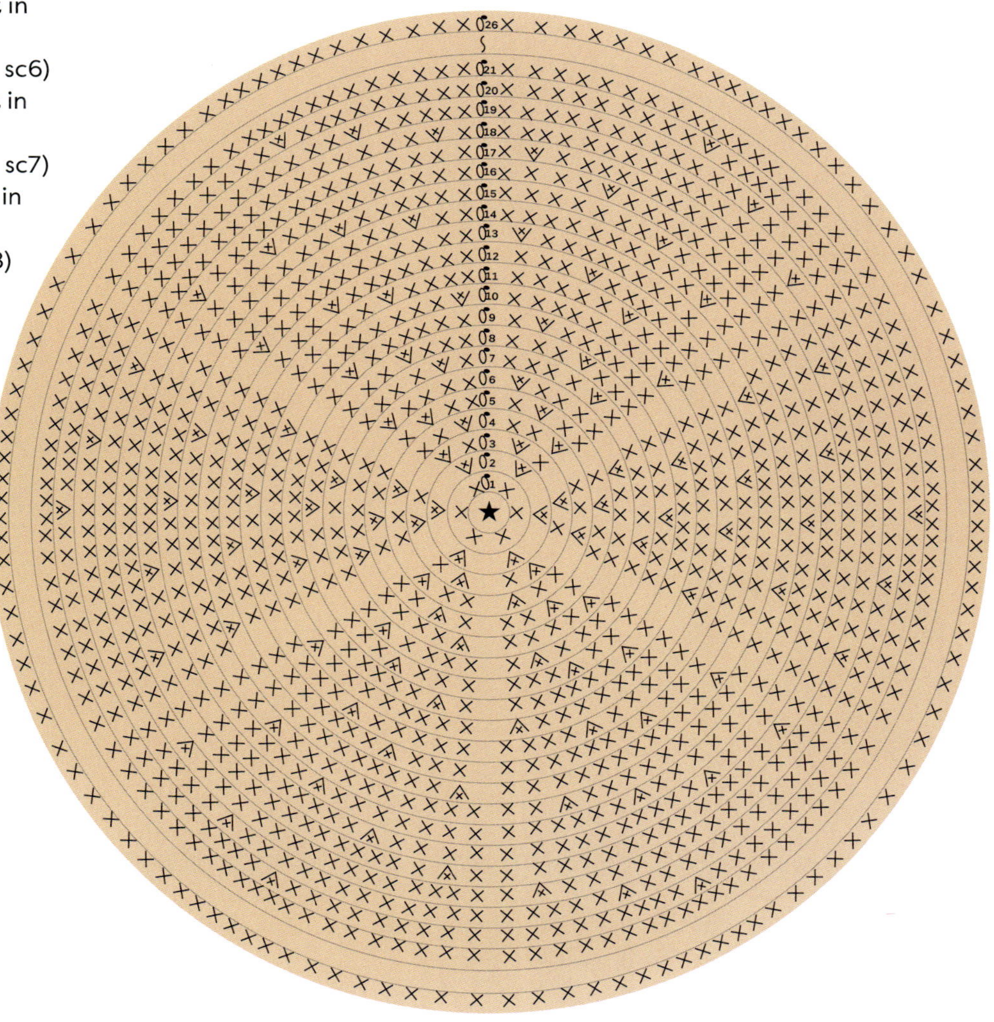

## Inside Buns (make 2)

With off-white and US L-11 hook, make a magic ring.
**Rnd 1:** ch1 (does not count as a st throughout), sc7 in magic ring, slst in beg ch1 [7]
Place stitch marker in first st of rnd 1 and move it up after each round
**Rnd 2:** ch1, (sc2 in next st) 7 times, slst in beg ch1 [14]
**Rnd 3:** ch1, (sc1, sc2 in next st) 7 times, slst in beg ch1 [21]
**Rnd 4:** ch1, (sc2 in next st, sc2) 7 times, slst in beg ch1 [28]
**Rnd 5:** ch1, sc2, (sc2 in next st, sc3) 6 times, sc2 in next st, sc1, slst in beg ch1 [35]
**Rnd 6:** ch1, (sc4, sc2 in next st) 7 times, slst in beg ch1 [42]
**Rnd 7:** ch1, sc1, (sc2 in next st, sc5) 6 times, sc2 in next st, sc4, slst in beg ch1 [49]
**Rnd 8:** ch1, sc3, (sc2 in next st, sc6) 6 times, sc2 in next st, sc3, slst in beg ch1 [56]
**Rnd 9:** ch1, sc6, (sc2 in next st, sc7) 6 times, sc2 in next st, sc1, slst in beg ch1 [63]
**Rnd 10:** ch1, (sc2 in next st, sc8) 7 times, slst in beg ch1 [70]
**Rnd 11:** ch1, sc4, (sc2 in next st, sc9) 6 times, sc2 in next st, sc5, slst in beg ch1 [77]
**Rnd 12:** ch1, sc7, (sc2 in next st, sc10) 6 times, sc2 in next st, sc3, slst in beg ch1 [84]
**Rnd 13:** ch1, sc6, (sc2 in next st, sc13) 5 times, sc2 in next st, sc7, slst in beg ch1 [90]
**Rnd 14:** ch1, sc10, (sc2 in next st, sc14) 5 times, sc2 in next st, sc4, slst in beg ch1 [96]
**Rnd 15:** ch1, sc14, (sc2 in next st, sc15) 5 times, sc2 in next st, sc1, slst in beg ch1 [102]
**Rnd 16:** ch1, sc1, (sc2 in next st, sc16) 5 times, sc2 in next st, sc15, slst in beg ch1 [108]
**Rnd 17:** ch1, sc5, (sc2 in next st, sc17) 5 times, sc2 in next st, sc12, slst in beg ch1 [114]
Change to golden brown.
**Rnd 18:** ch1, sc9, (sc2 in next st, sc18) 5 times, sc2 in next st, sc9, slst in beg ch1 [120]
Cut yarn and fasten off, leaving a 3 yard (2.6 m) long tail.

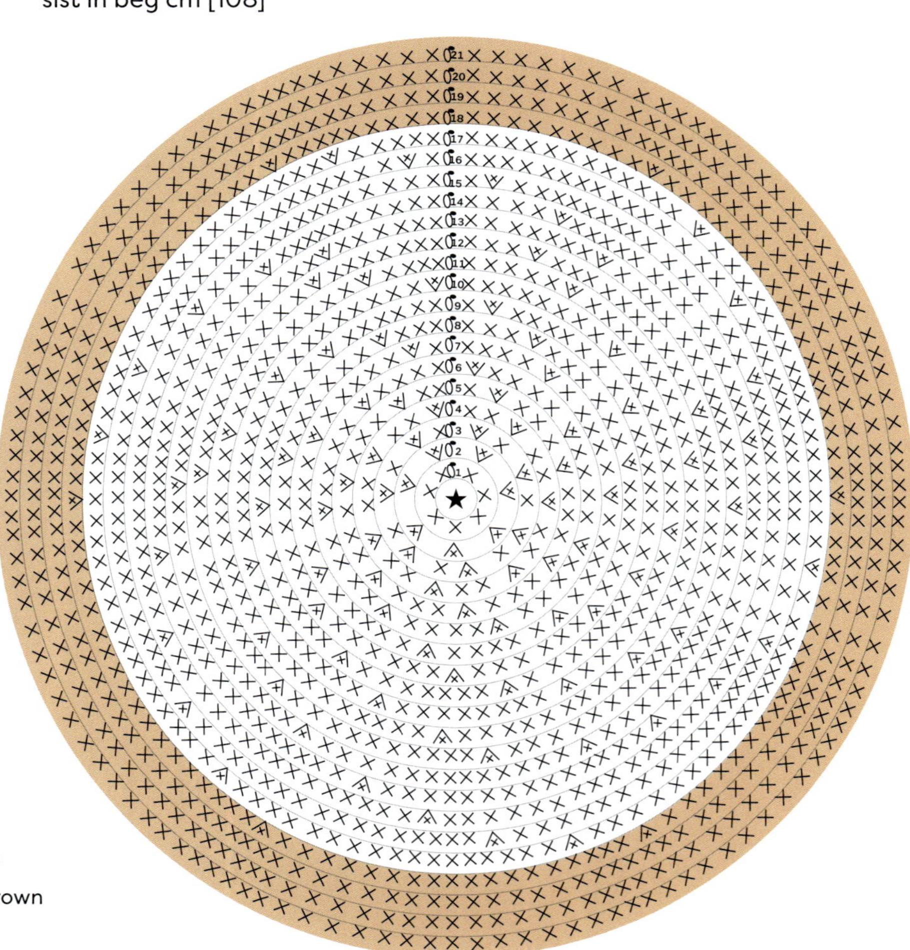


= Off-white
= Golden brown

## Bottom Outside Bun

With golden brown and US L-11 hook, make a magic ring.
Work as given for Inside Buns until end of rnd 18, using golden brown throughout [120]
**Rnds 19-21:** ch1, sc1 in each st, slst in beg ch1 (3 rnds)
Cut yarn and fasten off. Make up following step 2 instructions on page 76.

## Hamburger Patty (make 2)

With dark brown and US L-11 hook, make a magic ring.
Work as given for the Bottom Outside Bun until end of rnd 20, using dark brown throughout [120]
Cut yarn and fasten off, leaving a 3 yard (2.6 m) long tail. Make up following step 5 instructions on page 76.

## Tomato (make one smaller piece and one larger piece)

With rose pink and US L-11 hook, make a magic ring.

**Rnd 1:** ch1 (does not count as a st throughout), sc7 in magic ring, slst in beg ch1 [7]

Place stitch marker in first st of rnd 1 and move it up after each round

**Rnd 2:** ch1, (sc2 in next st) 7 times, slst in beg ch1 [14]

Join in cherry pink as needed.

**Rnd 3:** in off-white ch1, sc1, in cherry pink sc1 in next st, change to off-white and sc1 in same st (to increase), sc1 in next st, sc1 in next st, change to cherry pink and sc1 in same st, in off-white sc1, sc2 in next st, sc1, in cherry pink sc1 in next st, change to off-white and sc1 in same st, sc1 in next st, sc1 in next st, change to cherry pink and sc1 in same st, in off-white sc1, sc2 in next st, in cherry pink sc1, in off-white sc2 in next st, slst in beg ch1 [21]

**Rnd 4:** in off-white ch1, sc2 in first st, **in cherry pink sc1, in off-white sc1, sc2 in next st, sc1, in cherry pink sc1, sc1 in next st, change to off-white and sc1 in same st, sc2**, sc2 in next st; rep from ** to ** once more, in cherry pink sc2 in next st, in off-white sc2, slst in beg ch1 [28]

Join in red as needed.

**Rnd 5:** in off-white ch1, sc1, **in red sc1, in cherry pink sc2 in next st, in red sc1, in off-white sc2, sc1 in next st, change to red and sc1 in same st, in cherry pink sc2, in red sc1, in off-white sc2 in next st**, sc2; rep from ** to ** once more, in red sc1, in cherry pink sc2, in red sc1, change to off-white and sc1 in same st, sc1, slst in beg ch1 [35]

**Rnd 6:** in off-white ch1, sc1, **in red sc1, in cherry pink sc2, in red sc2 in next st, in off-white sc3, in red sc1, sc1 in next st, change to cherry pink and sc1 in same st, sc1**, in red sc2, in off-white sc1, sc2 in next st, sc1; rep from ** to ** once more, in red sc1, in off-white sc2, sc1 in next st, change to red and sc1 in same st, in cherry pink sc2, in red sc2, in off-white sc2 in next st, slst in beg ch1 [42]

**Rnd 7:** in off-white ch1, sc1, **in red sc2 in next st, in cherry pink sc2, in red sc2, in off-white sc1, sc2 in next st, sc1, in red sc2, in cherry pink sc2**, sc1 in next st, change to red and sc1 in same st, sc1, in off-white sc4; rep from ** to ** once more, in red sc2 in next st, in off-white sc3, in red sc1, in cherry pink sc1, sc2 in next st, in red sc2, in off-white sc2, slst in beg ch1 [49]

Cut off off-white.

**Rnd 8:** in red ch1, sc3, **in cherry pink sc2 in next st, sc1, in red sc5, sc2 in next st, sc2**, in cherry pink sc3, in red sc1, sc2 in next st, sc6; rep from ** to ** once more, in cherry pink sc2, in red sc2, sc2 in next st, sc3, in cherry pink sc3, in red sc2 in next st, sc3, slst in beg ch1 [56]

**Rnd 9:** in red ch1, sc3, in cherry pink sc3, in red sc2 in next st, sc7, sc2 in next st, in cherry pink sc3, in red sc4, sc2 in next st, sc4, in cherry pink sc3, sc1 in next st, change to red and sc1 in same st, sc7, sc2 in next st, in cherry pink sc2, in red sc5, sc2 in next st, sc1, in cherry pink sc3, in red sc3, sc2 in next st, sc1, slst in beg ch1 [63]

**Rnd 10:** in red ch1, sc2 in first st, sc2, in cherry pink sc3, in red sc3, sc2 in next st, sc7, in cherry pink sc1, sc2 in next st, sc1, in red sc7, sc2 in next st, sc2, in cherry pink sc4, in red sc2, sc2 in next st, sc7, in cherry pink sc1, sc2 in next st, in red sc8, sc1 in next st, change to cherry pink and sc1 in same st, sc2, in red sc6, slst in beg ch1 [70]

**Rnd 11:** in red ch1, sc4, sc1 in next st, change to cherry pink and sc1 in same st, sc2, in red sc7, sc2 in next st, sc4, in cherry pink sc4, in red sc1, sc2 in next st, sc9, sc1 in next st, change to cherry pink and sc1 in same st, sc3, in red sc6, sc2 in next st, sc4, in cherry pink sc3, in red sc2, sc2 in next st, sc6, in cherry pink sc3, sc1 in next st, change to red and sc1 in same st, sc5, slst in beg ch1 [77]

**Rnd 12:** in red ch1, sc5, in cherry pink sc2, sc2 in next st, in red sc10, sc2 in next st, sc2, in cherry pink sc4, in red sc4, sc2 in next st, sc8, in cherry pink sc2, sc2 in next st, sc1, in red sc9, sc2 in next st, sc2, in cherry pink sc3, in red sc5, sc2 in next st, sc4, in cherry pink sc4, in red sc2, sc2 in next st, sc3, slst in beg ch1 [84]

**Rnd 13:** in red ch1, sc5, in cherry pink sc1, sc2 in next st, sc2, in red sc11, sc2 in next st, sc2, in cherry pink sc4, in red sc7, sc2 in next st, sc6, in cherry pink sc5, in red sc2, sc2 in next st, sc10, in cherry pink sc3, in red sc2 in next st, sc11, in cherry pink sc2, sc2 in next st, in red sc7, slst in beg ch1 [90]

Cut off red. Continue in cherry pink.

**Rnd 14:** ch1, sc10, (sc2 in next st, sc14) 5 times, sc2 in next st, sc4, slst in beg ch1 [96]

**Rnd 15:** ch1, sc14, (sc2 in next st, sc15) 5 times, sc2 in next st, sc1, slst in beg ch1 [102]

**Rnd 16:** ch1, sc1, (sc2 in next st, sc16) 5 times, sc2 in next st, sc15, slst in beg ch1 [108]

Change to red orange.

**Rnd 17:** ch1, sc5, (sc2 in next st, sc17) 5 times, sc2 in next st, sc12, slst in beg ch1 [114]

**Rnd 18:** ch1, sc9, (sc2 in next st, sc18) 5 times, sc2 in next st, sc9, slst in beg ch1 [120]

Fasten off for smaller piece.

**Rnd 19:** ch1, sc1 BLO in each st, slst in beg ch1

**Rnd 20:** ch1, sc1 in each st, slst in beg ch1

Fasten off for larger piece. Make up following step 7 instructions on page 76.

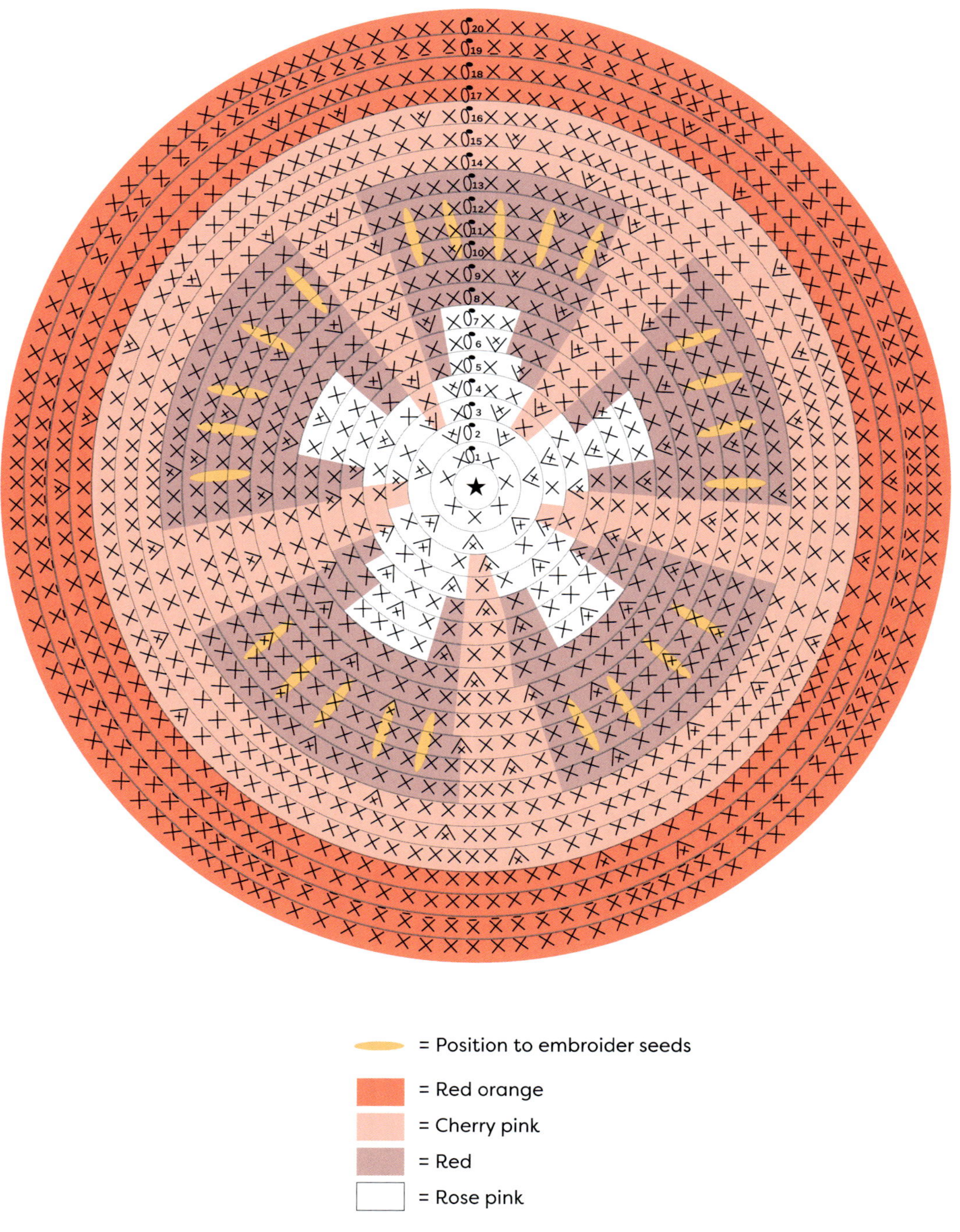
= Position to embroider seeds
= Red orange
= Cherry pink
= Red
= Rose pink

## Lettuce

With pistachio and US L-11 hook, ch14.

**Row 1:** sc1 in second ch from hook, sc11, sc4 in last ch, rotate and work along opposite side of ch, sc12, turn [28]

**Row 2:** ch1 (does not count as a st throughout), sc3, hdc3, dc6, (dc3 in next st) 4 times, dc6, hdc3, sc3, turn [36]

Change to lime green.

**Row 3:** ch1 (does not count as a st throughout), sc3, hdc3, dc5, tr1, (tr2 in next st) 12 times, tr1, dc5, hdc3, sc3, turn [48]

Change to pistachio +lime green

**Row 4:** ch1 (does not count as a st throughout), skip first st, slst in next st, sc1, hdc2, dc6, tr1, (tr2 in next st, tr1) 6 times, (tr1, tr2 in next st) 6 times, tr1, dc6, hdc2, sc1, slst2, fasten off, turn. [59]

**Row 5:** Rejoin yarn in last sc of row 4, ch1, sc1 in same st, hdc1, dc4, (tr2 in next st, tr1) 11 times, (tr1, tr2 in next st) 11 times, dc4, hdc1, sc1, fasten off, turn [78]

**Row 6:** skip last 3 sts made and rejoin yarn in fourth st at end of row 5, ch1, sc1 in same st, hdc1, dc1, (tr1, tr2 in next st) 16 times, tr2, (tr2 in next st, tr1) 16 times, dc1, hdc1, sc1, slst in next st, fasten off turn [105]

**Row 6:** skip last 3 sts made and rejoin yarn in fourth st at end of row 6 (this is the dc), ch1, sc1 in same st, hdc1, dc1, (tr1, tr2 in next st) 23 times, (tr2 in next st, tr1) 23 times, dc1, hdc1, sc1, slst in next st, fasten off [145]

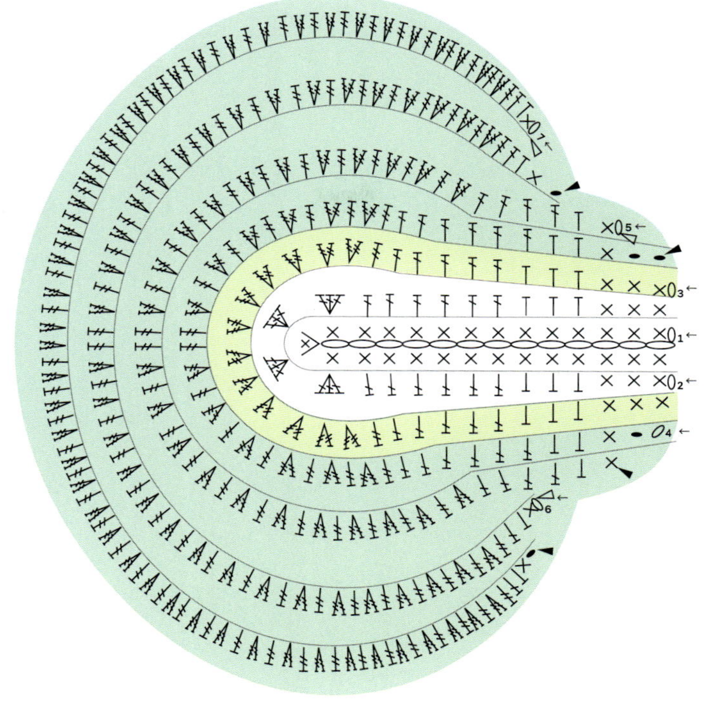

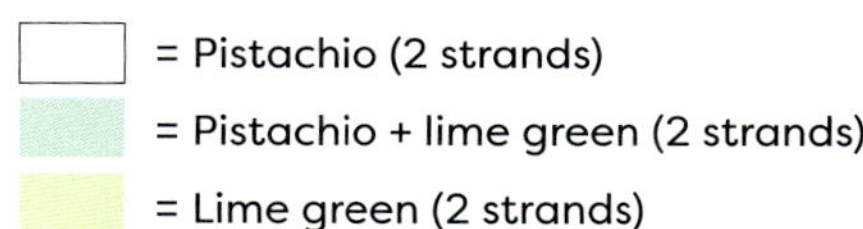


## Cheese

With lemon and US L-11 hook, ch37.

Work in rows.

**Row 1:** sc1 in second ch from hook, sc1 in each ch to end, turn [36]

**Row 2:** ch1 (does not count as a st throughout), sc1 in each st, turn

**Rows 3-40:** as row 2

Do not turn after row 40, continue with edge as follows: ch1, sc1 in each row-end (40 sts), continue along foundation chain working sc2 in first st, sc1 in each st to last st, sc2 in last st (38 sts), continue along next side working sc1 in each row-end (40 sts), finally work across top edge, working sc2 in first st, sc1 in each st to last st, sc2 in last st (38 sts), slst in beg ch1 and fasten off [156]

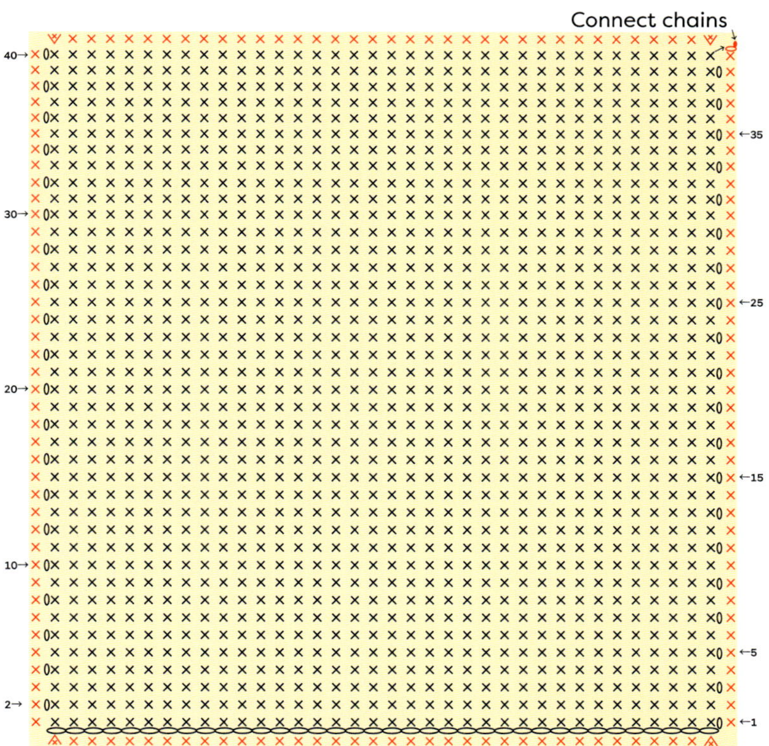

Finished Sizes for Each of the Components:

Top Bun: 16⅛" (41 cm) diameter x 5½" (14 cm) tall

Bottom Bun: 16⅛" (41 cm) diameter x 3" (7.5 cm) tall

Hamburger Patty: 16⅛" (41 cm) diameter x 3¾" (9.5 cm) tall

Tomato: 15½" (39.5 cm) diameter x 2½" (6 cm) tall

Lettuce: 13½" (34 cm) long x 15½" (39 cm) wide

Cheese: 15¾" (40 cm) long x 15¾" (40 cm) wide

15

# Hot Dog

**SHOWN ON PAGE 21**

*See page 86 for the finished sizes of the components.*

## TOOLS & MATERIALS

### Yarn

- 100% acrylic bulky-weight yarn
  - 407 yds (372 m) in dark beige
  - 144 yds (132 m) in off-white
  - 394 yds (360 m) in brown
  - 14 yds (12 m) in mustard
  - 14 yds (12 m) in red orange

### Other Materials

- 400 g of polyester stuffing (use 100 g for bun and 300 g for hot dog)

### Tools

- US L-11 (8 mm) crochet hook
- Yarn needle
- Felting needle

## CONSTRUCTION STEPS

Note: Use 2 strands of yarn throughout.

**1.** Crochet the bun outside: Make 28 foundation chains, and crochet until round 16, turning after each round. For odd rows after round 3, when the previous row is half double crochet, scoop front two loops (the back bump from previous row and front loop of the stitch) to crochet, and for even rows, scoop the top two loops of the stitch to crochet. Cut the yarn, leaving a 2¾ yard (2.5 m) long tail.

**2.** Crochet the bun inside: Work as given for Bun Outside until the end of round 6. Crochet round 7 as instructed for Bun Inside.

**3.** Assemble the bun: Align the bun inside on top of the bun outside. Sew together using the yarn tail from step 1. After sewing around ⅔ of the bun, fill with polyester stuffing. Position the majority of the stuffing on the sides and less in the center of the bun. Continue sewing to the end.

**4.** Adjust the shape of the bun: Adjust the stuffing as necessary so that the bun is concave in the center and raised on the sides. Use a felting needle to work the surface of the bun inside to set the shape (see **Figure A**).

**5.** Crochet the hot dog: Start with a magic ring and crochet until round 63, stuffing as you go. Gather half loops on round 63 using the remaining yarn. Cut yarn and fasten off, leaving a 12" (30 cm) long tail.

**6.** Use a felting needle to add ketchup and mustard to the hot dog (see **Figure B**).

**7.** Follow instructions on page 81 to make lettuce (optional). Layer the lettuce and hot dog on top of the bun.

*Figure A*

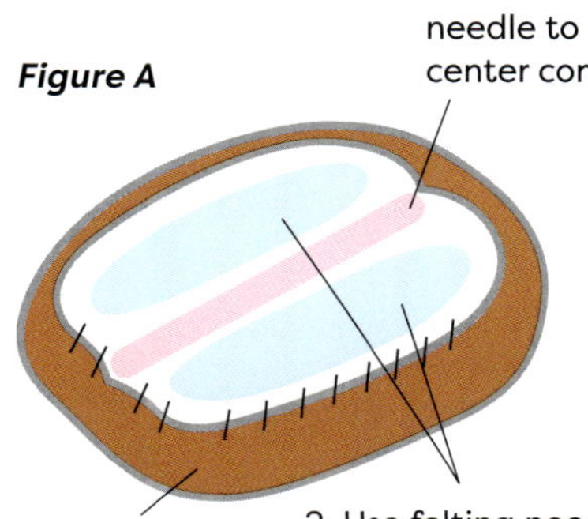


*Figure B*

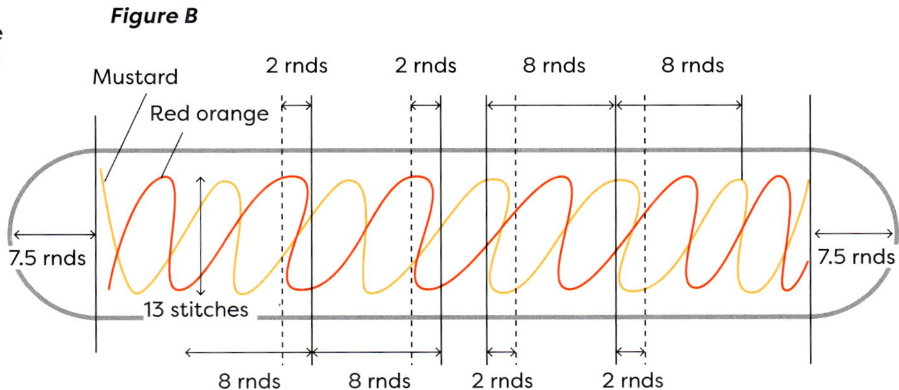


Arrange two strands of mustard yarn in a squiggly shape for the mustard, then secure in place using a felting needle. Follow the same process to attach two strands of red orange yarn for the ketchup.

## CROCHET INSTRUCTIONS

### Bun Outside

With dark beige and US L-11 hook, ch28.

**Rnd 1 (RS):** skip 2ch (counts as hdc), hdc2 in next ch, hdc24, hdc5 in last ch, rotate and work along opposite side of ch, hdc24, hdc2 in last ch, slst in top of skipped 2ch at beginning, turn [58]

**Rnd 2 (WS):** ch2 (counts as hdc1 throughout), hdc2 in first 2 sts, hdc24, hdc2 in next 2 sts, hdc1, hdc2 in next 2 sts, hdc24, hdc2 in last 2 sts, slst in top of beginning ch2, turn [66]

**Rnd 3:** ch2 (counts as hdc1 throughout), hdc2 in first st, hdc1, hdc2 in next st, hdc26, hdc2 in next st, (hdc1, hdc2 in next st) 3 times, hdc26, hdc2 in next st, hdc1, hdc2 in last st, slst in top of beginning ch2, turn [74]

**Rnd 4:** ch2 (counts as hdc1 throughout), hdc1, hdc2 in next st, hdc2, hdc2 in next st, hdc26, hdc2 in next st, hdc2, hdc2 in next st, hdc3, hdc2 in next st, hdc2, hdc2 in next st, hdc26, hdc2 in next st, hdc2, hdc2 in next st, hdc1 in last st, slst in top of beginning ch2, turn [82]

**Rnd 5:** ch2 (counts as hdc1 throughout), hdc2, hdc2 in next st, hdc2, hdc2 in next st, hdc28, hdc2 in next st, hdc2, hdc2 in next st, hdc5, hdc2 in next st, hdc2, hdc2 in next st, hdc28, hdc2 in next st, hdc2, hdc2 in next st, hdc2 in last st, slst in top of beginning ch2, turn [90]

**Rnd 6:** ch2 (counts as hdc1 throughout), hdc2, hdc2 in next st, hdc2, hdc2 in next st, hdc32, hdc2 in next st, hdc2, hdc2 in next st, hdc5, hdc2 in next st, hdc2, hdc2 in next st, hdc32, hdc2 in next st, hdc2, hdc2 in next st, hdc2 in last st, slst in top of beginning ch2, turn [98]

**Rnd 7:** ch1, sc1 in same st, sc4, hdc1, hdc2 in next st, hdc3, hdc2 in next st, hdc28, hdc2 in next st, hdc3, hdc2 in next st, hdc1, sc9, hdc1, hdc2 in next st, hdc3, hdc2 in next st, hdc28, hdc2 in next st, hdc3, hd2 in next st, hdc1, sc4, slst in beg ch1, turn [106]

**Rnd 8:** ch1, sc1 in same st, sc5, hdc2, hdc2 in next st, hdc2, hdc2 in next st, hdc30, hdc2 in next st, hdc2, hdc2 in next st, hdc2, sc11, hdc2, hdc2 in next st, hdc2, hdc2 in next st, hdc30, hdc2 in next st, hdc2, hdc2 in next st, hdc2, sc5, slst in beg ch1, turn [114]

**Rnd 9:** ch1, sc1 in same st, sc6, hdc1, hdc2 in next st, hdc2, hdc2 in next st, hdc34, hdc2 in next st, hdc2, hdc2 in next st, hdc1, sc13, hdc1, hdc2 in next st, hdc2, hdc2 in next st, hdc34, hdc2 in next st, hdc2, hdc2 in next st, hdc1, sc6, slst in beg ch1, turn [122]

**Rnds 10–11:** ch1, sc1 in same st, sc6, hdc48, sc13, hdc48, sc6, slst in beg ch1, turn [122]

**Rnds 12–13:** ch1, sc1 in same st, sc5, hdc50, sc11, hdc50, sc5, slst in beg ch1, turn [122]

**Rnd 14:** ch1, sc1 in same st, sc2tog, sc3, hdc50, sc3, sc2tog, sc1, sc2tog, sc3, hdc50, sc3, sc2tog, slst in beg ch1, turn [118]

**Rnd 15:** ch1, sc1 in same st, sc2tog, sc2, hdc6, hdc2tog, hdc34, hdc2tog, hdc6, sc2, sc2tog, sc1, sc2tog, sc2, hdc6, hdc2tog, hdc34, hdc2tog, hdc6, sc2, sc2tog, slst in beg ch1, turn [110]

**Rnd 16:** ch1, sc2tog, sc2, hdc5, hdc2tog, hdc34, hdc2tog, hdc5, sc2, sc3tog, sc2, hdc5, hdc2tog, hdc34, hdc2tog, hdc5, sc2, sc2tog over last st and first sc, slst in beg ch1 [102]

Cut yarn, leaving a 2¾ yard (2.5 m) long tail. Make up following step 3 instructions on page 83.

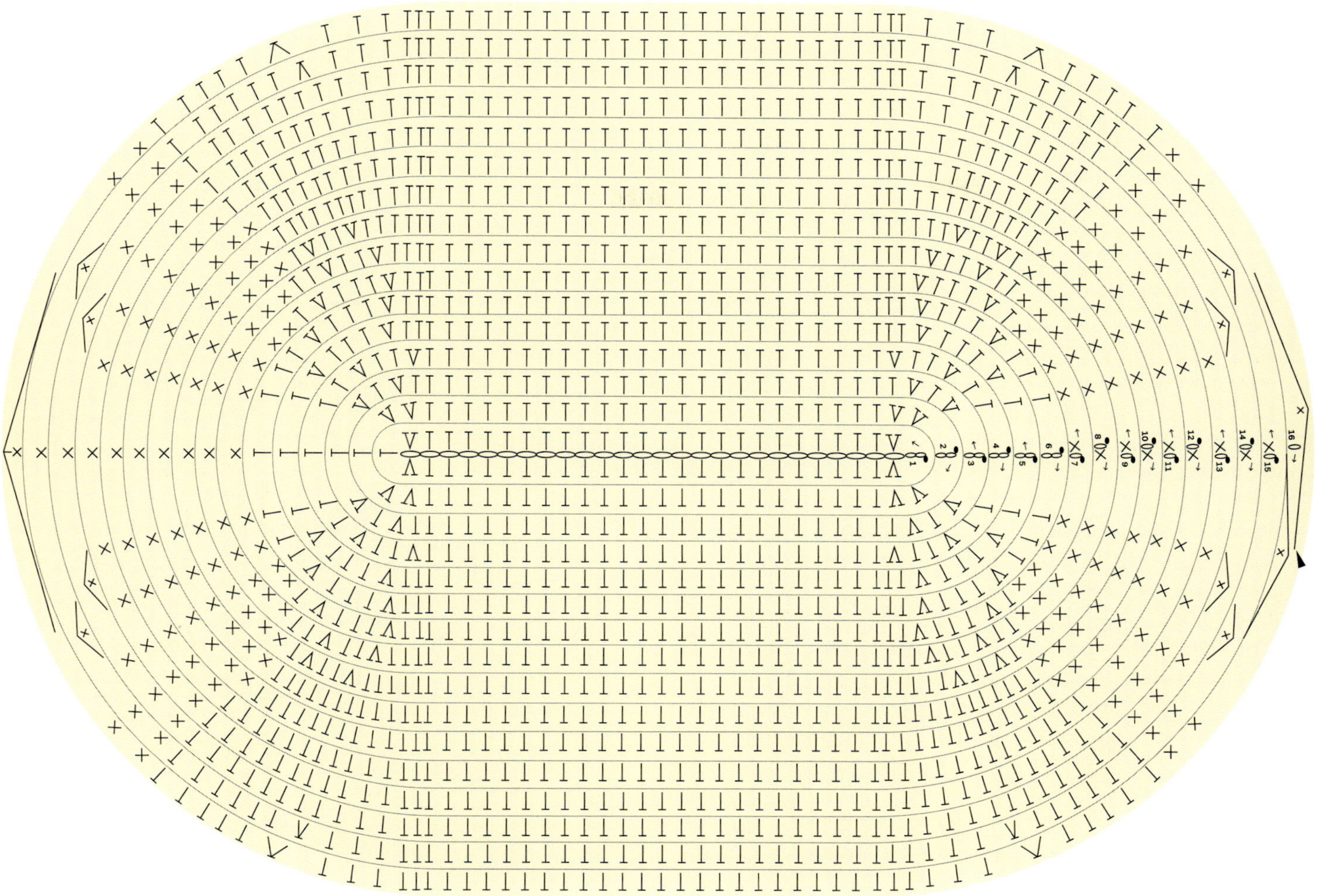

## Bun Inside

With off-white and US L-11 hook, work as given for Bun Outside to the end of rnd 6, turn [98]

**Rnd 7 (RS):** ch1 (does not count as a st), hdc1 in next st, hdc2, hdc2 in next st, hdc3, hdc2 in next st, hdc32, hdc2 in next st, hdc3, hdc2 in next st, hdc2, hdc3tog, hdc2, hdc2 in next st, hdc3, hdc2 in next st, hdc32, hdc2 in next st, hdc3, hdc2 in next st, hdc2, hdc2tog over last st and first hdc, slst in top of beginning ch2 [102]

Cut yarn, leaving a 2¾ yard (2.5 m) long tail. Make up following step 3 instructions on page 83.

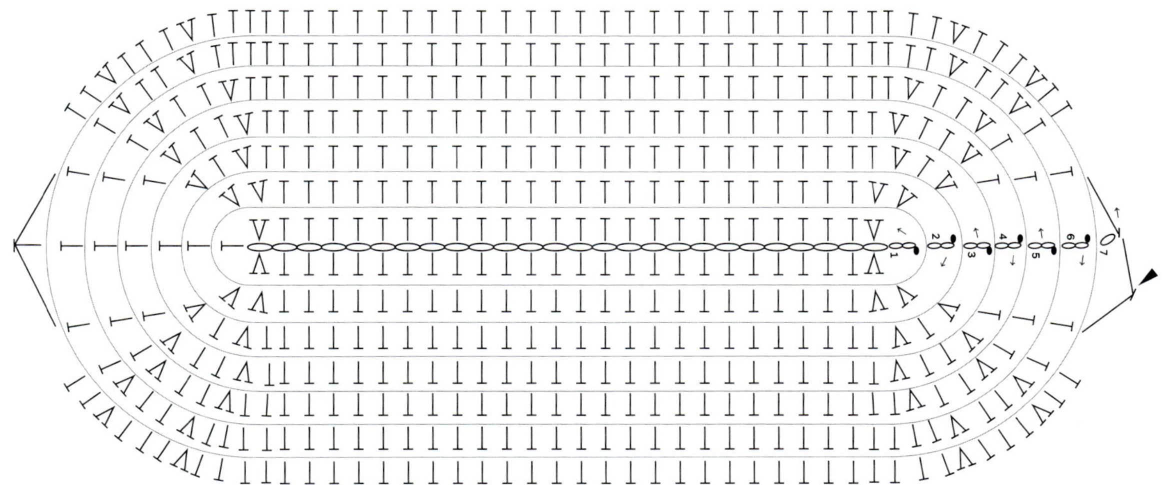

## Hot Dog

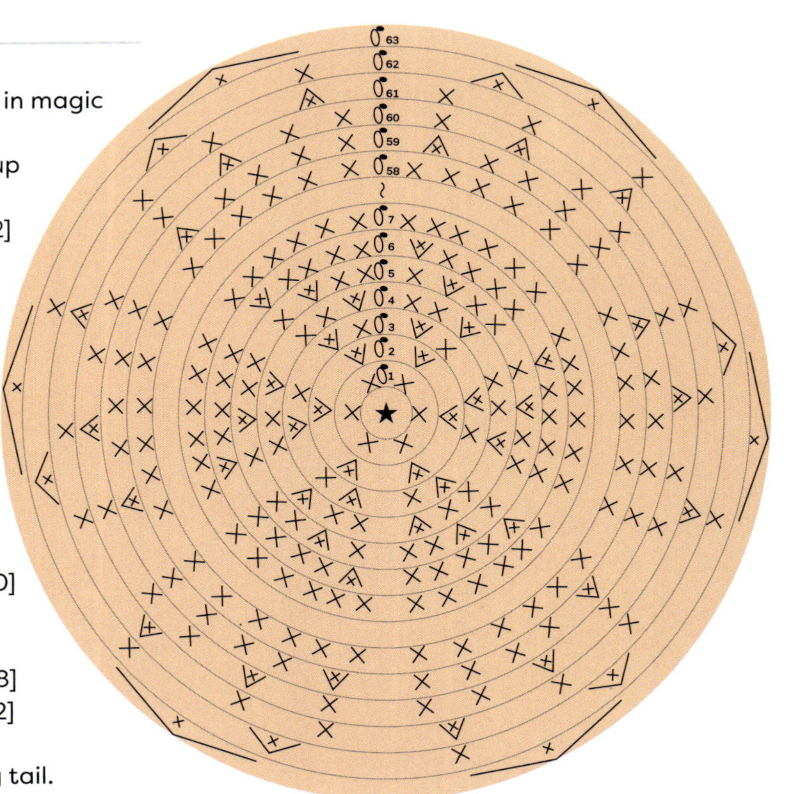

With brown and US L-11 hook, make a magic ring.

**Rnd 1:** ch1 (does not count as a st throughout), sc6 in magic ring, slst in beg ch1 [6]

Place stitch marker in first st of rnd 1 and move it up after each round

**Rnd 2:** ch1, (sc2 in next st) 6 times, slst in beg ch1 [12]

**Rnd 3:** ch1, (sc1, sc2 in next st) 6 times, slst in beg ch1 [18]

**Rnd 4:** ch1, (sc2 in next st, sc2) 6 times, slst in beg ch1 [24]

**Rnd 5:** ch1, sc2, (sc2 in next st, sc3) 5 times, sc2 in next st, sc1, slst in beg ch1 [30]

**Rnd 6:** ch1, (sc4, sc2 in next st) 6 times, slst in beg ch1 [36]

Fill with polyester stuffing as you crochet.

**Rnds 7–58:** ch1, sc1 in each st, slst in beg ch1

**Rnd 59:** ch1, (sc4, sc2tog) 6 times, slst in beg ch1 [30]

**Rnd 60:** ch1, sc2, sc2tog, (sc3, sc2tog) 5 times, sc1, slst in beg ch1 [24]

**Rnd 61:** ch1, (sc2tog, sc2) 6 times, slst in beg ch1 [18]

**Rnd 62:** ch1, (sc1, sc2tog) 6 times, slst in beg ch1 [12]

**Rnd 63:** ch1, (sc2tog) 6 times, slst in beg ch1 [6]

Cut yarn and fasten off, leaving a 12" (30 cm) long tail.

Make up following step 6 instructions on page 83.

Finished Sizes for Each of the Components:

Bun: 9½" (24 cm) wide x 19¾" (50 cm) long x 5½" (14 cm) tall

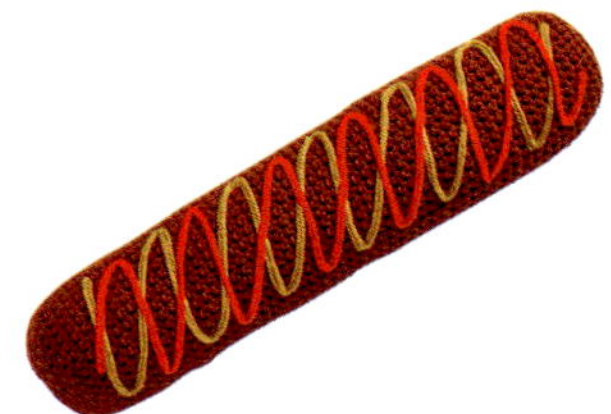

Hot Dog: 4¾" (12 cm) diameter x 25" (63 cm) long

16

# Egg on Toast

SHOWN ON PAGE 21

Finished Size:
Bread: 18½" (47 cm) wide x 18" (46 cm) long x 3½" (9 cm) tall
Egg: 15" (38 cm) diameter x 1¾" (4.5 cm) tall

## TOOLS & MATERIALS

### Yarn

#### For the Bread

- 100% acrylic bulky-weight yarn
  - 565 yds (516 m) in off-white
  - 263 yds (240 m) in golden brown

#### For the Egg

- 100% acrylic bulky-weight yarn
  - 197 yds (180 m) in white
  - 53 yds (48 m) in lemon
  - 27 yds (24 m) in dark beige

#### For the Lettuce

- 100% acrylic bulky-weight yarn
  - 197 yds (180 m) in lime green
  - 40 yds (36 m) in pistachio

### Other Materials

- 270 g of polyester stuffing (260 g for the bread and 10 g for the egg)

### Tools

- US L-11 (8 mm) crochet hook
- Yarn needle

## CONSTRUCTION STEPS

Note: Use 2 strands of yarn throughout.

**1.** Crochet the bread: Using off-white yarn, make 38 foundation chains and crochet through row 30. Change the yarn to golden brown and continue to crochet the edges of the bread, crocheting one piece through round 1 and another piece through round 7, following the diagram or written instructions. Cut yarn, leaving a 4½ yard (4 m) long tail.

**2.** Assemble the bread: Align the two crocheted pieces with wrong sides together. Use the yarn tail to whipstitch the two pieces together. After sewing around ⅔ of the bread, fill with polyester stuffing, and the continue sewing and stuffing to the end.

**3.** Crochet the egg white: Make 7 single crochet in a magic ring and continue through round 17.

**4.** Crochet the egg yolk: Make 6 single crochet in a magic ring and continue through round 8. Cut yarn, leaving a 1 yard (1 m) long tail.

**5.** Assemble the egg: Use the wrong side of both the egg white and egg yolk as the right side of the fabric. Sew the egg yolk to the egg white, making sure to scoop only the inside stitches of the egg yolk fabric so that the yarn is not visible from the front. After sewing around ⅔ of the egg yolk, fill with polyester stuffing, and the continue sewing and stuffing to the end (see **Figure A**).

**6.** Refer to page 81 to crochet the lettuce.

*Figure A*

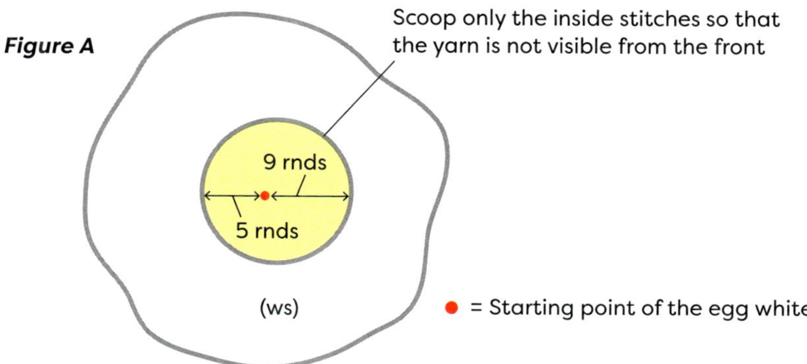

## CROCHET INSTRUCTIONS

### Bread (make one smaller piece and one larger piece)

With off-white and US L-11 hook, ch38.
Work in rows.
**Row 1:** skip 3ch (counts as first st), hdc1 in fourth ch from hook, hdc1 in each ch to end, turn [36]
**Row 2:** ch2 (counts as first hdc throughout), hdc1 in each st, turn
**Rows 3-23:** as row 2
**Row 24:** ch2, hdc2 in first st, hdc1 in each st to last st, hdc3 in last st, turn [40]
**Row 25:** ch2, hdc1 in first st, hdc1 in each st to last st, hdc2 in last st, turn [42]
**Rows 26-27:** as row 2 (2 rows)
**Row 28:** ch1 and hdc in next st (counts as hdc2tog), hdc1 in each st to last 2 sts, hdc2tog, turn [40]
**Rows 29-30:** as row 28 (2 rows) changing to golden brown on last st of row 30 [36]
Do not turn. Continue in golden brown and work in rounds.
**Rnd 1:** working along first side, ch1 (does not count as a st throughout), sc40 evenly along the side edge, working along bottom edge sc2 in first st, sc34, sc2 in last st, working along next side sc40 evenly, working along top sc2 in first st, sc34, sc2 in last st, slst in beg ch1 [156]
Cut yarn and fasten off here for smaller piece, leaving a 4½ yard (4 m) long tail.
**Rnd 2:** ch1 (does not count as a st throughout), sc40 along the side edge, working along bottom edge sc2 in first st, sc36, sc2 in last st, working along next side sc40 evenly, working along top sc2 in first st, sc36, sc2 in last st, slst in beg ch1 [160]
**Rnd 3:** ch1, sc1 BLO in each st, slst in beg ch1
**Rnds 4-7:** ch1, sc1 in each st, slst in beg ch1 (4 rnds)
Cut yarn and fasten off for larger piece, leaving a 4½ yard (4 m) long tail. Make up following step 2 on page 87.

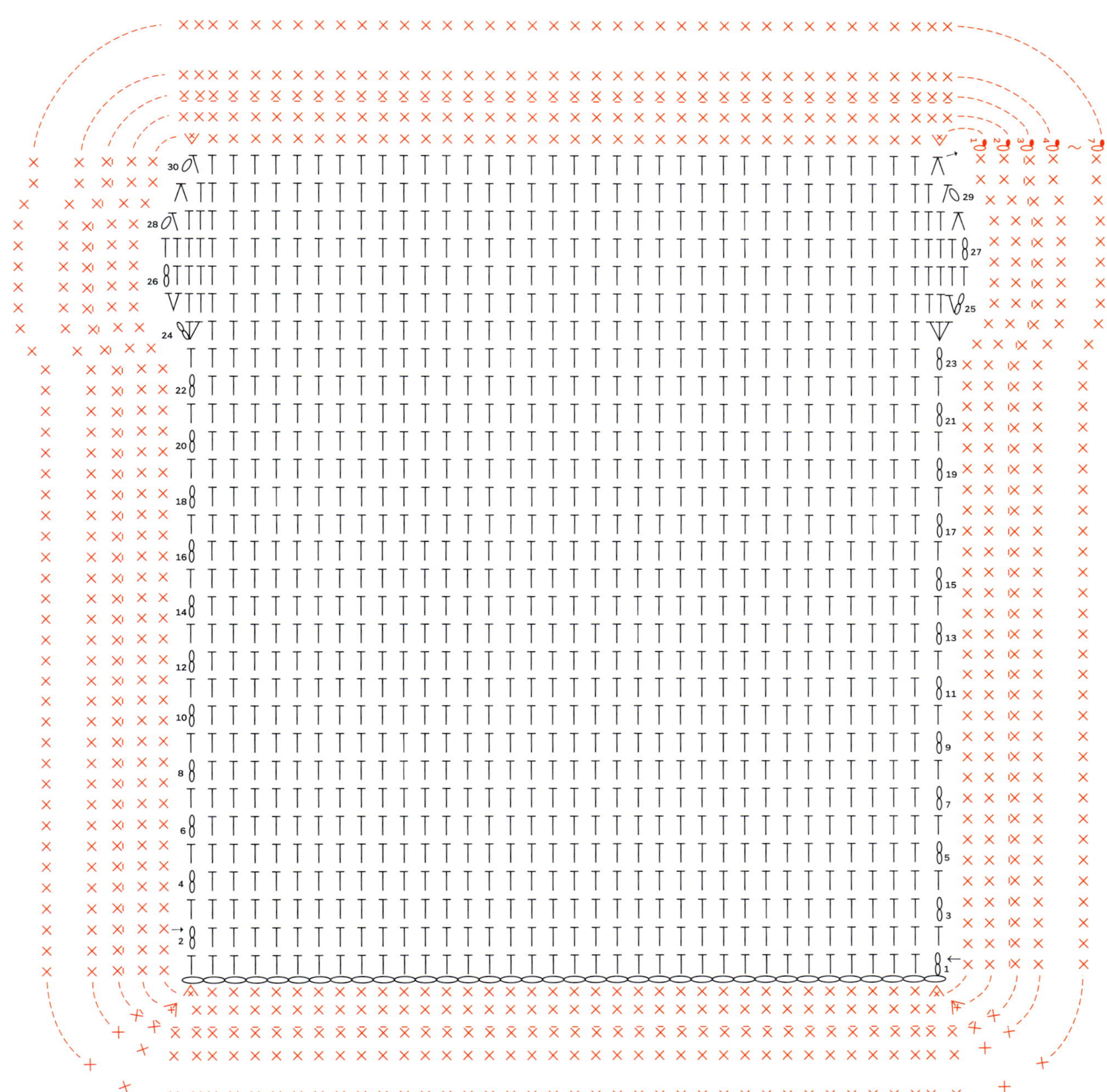

× = Golden brown

T = Off-white

## Egg White

With white and US L-11 hook, make a magic ring.

**Rnd 1:** ch1 (does not count as a st throughout), sc7 in magic ring, slst in beg ch1 [7]

Place stitch marker in first st of rnd 1 and move it up after each round

**Rnd 2:** ch1, (sc2 in next st) 7 times, slst in beg ch1 [14]

**Rnd 3:** ch1, (sc1, sc2 in next st) 7 times, slst in beg ch1 [21]

**Rnd 4:** ch1, (sc2 in next st, sc2) 7 times, slst in beg ch1 [28]

**Rnd 5:** ch1, sc2, (sc2 in next st, sc3) 6 times, sc2 in next st, sc1, slst in beg ch1 [35]

**Rnd 6:** ch1, (sc4, sc2 in next st) 7 times, slst in beg ch1 [42]

**Rnd 7:** ch1, sc1, (sc2 in next st, sc5) 6 times, sc2 in next st, sc4, slst in beg ch1 [49]

**Rnd 8:** ch1, sc3, (sc2 in next st, sc6) 6 times, sc2 in next st, sc3, slst in beg ch1 [56]

**Rnd 9:** ch1, sc6, (sc2 in next st, sc7) 6 times, sc2 in next st, sc1, slst in beg ch1 [63]

**Rnd 10:** ch1, (sc2 in next st, sc8) 7 times, slst in beg ch1 [70]

**Rnd 11:** ch1, sc4, (sc2 in next st, sc9) 6 times, sc2 in next st, sc5, slst in beg ch1 [77]

**Rnd 12:** ch1, sc7, (sc2 in next st, sc10) 6 times, sc2 in next st, sc3, slst in beg ch1 [84]

**Rnd 13:** ch2 (counts as first hdc), hdc1 in same st, hdc10, sc1, sc2 in next st, sc3, hdc7, sc1, sc2 in next st, sc4, hdc7, hdc2 in next st, hdc11, hdc2 in next st, hdc3, sc7, hdc1, hdc2 in next st, hdc5, sc6, sc2 in next st, sc1, hdc10, slst in top of beg ch2 [91]

**Rnd 14:** ch2 (counts as first hdc), hdc3, hdc2 in next st, hdc7, sc5, sc2 in next st, hdc7, sc5, sc2 in next st, sc1, hdc11, hdc2 in next st, hdc12, hdc2 in next st, sc7, hdc5, hdc2 in next st, hdc2, sc9, hdc1, hdc2 in next st, hdc8, slst in top of beg ch2 [98]

**Rnd 15:** ch2 (counts as first hdc), hdc7, hdc2 in next st, hdc4, sc7, hdc2, hdc2 in next st, hdc4, sc8, hdc1, hdc2 in next st, hdc13, hdc2 in next st, hdc11, sc2, sc2 in next st, sc4, hdc9, sc2 in next st, sc8, hdc5, hdc2 in next st, hdc5, slst in top of beg ch2 [105]

**Rnd 16:** ch2 (counts as first hdc), hdc12, hdc2 in next st, sc7, hdc7, hdc2 in next st, sc8, hdc6, hdc2 in next st, hdc14, hdc2 in next st, hdc7, sc7, sc2 in next st, hdc9, sc5, sc2 in next st, sc4, hdc10, hdc2 in next st, hdc1, slst in top of beg ch2 [112]

Change to dark beige.

**Rnd 17:** ch1 (does not count as a st), sc1 in each st, slst in beg ch1

Cut yarn and fasten off, leaving a 1 yard (1 m) long tail.

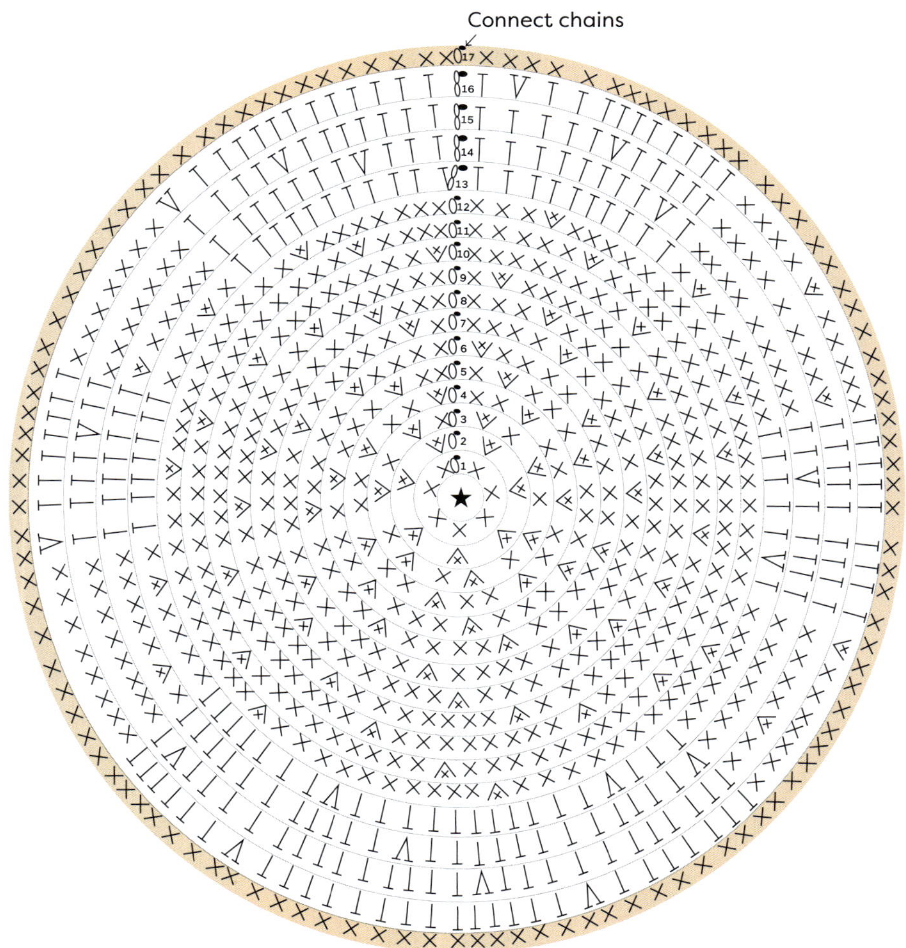

### Egg Yolk

With lemon and US L-11 hook, make a magic ring.

**Rnd 1:** ch1 (does not count as a st throughout), sc6 in magic ring, slst in beg ch1 [6]

Place stitch marker in first st of rnd 1 and move it up after each round

**Rnd 2:** ch1, (sc2 in next st) 6 times, slst in beg ch1 [12]

**Rnd 3:** ch1, (sc1, sc2 in next st) 6 times, slst in beg ch1 [18]

**Rnd 4:** ch1, (sc2 in next st, sc2) 6 times, slst in beg ch1 [24]

**Rnd 5:** ch1, sc2, (sc2 in next st, sc3) 5 times, sc2 in next st, sc1, slst in beg ch1 [30]

**Rnd 6:** ch1, (sc4, sc2 in next st) 6 times, slst in beg ch1 [36]

**Rnd 7:** ch1, sc1, (sc2 in next st, sc5) 5 times, sc2 in next st, sc4, slst in beg ch1 [42]

**Rnd 8:** ch1, sc1 in each st, slst in beg ch1

Cut yarn and fasten off, leaving a 1 yard (1 m) long tail.

Make up following step 5 instructions on page 87.

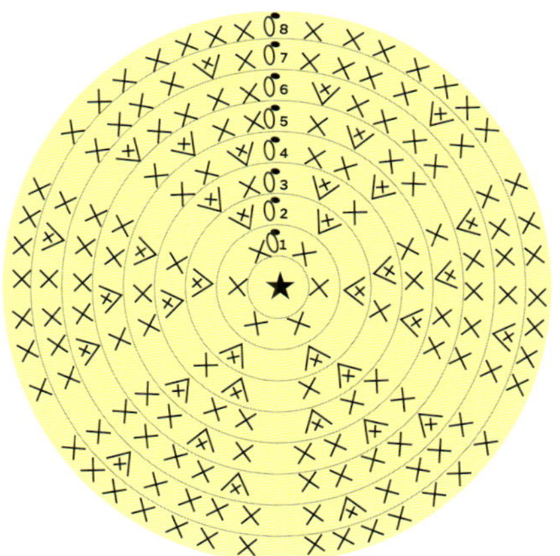

17

# Naked Cake

SHOWN ON PAGE 24

Finished Size:
15¾" (40 cm) diameter x
15¾" (40 cm) tall

## TOOLS & MATERIALS

### Yarn

- 100% acrylic bulky-weight yarn
  - 657 yds (600 m) in white
  - 539 yds (492 m) in golden brown
  - 289 yds (264 m) in red orange
  - 105 yds (96 m) in cherry pink
  - 79 yds (72 m) in red purple
  - 73 yds (66 m) in eggplant navy
  - 66 yds (60 m) in red
  - 33 yds (30 m) in yellow green
  - 33 yds (30 m) in grass green

### Other Materials

- 750 g of polyester stuffing

### Tools

- US L-11 (8 mm) crochet hook
- Yarn needle

## CONSTRUCTION STEPS

Note: Use 2 strands of yarn throughout.

**1.** Crochet the top and sides of the lower tier: Make 9 half double crochet in magic ring and crochet until round 23, following the written instructions or diagram. Note: For round 14, work into the back loop and back bump of the stitch. Cut the yarn, leaving a 3 yard (2.6 m) long tail.

**2.** Repeat rounds 1–13 to crochet the bottom of the lower tier. Fill the piece from step 1 with polyester stuffing. Use the yarn tail from step 1 to whipstitch the bottom in place.

**3.** With the top facing up, scoop the remaining loop on round 13 from below and crochet the cream.

**4.** Crochet the upper tier: Crochet until round 20, following the written instructions or diagram. Note: For round 11, work into the back loop and back bump of the stitch. Cut the yarn, leaving a 2¼ yard (2 m) long tail.

**5.** Fill the upper tier with polyester stuffing. Use the yarn tail from step 4 to sew the upper tier to the lower tier, scooping the spare loop on round 10 on the surface of the lower tier (see **Figure A**).

**6.** As in step 3, scoop the spare loop on round 13 of the upper tier from below and crochet the cream (see **Figure A**).

**7.** Crochet the berries and leaves. Cut the yarn, leaving a 12" (30 cm) long tail for the strawberries, an 8" (20 cm) long tail for the other berries, and a 6" (15 cm) long tail for the leaves. Use the wrong side of the crocheted fabric as the right side for berries other than the strawberries.

**8.** Fill each berry with polyester stuffing and sew to the upper and lower tiers of the cake as desired. Sew the leaves in place between the berries, using the photos as a guide.

*Figure A*

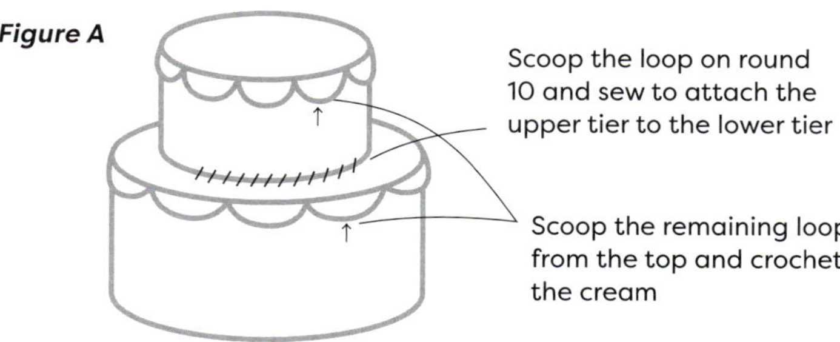

## CROCHET INSTRUCTIONS

### Lower Tier: Top and Sides

With white and US L-11 hook, make a magic ring.

**Rnd 1:** ch2 (counts as first hdc throughout), hdc8 in magic ring, slst in top of beg ch2 [9]

Place stitch marker in first st of rnd 1 and move it up after each round

**Rnd 2:** ch2, hdc1 in same st at base of ch2, (hdc2 in next st) 8 times, slst in top of beg ch2 [18]

**Rnd 3:** ch2, (hdc2 in next st, hdc1) 8 times, hdc2 in next st, slst in top of beg ch2 [27]

**Rnd 4:** ch2, hdc1 in same st at base of ch2, (hdc2, hdc2 in next st) 8 times, hdc2, slst in top of beg ch2 [36]

**Rnd 5:** ch2, hdc1, (hdc2 in next st, hdc3) 8 times, hdc2 in next st, hdc1, slst in top of beg ch2 [45]

**Rnd 6:** ch2, hdc3, (hdc2 in next st, hdc4) 8 times, hdc2 in next st, slst in top of beg ch2 [54]

**Rnd 7:** ch2, (hdc2 in next st, hdc5) 8 times, hdc2 in next st, hdc4, slst in top of beg ch2 [63]

**Rnd 8:** ch2, hdc3, (hdc2 in next st, hdc6) 8 times, hdc2 in next st, hdc2, slst in top of beg ch2 [72]

**Rnd 9:** ch2, hdc1 in same st at base of ch2, (hdc7, hdc2 in next st) 8 times, hdc7, slst in top of beg ch2 [81]

**Rnd 10:** ch2, hdc3, (hdc2 in next st, hdc8) 8 times, hdc2 in next st, hdc4, slst in top of beg ch2 [90]

**Rnd 11:** ch2, hdc8, (hdc2 in next st, hdc9) 8 times, hdc2 in next st, slst in top of beg ch2 [99]

**Rnd 12:** ch2, hdc2, (hdc2 in next st, hdc10) 8 times, hdc2 in next st, hdc7, slst in top of beg ch2 [108]

**Rnd 13:** ch2, hdc1 in each st, slst in top of beg ch2

Change to golden brown.

**Rnd 14:** ch2, hdc1 in BLO + back bump of each st, slst in top of beg ch2

**Rnd 15:** ch2, hdc1 in each st, slst in top of beg ch2

Change to white.

**Rnds 16–17:** ch2, hdc1 in each st, slst in top of beg ch2

Change to golden brown.

**Rnds 18–19:** ch2, hdc1 in each st, slst in top of beg ch2

Change to white.

Rep rnds 16–19 once more

Cut yarn and fasten off, leaving a 3 yard (2.6 m) long tail.

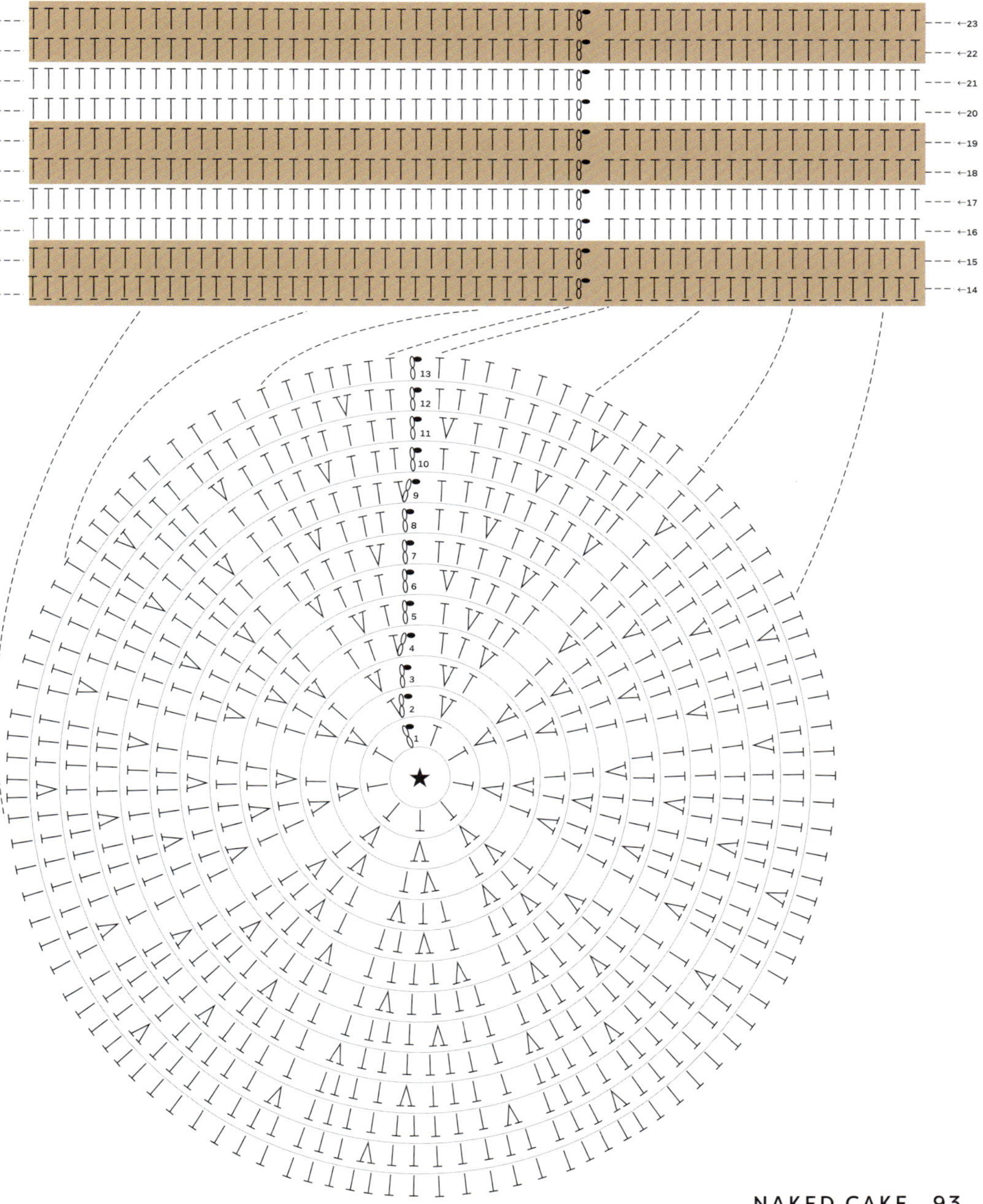

## Lower Tier: Bottom

Work a given for top and sides, to end of rnd 13. Make up following step 2 on page 92, then attach the cream.

## Lower Tier: Cream

With white, join yarn to spare front loop of rnd 13, ch1 (does not count as a st), *sc1, hdc1, dc1, (dc2 in next st) twice, dc1, hdc1, sc1, dc2, (dc2 in next st) 4 times, dc2, hdc1, sc1*; rep from * 5 times more, slst in beg ch1, fasten off and weave in ends [144]

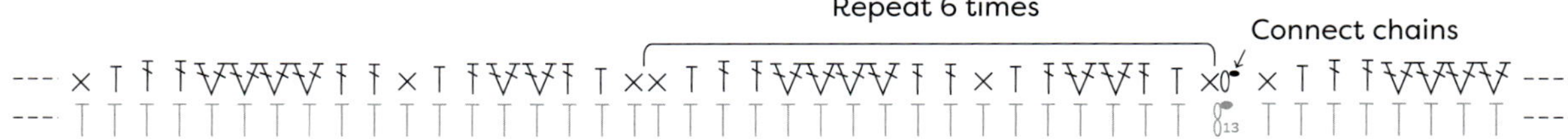


## Upper Tier

Work as given for Lower Tier: Top and Sides to end of rnd 9 [81]

**Rnd 10:** ch2, hdc1 in each st, slst in top of beg ch2

Change to golden brown.

**Rnd 11:** ch2, hdc1 in BLO + back bump of each st, slst in top of beg ch2

**Rnd 12:** ch2, hdc1 in each st, slst in top of beg ch2

Change to white.

**Rnds 13–14:** ch2, hdc1 in each st, slst in top of beg ch2

Change to golden brown.

**Rnds 15–16:** ch2, hdc1 in each st, slst in top of beg ch2

Change to white.

Rep rnds 13–16 once more

Cut yarn and fasten off, leaving a 2¼ yard (2 m) long tail. Make up following step 5 on page 92, then attach the cream.

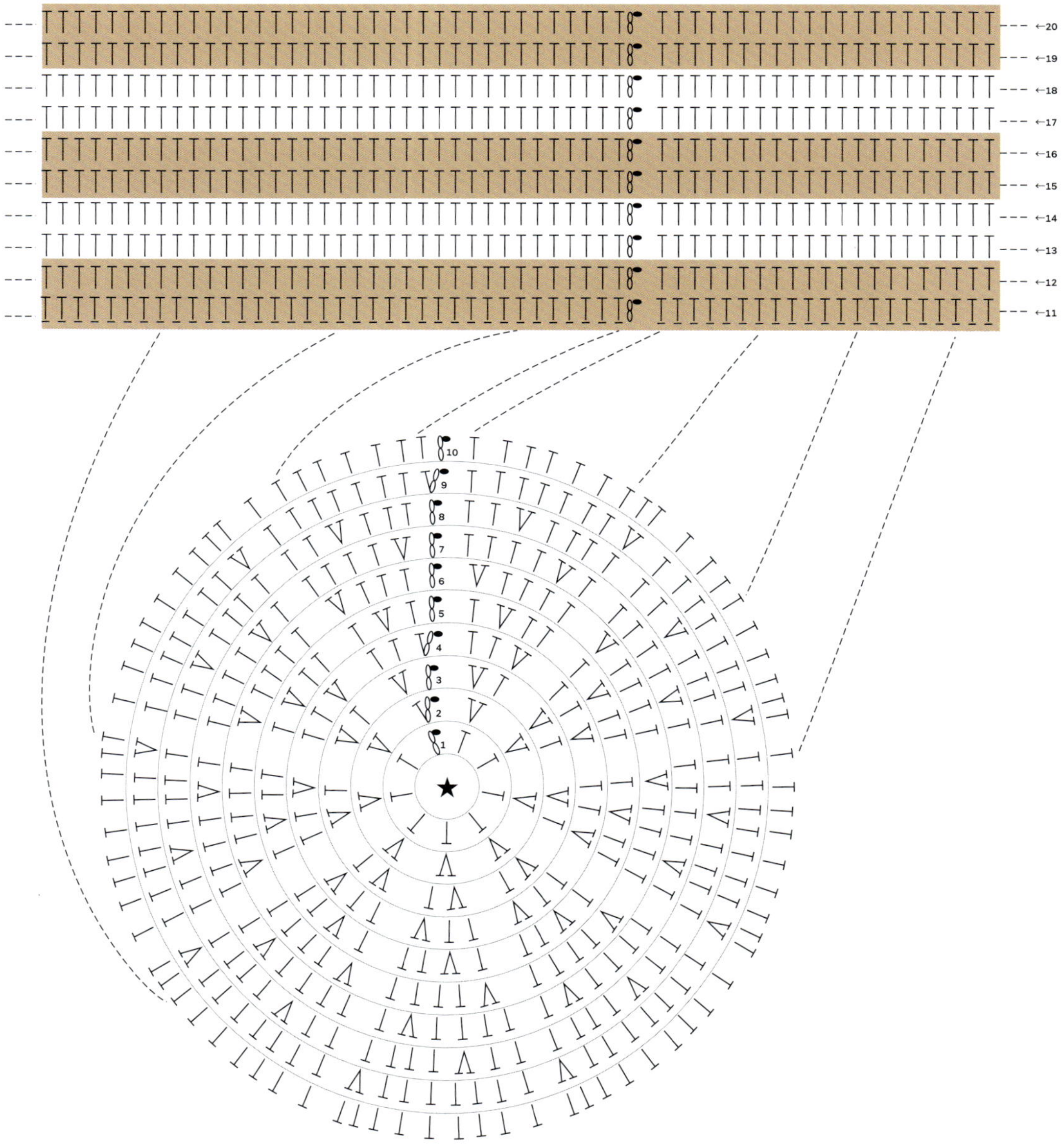

### Upper Tier: Cream

With white, join yarn to spare front loop of rnd 10, ch1 (does not count as a st), *sc1, hdc1, dc1, (dc2 in next st) 3 times, dc1, hdc1, sc1*; rep from * 8 times more, slst in beg ch1, fasten off and weave in ends [108]

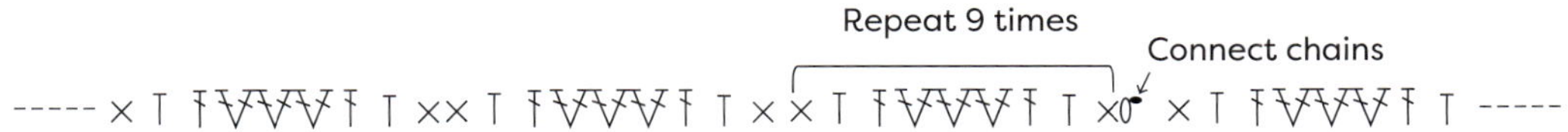


### Strawberries (make 20)

With red orange and US L-11 hook, make a magic ring.

**Rnd 1:** ch1 (does not count as a st throughout), sc6 in magic ring, slst in beg ch1 [6]

Place stitch marker in first st of rnd 1 and move it up after each round

**Rnd 2:** ch1, (sc1, sc2 in next st) 3 times, slst in beg ch1 [9]

**Rnd 3:** ch1, (sc2 in next st, sc2) 3 times, slst in beg ch1 [12]

**Rnd 4:** ch1, sc2, (sc2 in next st, sc3) twice, sc2 in next st, sc1, slst in beg ch1 [15]

**Rnd 5:** ch1, sc1 in each st, slst in beg ch1

**Rnd 6:** ch1, (sc1, sc2tog) 5 times, slst in beg ch1 [10]

Cut yarn and fasten off, leaving a 12" (30 cm) long tail.

Make up following steps 7–8 on page 92.

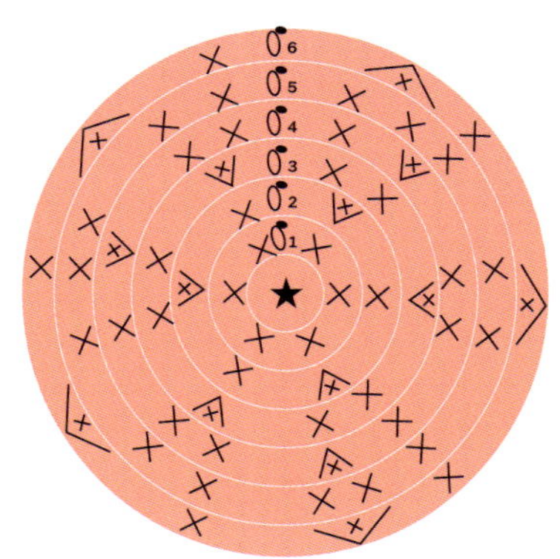

### Blueberries (make 12)

With eggplant navy and US L-11 hook, make a magic ring.

**Rnd 1:** ch1 (does not count as a st throughout), sc5 in magic ring, slst in beg ch1 [5]

Place stitch marker in first st of rnd 1 and move it up after each round

**Rnd 2:** ch1, (sc2 in next st) 5 times, slst in beg ch1 [10]

**Rnd 3:** ch1, (sc2tog) 5 times, slst in beg ch1 [5]

Cut yarn and fasten off, leaving an 8" (20 cm) long tail. Make up following steps 7–8 on page 92.

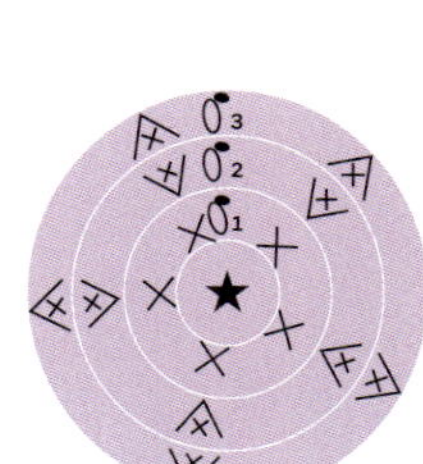

### Black Currants (make 13)

With red purple, follow instructions for Blueberries.

### Cranberries (make 11)

With red, follow instructions for Blueberries.

## Raspberries (make 12)

With cherry pink and US L-11 hook, make a magic ring.
**Rnd 1:** ch1 (does not count as a st throughout), sc6 in magic ring, slst in beg ch1 [6]
Place stitch marker in first st of rnd 1 and move it up after each round
**Rnd 2:** ch1, (sc2 in next st) 6 times, slst in beg ch1 [12]
**Rnds 3–4:** ch1, sc1 in each st, slst in beg ch1 (2 rnds)
**Rnd 5:** ch1, (sc2tog) 6 times, slst in beg ch1 [6]
Cut yarn and fasten off, leaving an 8" (20 cm) long tail.
Make up following steps 7–8 on page 92.

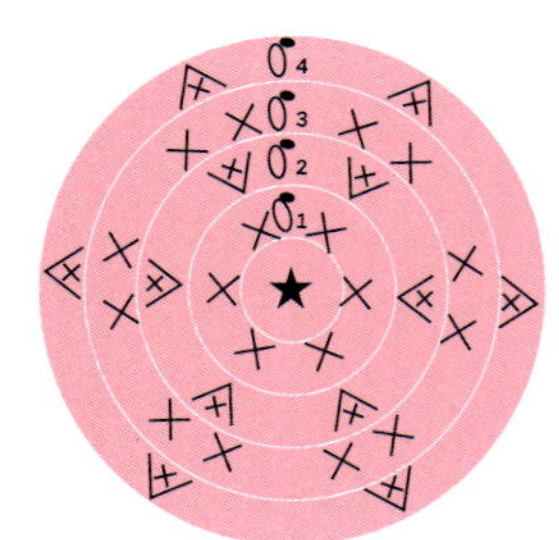

## Leaves (make 8 in yellow green, 8 in grass green)

With chosen color and US L-11 hook, ch7.
**Rnd 1:** dc1 in fourth ch from hook, hdc1 in next ch, sc1 in next ch, 3slst in last ch, rotate and work along opposite side of ch, sc1 in next ch, hdc1 in next ch, dc1 in next ch, (hdc1 in next ch) twice.
Fasten off, leaving a 6" (15 cm) long tail. Make up following steps 7–8 on page 92.

Start

18

# Strawberry Cupcake

**SHOWN ON PAGE 31**

Finished Size:
5¼" (13 cm) diameter x
7" (17.5 cm) tall

## TOOLS & MATERIALS

### Yarn

- 100% acrylic bulky-weight yarn
  - 53 yds (48 m) in light pink
  - 33 yds (30 m) in white
  - 27 yds (24 m) in ice green
  - 14 yds (12 m) in dark brown
  - 6 yds (5 m) in red orange

### Other Materials

- 35 g of polyester stuffing
- 12 heart-shaped beads in light blue, pink, yellow, light pink, and white
- White sewing thread

### Tools

- US 7 (4.5 mm) crochet hook
- Yarn needle
- Sewing needle
- Tweezers

## CONSTRUCTION STEPS

Note: Use one strand of yarn throughout.

**1.** Crochet the cake body: Start with a magic ring and crochet until round 25. Turn the fabric inside out, fill with polyester stuffing, then continue crocheting until round 27. Add more polyester stuffing then fasten off, leaving an 8" (20 cm) long tail. Gather the final stitches on round 27 using a yarn needle, pull tight to close, then fasten off.

**2.** Crochet the cream: Make 19 foundation chains and work flat in rows until row 24, then fasten off, leaving a 20" (50 cm) long tail. Align the first and 24th rows together to make a tube, then join with whipstitch. Sew running stitch around both ends, pull tight to gather, then fasten off at the center. Sew the cream portion to the cake body (see **Figure A**).

**3.** Crochet the strawberry and fasten off, leaving an 8" (20 cm) long tail. Fill with polyester stuffing, then sew to the center of the cream.

**4.** Crochet the cup bottom and fasten off. Crochet the cup side and fasten off, leaving a 1 yard (1 m) long tail.

**5.** Align row ends of the cup side with the bottom so the wrong side of the cup is facing out and the right side of the bottom is facing out. Whipstitch together, skipping a stitch every fifth row on the cup side. Finally, sew the seam of the cup side, from row 52 to the foundation row using whipstitch (see **Figure B**).

**6.** Use a sewing needle and thread to attach candy beads to the cream portion.

***Figure A***

Running stitch
Wrong side
Whipstitch together
Sew running stitch on both ends
Gather
Fasten off

***Figure B***

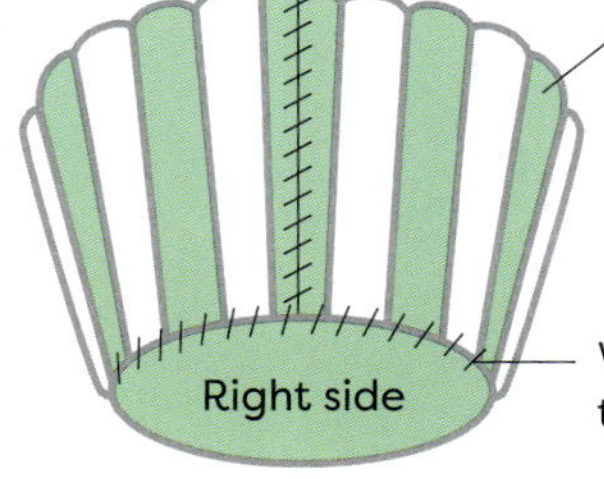

## CROCHET INSTRUCTIONS

### Cake Body

With light pink and US 7 hook, make a magic ring.

**Rnd 1:** ch1 (does not count as a st throughout), sc6 in magic ring, slst in beg ch1 [6]

Place stitch marker in first st of rnd 1 and move it up after each round

**Rnd 2:** ch1, (sc2 in next st) 6 times, slst in beg ch1 [12]

**Rnd 3:** ch1, (sc1, sc2 in next st) 6 times, slst in beg ch1 [18]

**Rnd 4:** ch1, (sc2 in next st, sc2) 6 times, slst in beg ch1 [24]

**Rnd 5:** ch1, sc2, (sc2 in next st, sc3) 5 times, sc2 in next st, sc1, slst in beg ch1 [30]

**Rnd 6:** ch1, (sc4, sc2 in next st) 6 times, slst in beg ch1 [36]

**Rnd 7:** ch1, sc1, (sc2 in next st, sc5) 5 times, sc2 in next st, sc4, slst in beg ch1 [42]

**Rnd 8:** ch1, sc3, (sc2 in next st, sc6) 5 times, sc2 in next st, sc3, slst in beg ch1 [48]

**Rnd 9:** ch1, sc6, (sc2 in next st, sc7) 5 times, sc2 in next st, sc1, slst in beg ch1 [54]

**Rnd 10:** ch1, (sc2 in next st, sc8) 6 times, slst in beg ch1 [60]

**Rnd 11:** ch1, sc1 in each st, slst in beg ch1

**Rnd 12:** ch1, (sc2tog, sc8) 6 times, slst in beg ch1 [54]

**Rnd 13:** as rnd 11

**Rnd 14:** ch1, (sc6, sc2tog, sc1) 6 times, slst in beg ch1 [48]

**Rnd 15:** as rnd 11

**Rnd 16:** ch1, (sc3, sc2tog, sc3) 6 times, slst in beg ch1 [42]

**Rnd 17:** as rnd 11

**Rnd 18:** ch1, (sc1, sc2tog, sc4) 6 times, slst in beg ch1 [36]

**Rnds 19–21:** as rnd 11 (3 rnds)

**Rnd 22:** ch1, (sc4, sc2tog) 6 times, slst in beg ch1 [30]

**Rnd 23:** as rnd 11

**Rnd 24:** ch1, (sc2, sc2tog, sc1) 6 times, slst in beg ch1 [24]

**Rnd 25:** ch1, (sc2, sc2tog) 6 times, slst in beg ch1 [18]

Turn fabric inside out, add polyester stuffing, then continue crocheting.

**Rnd 26:** ch1, (sc1, sc2tog) 6 times, slst in beg ch1 [12]

**Rnd 27:** ch1, (sc2tog) 6 times, slst in beg ch1 [6]

Add more stuffing if needed, then cut yarn, leaving an 8" (20 cm) long tail. Make up following step 1 instructions on page 97.

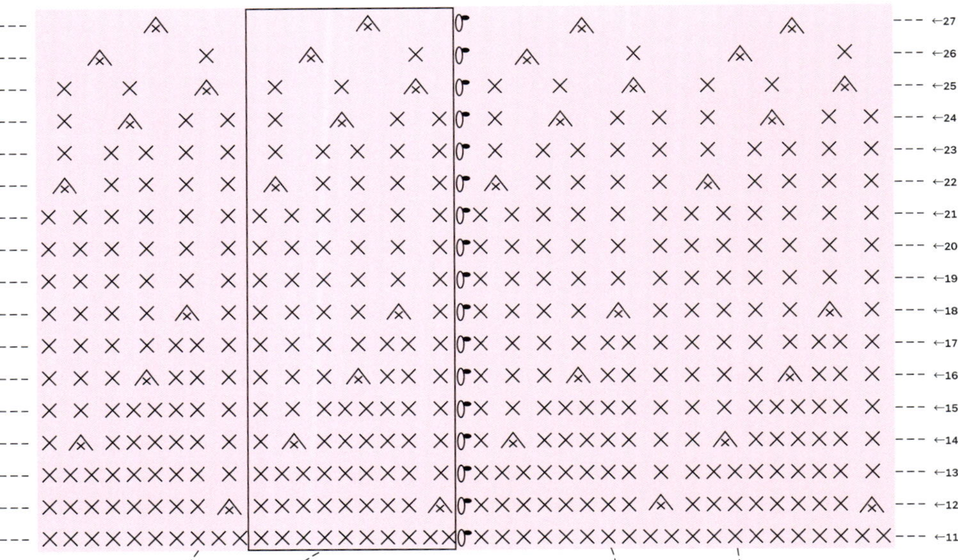


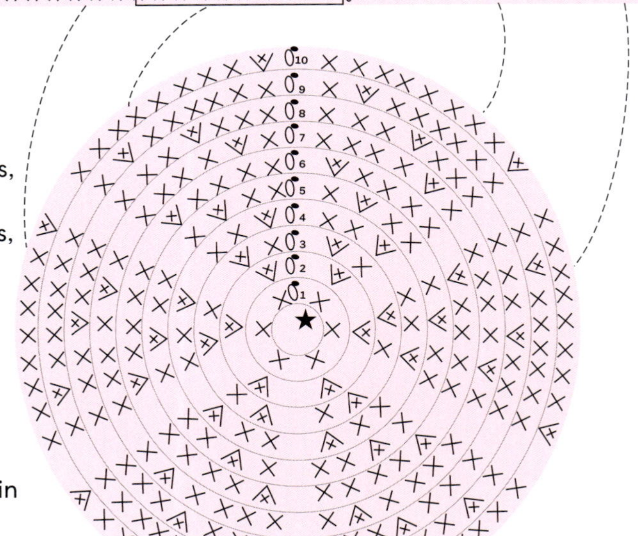

## Cream

With white and US 7 hook, ch19.
**Row 1:** sc1 in second ch from hook, sc1 in each ch to the end, turn [18]
**Row 2:** ch1 (does not count as a st throughout), sc2tog BLO, sc15 BLO, sc2 in BLO of last st, turn [18]
*Change to dark brown
**Row 3:** ch1, sc2 in BLO of first st, sc15 BLO, sc2tog BLO, turn [18]
**Row 4:** ch1, sc2tog BLO, sc15 BLO, sc2 in BLO of last st, turn [18]
Change to white
**Row 5:** ch1, sc2 in BLO of first st, sc15 BLO, sc2tog BLO, turn [18]
**Row 6:** ch1, sc2tog BLO, sc15 BLO, sc2 in BLO of last st, turn [18]*
**Rows 7–22:** rep from * to * 4 times more
Change to dark brown
**Rows 23–24:** rep rows 3 and 4
Cut yarn and fasten off, leaving a 20" (50 cm) long tail. Make up following step 2 instructions on page 97.

Alternate white and brown every two rows

## Strawberry

With red orange and US 7 hook, make a magic ring.
**Rnd 1:** ch1 (does not count as a st throughout), sc6 in magic ring, slst in beg ch1 [6]
Place stitch marker in first st of rnd 1 and move it up after each round
**Rnd 2:** ch1, (sc1, sc2 in next st) 3 times, slst in beg ch1 [9]
**Rnd 3:** ch1, (sc2 in next st, sc2) 3 times, slst in beg ch1 [12]

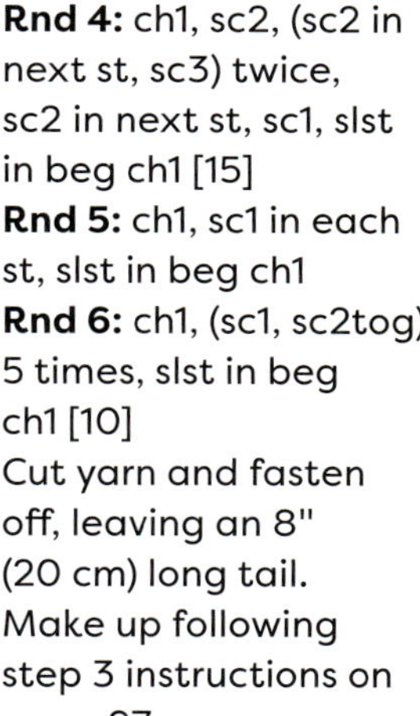

**Rnd 4:** ch1, sc2, (sc2 in next st, sc3) twice, sc2 in next st, sc1, slst in beg ch1 [15]
**Rnd 5:** ch1, sc1 in each st, slst in beg ch1
**Rnd 6:** ch1, (sc1, sc2tog) 5 times, slst in beg ch1 [10]
Cut yarn and fasten off, leaving an 8" (20 cm) long tail.
Make up following step 3 instructions on page 97.

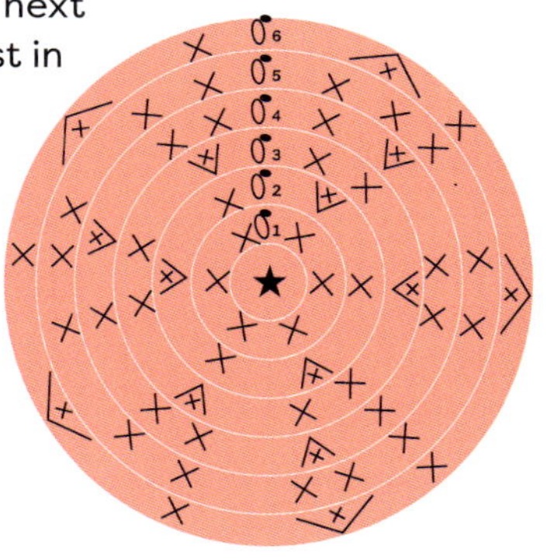

## Cup Bottom

With ice green and US 7 hook, make a magic ring.
**Rnd 1:** ch1 (does not count as a st throughout), sc7 in magic ring, slst in beg ch1 [7]
Place stitch marker in first st of rnd 1 and move it up after each round
**Rnd 2:** ch1, (sc2 in next st) 7 times, slst in beg ch1 [14]
**Rnd 3:** ch1, (sc1, sc2 in next st) 7 times, slst in beg ch1 [21]
**Rnd 4:** ch1, (sc2 in next st, sc2) 7 times, slst in beg ch1 [28]
**Rnd 5:** ch1, sc2, (sc2 in next st, sc3) 6 times, sc2 in next st, sc1, slst in beg ch1 [35]
**Rnd 6:** ch1, (sc4, sc2 in next st) 7 times, slst in beg ch1 [42]
Cut yarn and fasten off.

## Cup Side

With ice green and US 7 hook, ch12.
Bring previous yarn to the front when changing colors.
**Row 1:** sc1 in second ch from hook, sc1 in each ch to the end, turn [11]
*Change to white
**Row 2:** ch1 (does not count as a st throughout), sc11 BLO, turn
**Row 3:** ch1 (does not count as a st throughout), sc11, turn. Change to ice green
**Row 4:** ch1 (does not count as a st throughout), sc11 BLO, turn
**Row 5:** ch1 (does not count as a st throughout), sc11, turn*
**Rows 6–49:** rep from * to * 11 times more
Change to white
**Rows 50–51:** rep rows 2 and 3.
Change to ice green
**Row 52:** ch1 (does not count as a st throughout), sc11 BLO
Cut yarn and fasten off, leaving a 1 yard (1 m) long tail. Make up following step 5 instructions on page 97.

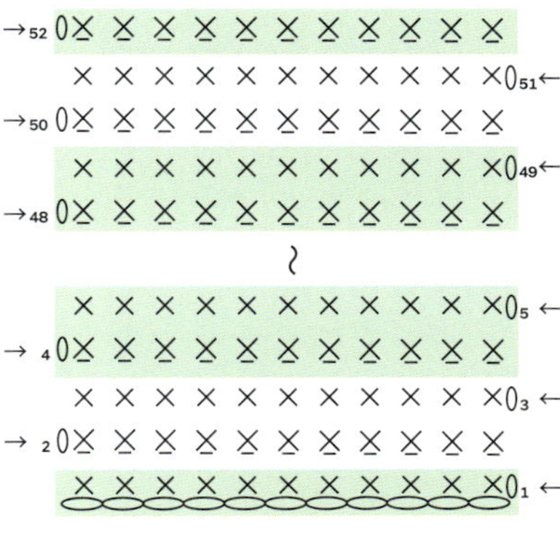

Alternate white and ice green every two rows for rows 2 to 51. Bring the previous yarn to the front when changing colors.

19

# Chocolate Roll Cake

SHOWN ON PAGE 31

Finished Size:
5¼" (13 cm) wide x 2" (5 cm) deep x 6¼" (16 cm) tall

## TOOLS & MATERIALS

### Yarn

- 100% acrylic bulky-weight yarn
  - 46 yds (42 m) in dark brown
  - 27 yds (24 m) in light brown
  - 20 yds (18 m) in light pink
  - 11 yds (10 m) in white
  - 6 yds (5 m) in red orange

### Other Materials

- 15 g of polyester stuffing
- 6 beads
- White sewing thread

### Tools

- US 7 (4.5 mm) crochet hook
- US K-10.5 (7 mm) crochet hook
- Yarn needle
- Sewing needle

## CONSTRUCTION STEPS

Note: Crochet body A, body B, and whipped cream using two strands of yarn with US K-10.5 crochet hook. Crochet the strawberry using one strand of yarn with US 7 crochet hook.

Refer to page 48 for crochet technique photos for this project.

**1.** Crochet body A: Make a magic ring and crochet until round 9, changing colors as noted. Cut the yarn, leaving a 1 yard (1 m) long tail.

**2.** Crochet body B working as given for body A through round 5.

**3.** Whipstitch body B to body A, filling with polyester stuffing as you sew.

**4.** Crochet the strawberry and whipped cream, following written instructions or diagrams. Cut the yarn, leaving a 12" (30 cm) long tail for each.

**5.** Fill the strawberry with polyester stuffing and sew to the roll cake (see **Figure A** for placement).

**6.** Use the yarn tails to tie the whipped cream into a loop (see **Figure B**). Sew the whipped cream in place around the strawberry.

**7.** Sew the beads to the whipped cream.

*Figure A*

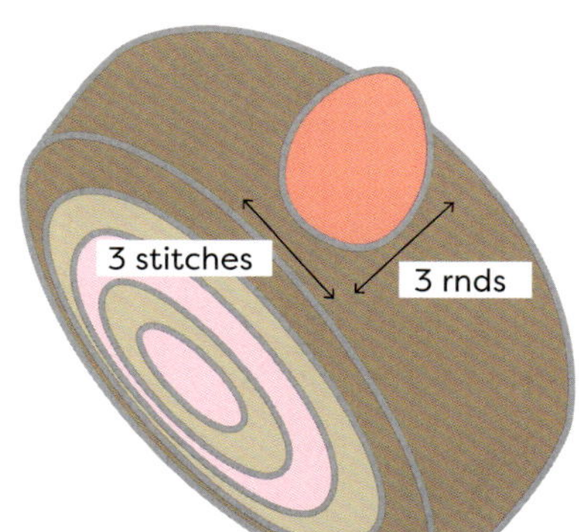


*Figure B*

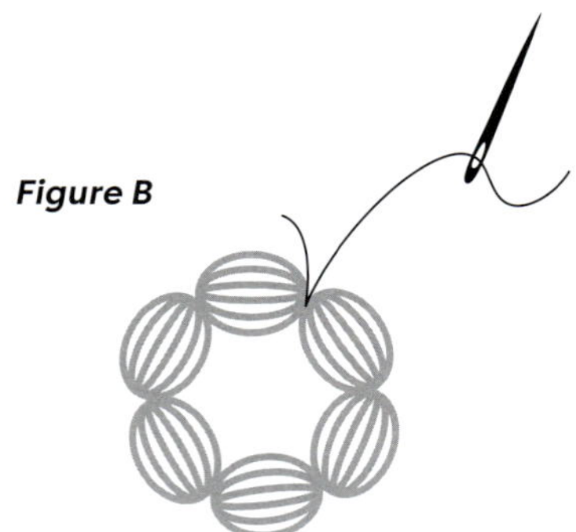

Tie the starting and ending yarn tails together firmly to make a loop. Sew around the strawberry using the remaining yarn.

## CROCHET INSTRUCTIONS

### Body A

With light pink and US K-10.5 hook, make a magic ring.
The spirals are crocheted by working into some of the stitches from the beginning of that round and changing color when indicated. Keep yarns not in use along back of work.

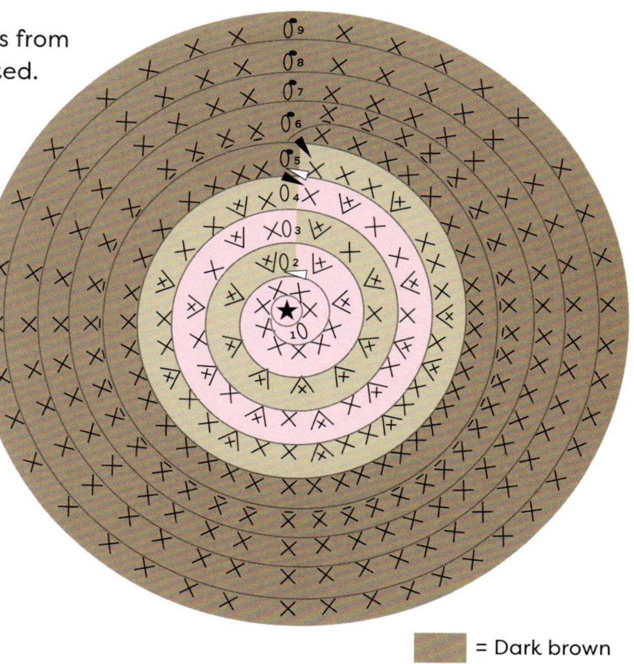


**Rnd 1:** ch1 (does not count as a st throughout), sc9 in magic ring, (sc2 in next st) 2 times [13]
Take light pink off the hook and place stitch marker in the loop. Join in light brown in the next st.
**Rnd 2:** ch1, (sc2 in next st) 7 times, (sc1, sc2 in next st) twice [20]
Take light brown off the hook and place stitch marker in the loop. Place pink loop back on the hook.
**Rnd 3:** ch1, (sc1, sc2 in next st) 8 times, sc2, sc2 in next st, sc1 [29]
Cut pink and fasten off. Place light brown loop back on the hook.
**Rnd 4:** ch1, sc1, (sc2 in next st, sc2) 6 times, sc2 in next st, sc1, (sc2 in next st, sc3) twice [38]
Cut light brown and fasten off. Join dark brown in next st.
**Rnd 5:** ch1, sc1 in each st, slst in beg ch1.
**Rnd 6:** ch1, sc1 BLO in each st, slst in beg ch1
**Rnds 7–9:** as rnd 5 (3 rnds)
Cut yarn and fasten off, leaving a 1 yard (1 m) long tail.

### Body B

Work as given for Body A, ending after rnd 5.
Make up following step 3 instructions on page 100.

### Strawberry

With red orange and US 7 hook, make a magic ring.
**Rnd 1:** ch1 (does not count as a st throughout), sc6 in magic ring, slst in beg ch1 [6]
Place stitch marker in first st of rnd 1 and move it up after each round
**Rnd 2:** ch1, (sc1, sc2 in next st) 3 times, slst in beg ch1 [9]
**Rnd 3:** ch1, (sc2 in next st, sc2) 3 times, slst in beg ch1 [12]
**Rnd 4:** ch1, sc2, (sc2 in next st, sc3) twice, sc2 in next st, sc1, slst in beg ch1 [15]
**Rnd 5:** ch1, sc1 in each st, slst in beg ch1
**Rnd 6:** ch1, (sc1, sc2tog) 5 times, slst in beg ch1 [10]
Cut yarn and fasten off, leaving a 12" (30 cm) long tail. Make up following step 5 instructions on page 100.

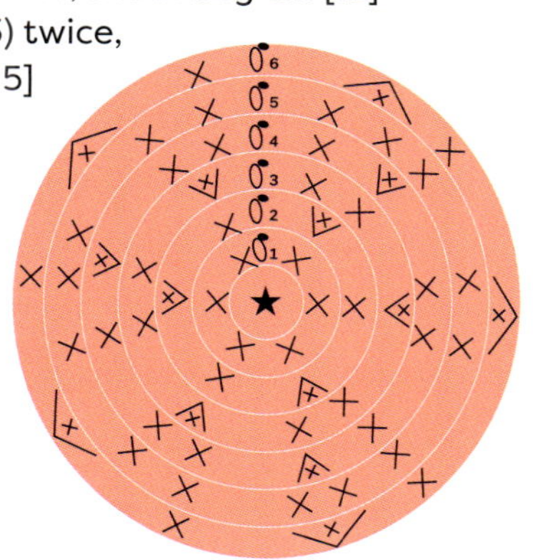

### Whipped Cream

With white and US K-10.5 hook, ch4
**Row 1:** 5dc-cl in fourth ch from hook
**Row 2:** ch4, 5dc-cl in fourth ch from hook
**Rows 3–6:** as row 2 (4 rows)
Cut yarn and fasten off, leaving a 12" (30 cm) long tail. Make up following step 6 instructions on page 100.

20

# Strawberry Shortcake

SHOWN ON PAGE 31

Finished Size:
5¾" (14.5 cm) wide x 4" (10 cm) deep x 5¼" (13.5 cm) tall

## TOOLS & MATERIALS

### Yarn

- 100% acrylic bulky-weight yarn
  - 53 yds (48 m) in white
  - 33 yds (30 m) in cream
  - 10 yds (9 m) in red orange
  - 5 yds (4 m) in eggplant navy
  - 4 yds (3 m) in light pink

### Other Materials

- 30 g of polyester stuffing
- 6 beads
- White sewing thread

### Tools

- US 7 (4.5 mm) crochet hook
- US N-15 (10 mm) crochet hook
- Yarn needle
- Felting needle

## CONSTRUCTION STEPS

Note: Crochet the body, strawberry, and blueberries using one strand of yarn with US 7 crochet hook. Crochet whipped cream A and B using 2 strands of yarn with US N-15 crochet hook.
Note: Crochet straight as much as possible so that each single crochet stitch aligns with the corresponding single crochet stitch of the previous row.

**1.** Crochet the top and sides of the body: Start with a magic ring and crochet in rows through row 22, as you increase. Continue crocheting the sides in the round, as shown, then cut the yarn, leaving a 1½ yard (1.3 m) long tail.

**2.** Crochet the bottom, working as given for the top through row 22.

**3.** Fill the body with polyester stuffing. Cover with the bottom and whipstitch closed. Use white yarn to sew the white area of the sides.

**4.** Adjust the shape using a felting needle.

**5.** Crochet the strawberry, blueberries, and whipped cream A and B. Cut the yarn, leaving a 12" (30 cm) long tail for each. Sew to the top of the cake (refer to **Figure A** for placement).

***Figure A***

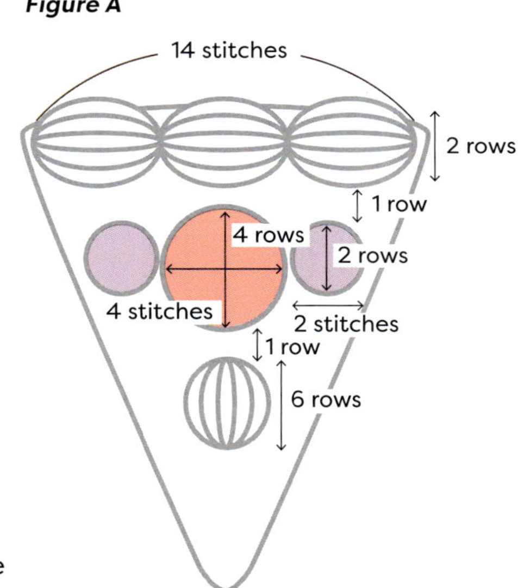

## CROCHET INSTRUCTIONS

### Body: Top

With white and US 7 hook, make a magic ring.
**Row 1:** ch1 (does not count as a st throughout), sc2 in magic ring, turn [2]
Work in rows.
**Row 2:** ch1, sc1, sc2 in next st, turn [3]
**Row 3:** ch1, sc2, sc2 in last st, turn [4]
**Row 4:** ch1, sc1 in each st to last st, sc2 in last st, turn [5]
**Row 5:** ch1, sc1 in each st, turn
**Rows 6–21:** rep rows 4–5 a further 8 times [13]
**Row 22:** ch1, sc12, sc2 in last st [14]

### Body: Sides

Rejoin white to ch1 of row 22. Work around the top as follows:
**Rnd 1:** ch1 (does not count as a st throughout), sc1 in each row-end of first side, to last row-end, sc2 in last row-end to make 23 sts, ch1, working along next side, sc2 in first row-end, sc1 in each of 21 row-ends, sc14 across straight edge (the stitches of row 22), slst in beg ch1.
Place stitch marker in first st of rnd 1 and move it up after each round
**Rnd 2:** ch1, sc1 in each st and into the ch1-sp at the tip, slst in beg ch1 [61]
Change to cream
**Rnds 3–4:** in cream, ch1, sc1 in each st to end, slst in beg ch1
Change to white
**Rnd 5:** in white, ch1, sc1 in each st to end, slst in beg ch1
Join in red orange as needed
**Rnd 6:** ch1, sc3 in white, sc3 in red orange, (sc4 in white, sc3 in red orange) twice, sc7 in white, (sc3 in red orange, sc4 in white) twice, sc3 in red orange, sc17 in white, slst in beg ch1
Join light pink as needed
**Rnd 7:** ch1, (sc2 in white, sc1 in red orange, sc3 in light pink, sc1 in red orange) 3 times, sc5 in white, (sc1 in red orange, sc3 in light pink, sc1 in red orange, sc2 in white) 3 times, sc14 in white, slst in beg ch1
Change to cream
**Rnds 8–12:** as rnds 3–7
Change to cream
**Rnds 13–14:** as rnds 3–4
Fasten off, leaving a 1½ yard (1.3 m) long tail.

### Body: Bottom

Work as given for Top, ending after row 22.
Make up following step 3 instructions on page 102.

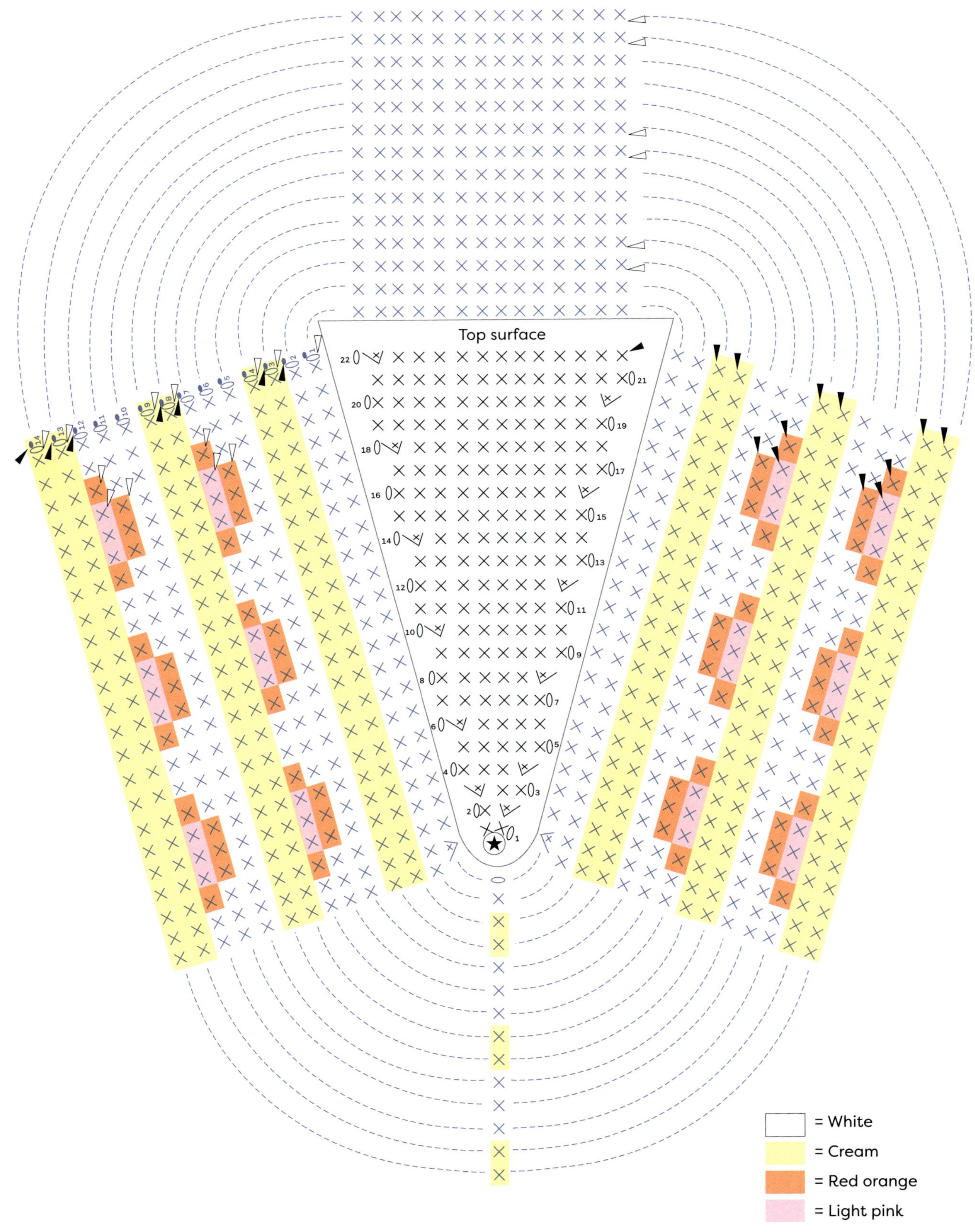
Top surface
= White
= Cream
= Red orange
= Light pink

## Strawberry

With red orange and US 7 hook, work as given for Chocolate Roll Cake Strawberry on page 101.
Cut yarn and fasten off, leaving a 12" (30 cm) long tail.

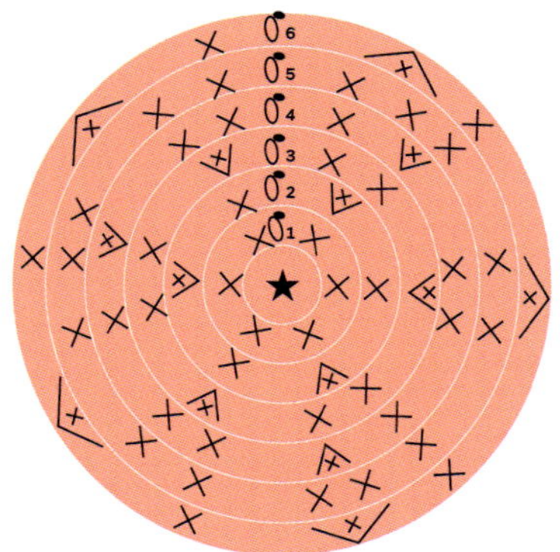

## Blueberries (make 2)

With eggplant navy and US 7 hook, work as given for Naked Cake Blueberry on page 95.
Cut yarn and fasten off, leaving a 12" (30 cm) long tail.

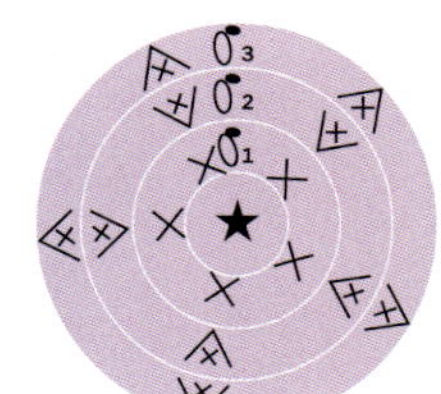

## Whipped Cream A

With white and US N-15 hook, ch4
**Row 1:** 5dc-cl in fourth ch from hook
**Row 2:** ch4, 5dc-cl in fourth ch from hook
**Rows 3:** as row 2
Cut yarn and fasten off, leaving a 12" (30 cm) long tail.

## Whipped Cream B

With white and US N-15 hook, ch4
**Row 1:** 5dc-cl in fourth ch from hook
Cut yarn and fasten off, leaving a 12" (30 cm) long tail.
Make up following step 5 instructions on page 102.

21

# Fruit Tarte

SHOWN ON PAGE 30

Finished Size:
5" (13 cm) diameter x
5" (13 cm) tall

## TOOLS & MATERIALS

### Yarn

- 100% acrylic bulky-weight yarn
  - 40 yds (36 m) in golden brown
  - 40 yds (36 m) in lime green
  - 33 yds (30 m) in red purple
  - 20 yds (18 m) in eggplant navy
  - 14 yds (12 m) in cream

### Other Materials

- 21 g of polyester stuffing

### Tools

- US 7 (4.5 mm) crochet hook
- Yarn needle
- Tweezers

## CONSTRUCTION STEPS

Note: Use one strand of yarn throughout.

**1.** Crochet the tarte crust: Make 7 single crochet in a magic ring and crochet until round 11 as indicated in the diagram or written instructions.

**2.** Crochet the cream: Work as given for the tarte crust through round 7. Cut yarn and fasten off, leaving a 20" (50 cm) long tail.

**3.** Sew the cream to the tarte crust, using the remaining yarn tail from step 2 and scooping inside loop at round 9 of the tarte. After sewing around ⅔ of the tarte, fill with polyester stuffing, and then continue sewing and stuffing to the end.

**4.** Crochet the grapes as indicated in the diagram or written instructions, following the colors, sizes, and quantities listed in the chart. To finish each grape, turn inside out and fill with polyester stuffing. Cut the yarn, leaving a 10" (25 cm) long tail. Use a yarn needle to scoop one side of the loop at the last round to gather the grape closed.

**5.** Crochet the blueberries as indicated in the diagram or written instructions. Follow the same process used in step 4 to finish each blueberry.

**6.** Sew the grapes and blueberries to the tarte (refer to **Figure A** for placement).

***Figure A***

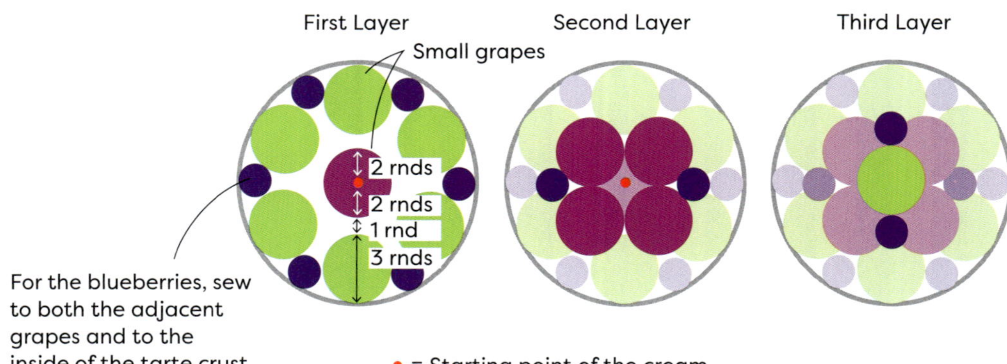

## CROCHET INSTRUCTIONS

### Tarte Crust

With golden brown and US 7 hook, make a magic ring.

**Rnd 1:** ch1 (does not count as a st throughout), sc7 in magic ring, slst in beg ch1 [7]

Place stitch marker in first st of rnd 1 and move it up after each round

**Rnd 2:** ch1, (sc2 in next st) 7 times, slst in beg ch1 [14]

**Rnd 3:** ch1, (sc1, sc2 in next st) 7 times, slst in beg ch1 [21]

**Rnd 4:** ch1, (sc2 in next st, sc2) 6 times, slst in beg ch1 [28]

**Rnd 5:** ch1, sc2, (sc2 in next st, sc3) 6 times, sc2 in next st, sc1, slst in beg ch1 [35]

**Rnd 6:** ch1, (sc4, sc2 in next st) 7 times, slst in beg ch1 [42]

**Rnd 7:** ch1, sc1, (sc2 in next st, sc5) 6 times, sc2 in next st, sc4, slst in beg ch1 [49]

**Rnd 8:** ch3 (counts as first dc), dc2, (dc2 in next st, dc6) 6 times, dc2 in next st, dc3, slst in top of beg ch3 [56]

**Rnds 9–12:** ch3 (counts as first dc), dc1, (FPdc2, dc2) 13 times, FPdc2, slst in top of beg ch3 (4 rnds)

Cut yarn and fasten off.

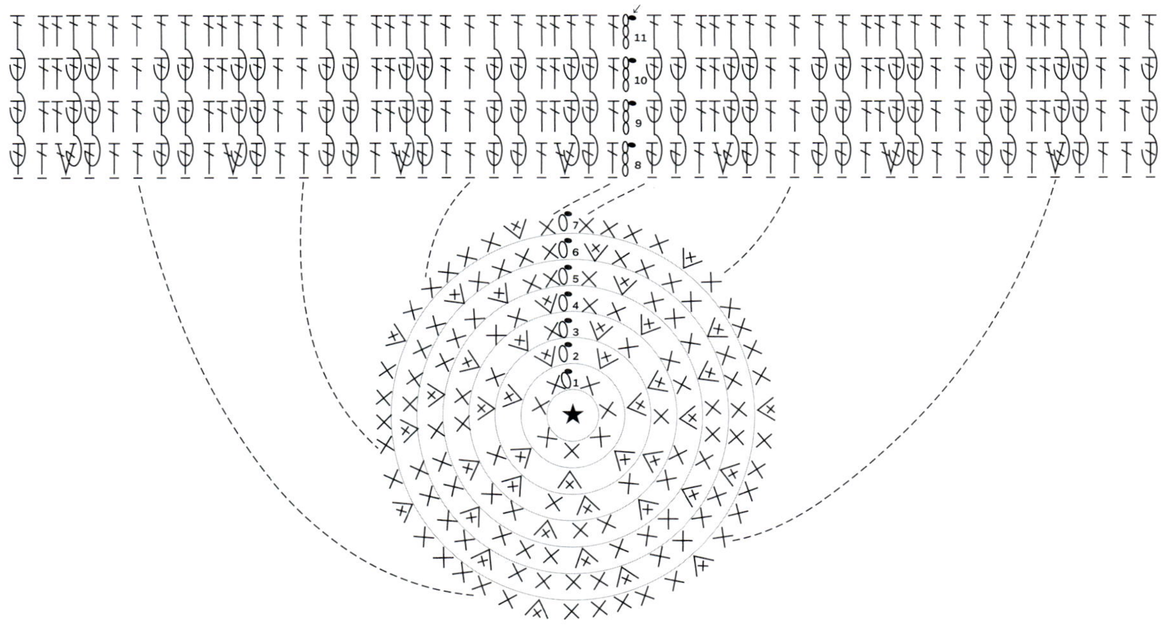


### Cream

With cream and US 7 hook, work as given for the Tarte Crust through round 7.

Cut yarn and fasten off, leaving a 20" (50 cm) long tail.

Follow step 3 on page 106 to attach the cream to the tarte crust.

## Grapes (make 17 in colors and sizes noted in chart below)

With US 7 hook, make a magic ring.
**Rnd 1:** ch1 (does not count as a st throughout), sc6 in magic ring, slst in beg ch1 [6]
Place stitch marker in first st of rnd 1 and move it up after each round
**Rnd 2:** ch1, (sc2 in next st) 6 times, slst in beg ch1 [12]
**Rnd 3:** ch1, (sc3, sc2 in next st) 3 times, slst in beg ch1 [15]
**Rnds 4–5:** ch1, sc1 in each st, slst in beg ch1 (2 rnds)
**Rnd 6:** ch1, (sc1, sc2tog) 5 times, slst in beg ch1 [10]
**Rnd 7:** ch1, (sc2tog) 5 times, slst in beg ch1 [5]
Cut yarn and fasten off, leaving a 10" (25 cm) long tail.
Follow step 4 on page 106 to finish.

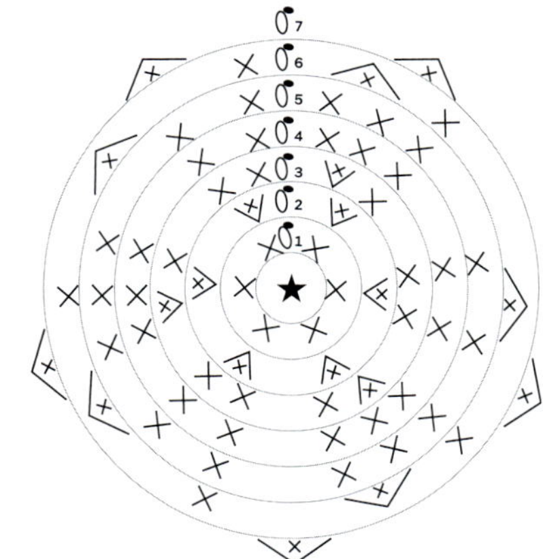

| Yarn Color | Size | Quantity |
|---|---|---|
| Lime green | Small (crochet rounds 1–6) | 6 |
| Lime green | Large (crochet rounds 1–7) | 1 |
| Red purple | Small (crochet rounds 1–6) | 6 |
| Red purple | Large (crochet rounds 1–7) | 4 |

## Blueberries

With eggplant navy and US 7 hook, make a magic ring.
**Rnd 1:** ch1 (does not count as a st throughout), sc5 in magic ring, slst in beg ch1 [5]
Place stitch marker in first st of rnd 1 and move it up after each round
**Rnd 2:** ch1, (sc2 in next st) 5 times, slst in beg ch1 [10]
**Rnd 3:** ch1, (sc2tog) 5 times, slst in beg ch1 [5]
Cut yarn and fasten off, leaving a 10" (25 cm) long tail.
Follow the same process used in step 4 to finish.

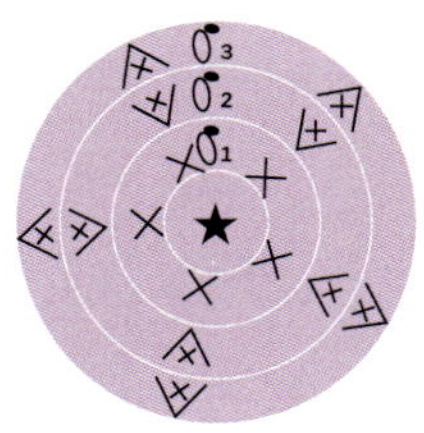

22

# Mousse au Citron

SHOWN ON PAGE 30

Finished Size:
4" (10 cm) diameter x
7" (17.5 cm) tall

## TOOLS & MATERIALS

### Yarn

- 100% acrylic bulky-weight yarn
  - 20 yds (18 m) in lemon
  - 20 yds (18 m) in light orange
  - 20 yds (18 m) in cream
  - 14 yds (12 m) in dark beige
  - 14 yds (12 m) in white
  - 4 yds (3 m) in bright orange
  - 4 yds (3 m) in orange
  - 4 yds (3 m) in off-white
  - 4 yds (3 m) in yellow green

### Other Materials

- 30 g of polyester stuffing
- 32" (80) cm of lace trim
- Craft glue

### Tools

- US 7 (4.5 mm) crochet hook
- US L-11 (8 mm) crochet hook
- Yarn needle
- Felting needle

## CONSTRUCTION STEPS

Note: Crochet the body, orange slice, lemon slice, and mint leaves using one strand of yarn with US 7 crochet hook. Crochet the whipped cream using two strands of yarn with US L-11 crochet hook.

**1.** Crochet the body: Start with a magic ring and crochet as indicated in the diagram or written instructions through round 19. Fill with polyester stuffing, then continue crocheting through round 20. Add more polyester stuffing until firm and cut the yarn, leaving an 8" (20 cm) long tail.

**2.** Gather the final stitches of round 20 using the remaining yarn tail from step 1, then pull tight and fasten off.

**3.** Use a felting needle to make both the top and bottom surfaces flat.

**4.** Crochet the orange and lemon slices as indicated in the diagram or written instructions.

**5.** Cut the yarn, leaving a 16" (40 cm) long tail. Embroider as indicated in the diagram, then fold each piece in half with wrong sides together and whipstitch together (see **Figure A**).

**6.** Crochet the whipped cream as indicated in the diagram or written instructions. Cut the yarn, leaving a 12" (30 cm) long tail. Fill with polyester stuffing and gather by pulling the yarn through the stitches indicated by the light blue dots in the diagram on page 111.

**7.** Crochet the mint leaves as indicated in the diagram or written instructions. Cut yarn and fasten off, leaving a 6" (15 cm) long tail.

**8.** Sew the orange slice, lemon slice, whipped cream, and mint leaves to the body (see **Figure B**).

**9.** Apply craft glue to the wrong side of the lace, then adhere to the side (refer to **Figure C** for placement).

***Figure A***

Fold in half and whipstitch together around curved edge

***Figure B***

View from Above

Whipped cream
5 rnds
Mint leaves
1 rnd
Orange slice
1 rnd
Lemon slice

Arrange whipped cream, orange slice, and lemon slice in a diagonal line along top surface

***Figure C***

Whipped cream
5 rnds
4 rnds
4 rnds
3 rnds
Position to attach lace

● = Starting point of body

## CROCHET INSTRUCTIONS

### Body

With light orange and US 7 hook, make a magic ring.

**Rnd 1:** ch2 (counts as first hdc here and throughout), hdc8 in magic ring, slst in top of beg ch2 [9]

Place stitch marker in first st of rnd 1 and move it up after each round

**Rnd 2:** ch2, hdc1 in same st at base of ch2, (hdc2 in next st) 8 times, slst in top of beg ch2 [18]

**Rnd 3:** ch2, hdc2 in next st, (hdc1, hdc2 in next st) 8 times, slst in top of beg ch2 [27]

**Rnd 4:** ch2, hdc1 in same st at base of ch2, hdc2, (hdc2 in next st, hdc2) 8 times, slst in top of beg ch2 [36]

**Rnd 5:** ch2, hdc1 in next st, hdc2 in next st, (hdc3, hdc2 in next st) 8 times, hdc1, slst in top of beg ch2 [45]

**Rnds 6-7:** ch2, hdc1 in each st, slst in top of beg ch2

Change to lemon.

**Rnds 8-11:** ch2, hdc1 in each st, slst in top of beg ch2

Change to cream.

**Rnds 12-15:** ch2, hdc1 in each st, slst in top of beg ch2

Change to light beige.

**Rnd 16:** ch2, hdc1 in each st, slst in top of beg ch2

**Rnd 17 (BLO):** ch2, hdc1 blo, (hdc2tog blo, hdc3 blo) 8 times, hdc2tog blo, hdc1 blo, slst in top of beg ch2 [36]

**Rnd 18:** ch1, hdc in next st (counts as hdc2tog), hdc2, (hdc2tog, hdc2) 8 times, slst in top of beg hdc2tog [27]

**Rnd 19:** ch2, (hdc2tog, hdc1) 8 times, hdc2tog, slst in top of beg ch2 [18]

**Rnd 20:** ch1, hdc in next st (counts as hdc2tog), (hdc2tog) 8 times, slst in top of beg ch2 [9]

Cut yarn and fasten off, leaving an 8" (20 cm) long tail. Fill firmly with polyester stuffing and make up following steps 2–3 on page 109.

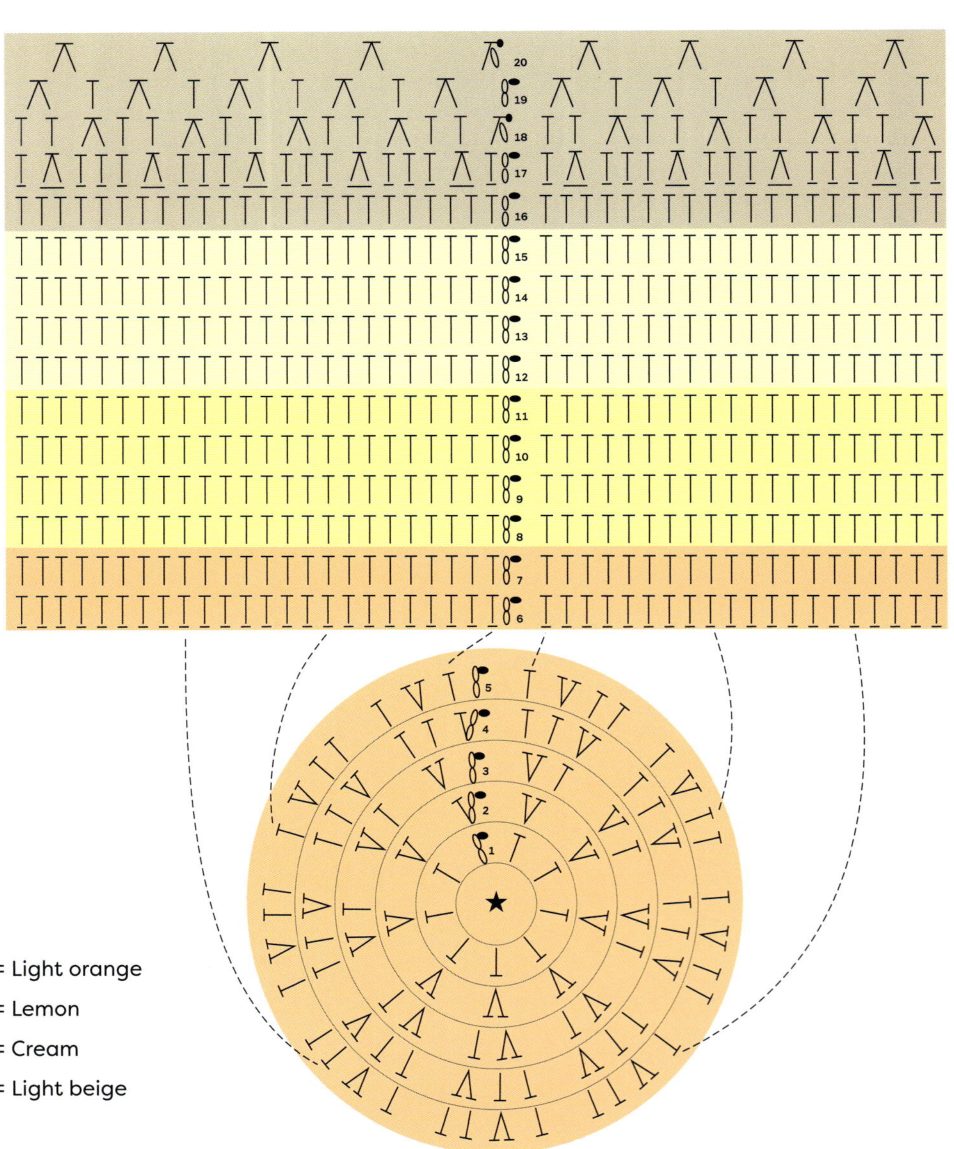

## Orange Slice (make 1)

With cream and US 7 hook, make a magic ring.

**Rnd 1:** ch1 (does not count as a st here and throughout), sc6 in magic ring, slst in beg ch1 [6]

Place stitch marker in first st of rnd 1 and move it up after each round

Change to orange

**Rnd 2:** ch2, hdc1 in same st at base of ch2, (hdc2 in next st) 5 times, slst in top of beg ch2 [12]

**Rnd 3:** ch2, hdc1 in same st at base of ch2, (hdc2 in next st) 11 times, slst in top of beg ch2 [24]

Change to cream

**Rnd 4:** ch1, sc1 in same st at base of ch1, sc2, sc2 in next st, (sc3, sc2 in next st) 5 times, slst in beg ch1 [30]

Change to bright orange

**Rnd 5:** ch1, sc1 in same st at base of ch1, sc1, sc2 in next st, (sc4, sc2 in next st) 5 times, sc2, slst in beg ch1 [36]

Cut yarn and fasten off, leaving a 16" (40 cm) long tail. Embroider as shown in the diagram at right, then make up following step 5 instructions on page 109.

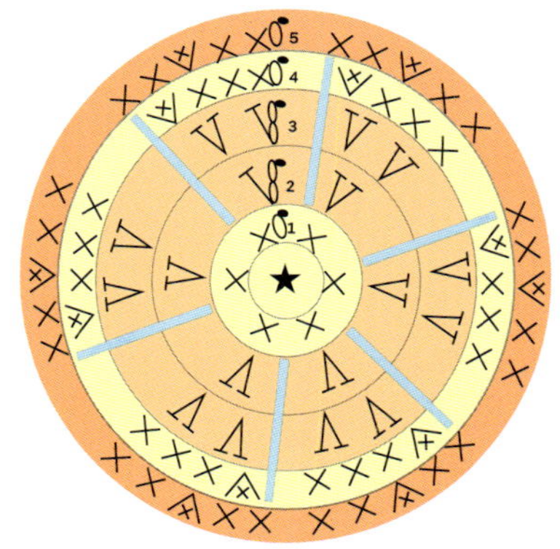

= Straight stitch (1 strand)

Use cream yarn to embroider the orange slice and off-white yarn to embroider the lemon slice.

## Lemon Slice (make 1)

Work as given for Orange Slice, but use off-white yarn in place of the cream yarn and lemon yarn in place of both the orange and bright orange yarn.

## Whipped Cream (make 1)

With white and US L-11 hook, make a magic ring.

**Rnd 1:** ch1 (does not count as a st throughout), sc7 in magic ring, slst in beg ch1 [7]

Place stitch marker in first st of rnd 1 and move it up after each round

**Rnd 2:** ch1, (sc2 in next st) 7 times, slst in beg ch1 [14]

**Rnd 3:** ch8 (counts as 1dc and ch5), skip first st, slst in next st, (ch2, dc1 in next st, ch5, slst in next st) 6 times, ch2, slst in third of beg ch8

Cut yarn and fasten off, leaving an 8" (20 cm) long tail. Make up following step 6 instructions on page 109.

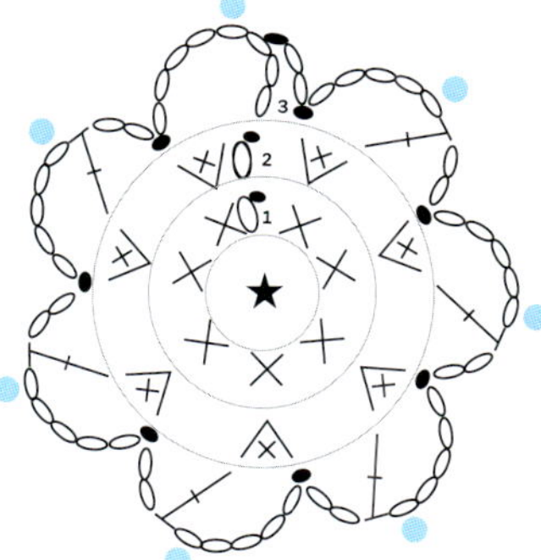

After crocheting round 3, cut the yarn, leaving an 8" (20 cm) long tail. Fill with polyester stuffing and gather by pulling the yarn through the stitches marked by ●.

## Mint Leaves (make 2)

With yellow green and US 7 hook, ch6.

**Rnd 1:** sc1 in third ch from hook, hdc1 in next ch, sc1 in next ch, 2slst in last ch, rotate and work along opposite side of ch, sc1 in next ch, hdc1 in next ch, sc1 in next ch, slst in next ch

Cut yarn and fasten off, leaving a 6" (15 cm) long tail.

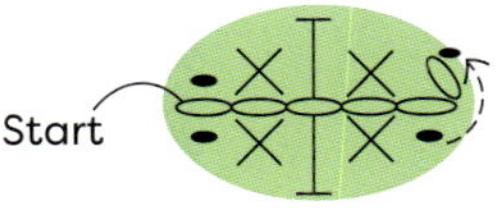

23

# Charlotte Cake

SHOWN ON PAGE 30

Finished Size:
5" (13 cm) diameter x 5" (13 cm) tall

## TOOLS & MATERIALS

### Yarn

- 100% acrylic bulky-weight yarn
  - 112 yds (102 m) in dark beige
  - 33 yds (30 m) in light pink
  - 27 yds (24 m) in pink
  - 14 yds (12 m) in white
  - 7 yds (6 m) in lime green

### Other Materials

- 35 g of polyester stuffing
- 1 yard (1 m) of ¾" (2 cm) wide white frilled ribbon

### Tools

- US 7 (4.5 mm) crochet hook
- Yarn needle

## CONSTRUCTION STEPS

Note: Use one strand of yarn throughout.

**1.** Crochet the biscuits: Start with a magic ring and crochet until round 13. Fasten off, leaving a 12" (30 cm) long tail. Make 14 biscuits.

**2.** Whipstitch the sides of the biscuits together along what will become the inside of the cake, then fill each biscuit with polyester stuffing (see **Figure A**).

**3.** Crochet the cake bottom and fasten off, leaving a 1 yard (1 m) long tail. Align the assembled biscuits with the wrong side of the cake bottom and whipstitch together (see **Figure B**).

**4.** Crochet the cake top which ends at round 7. Fasten off, leaving a 32" (80 cm) long tail.

**5.** Whipstitch the cake top to the assembled biscuits (see **Figure C**). After sewing around ⅔ of the cake, fill with polyester stuffing, and then continue sewing and stuffing to the end.

**6.** Crochet the leaves.

**7.** Crochet the rolled roses (both large and small). Fasten off, leaving 8" (20 cm) long tails, then roll into shape as shown in the diagram on page 114.

**8.** Sew the leaves and roses to the top of the cake (see **Figure D**).

**9.** Tie the ribbon around the cake.

***Figure A***

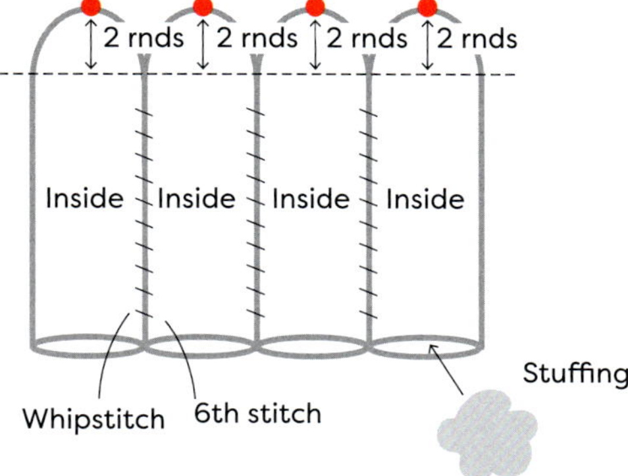


● = Starting point of each biscuit

***Figure B***

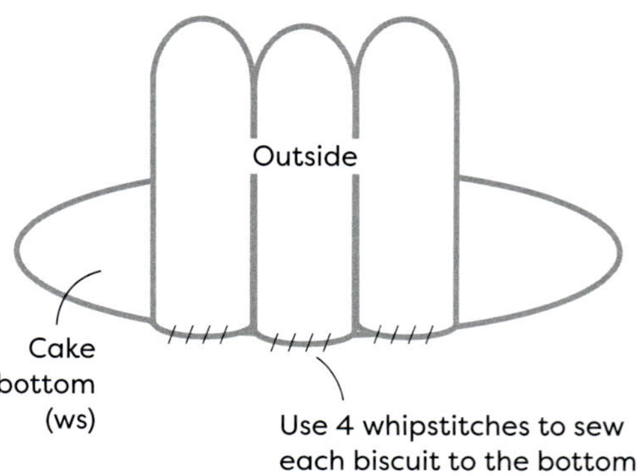

*Figure C*

Stuffing

Whipstitch the cake top to the 4th round of the biscuits

4 rnds

Cake top (rs)

*Figure D*

Sew one leaf to the center/ starting point of the cake top, then sew the other four leaves to the 6th round

Cake top (rs)

6 rnds

5 rnds

Sew the large and small roses to the 5th round, alternating sizes

## CROCHET INSTRUCTIONS

### Biscuits (make 14)

With dark beige and US 7 hook, make a magic ring.

**Rnd 1:** ch1 (does not count as a st throughout), sc6 in magic ring, slst in beg ch1 [6]

Place stitch marker in first st of rnd 1 and move it up after each round

**Rnd 2:** ch1, (sc2, sc2 in next st) twice, slst in beg ch1 [8]

**Rnds 3–13:** ch1, sc1 in each st, slst in beg ch1 (11 rounds)

Cut yarn and fasten off, leaving a 12" (30 cm) long tail. Make up following step 2 instructions on page 112.

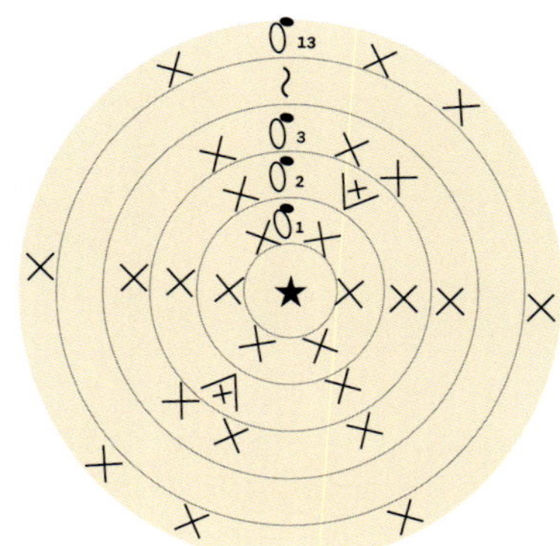

### Cake Bottom

With dark beige and US 7 hook, make a magic ring.

**Rnd 1:** ch1 (does not count as a st throughout), sc7 in magic ring, slst in beg ch1 [7]

Place stitch marker in first st of rnd 1 and move it up after each round

**Rnd 2:** ch1, (sc2 in next st) 7 times, slst in beg ch1 [14]

**Rnd 3:** ch1, (sc1, sc2 in next st) 7 times, slst in beg ch1 [21]

**Rnd 4:** ch1, (sc2 in next st, sc2) 7 times, slst in beg ch1 [28]

**Rnd 5:** ch1, sc2, (sc2 in next st, sc3) 6 times, sc2 in next st, sc1, slst in beg ch1 [35]

**Rnd 6:** ch1, (sc4, sc2 in next st) 7 times, slst in beg ch1 [42]

**Rnd 7:** ch1, sc1, (sc2 in next st, sc5) 6 times, sc2 in next st, sc4, slst in beg ch1 [49]

**Rnd 8:** ch1, sc3, (sc2 in next st, sc6) 6 times, sc2 in next st, sc3, slst in beg ch1 [56]

Cut yarn and fasten off, leaving a 1 yard (1 m) long tail.

Make up following step 3 instructions on page 112.

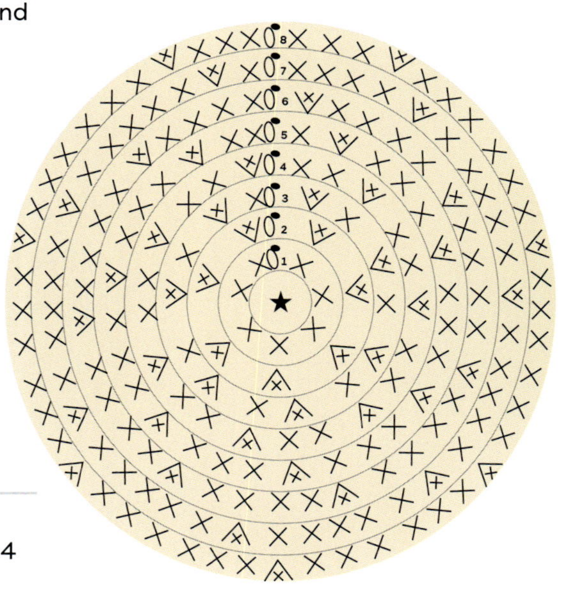

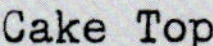

### Cake Top

Work as given for the Cake Bottom through round 7. Cut yarn and fasten off, leaving a 32" (80 cm) long tail. Make up following steps 4 and 5 on page 112.

## Leaves (make 5)

With lime green and US 7 hook, ch7.

**Rnd 1:** dc1 in fourth ch from hook, hdc1 in next ch, sc1 in next ch, 3slst in last ch, rotate and work along opposite side of ch, sc1 in next ch, hdc1 in next ch, dc1 in next ch, hdc1 in next ch.

Cut yarn and fasten off, leaving an 8" (20 cm) long tail.

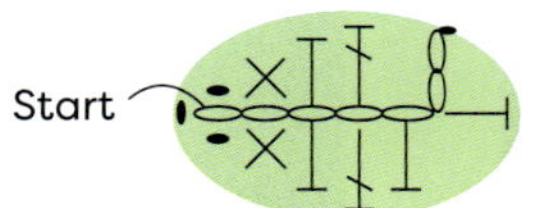


## Large Rolled Roses (make 3)

With light pink and US 7 hook, ch17.

**Row 1:** dc1 in fourth ch from hook (counts as 2dc), (dc2 in next ch) to end, turn [28]

**Row 2:** ch2 (counts as hdc), (hdc2 in next st) twice, ch2, slst in next st, ch2, (dc2 in next st, dc1 in next st, dc2 in next st, ch2, slst in next st, ch2) 3 times, ch1, (tr2 in next st, tr1 in next st, tr2 in next st, ch3, slst in next st, ch3) 3 times, omitting ch3 on last repeat.

Cut yarn and fasten off, leaving an 8" (20 cm) long tail, then roll into shape as shown in the diagram below.

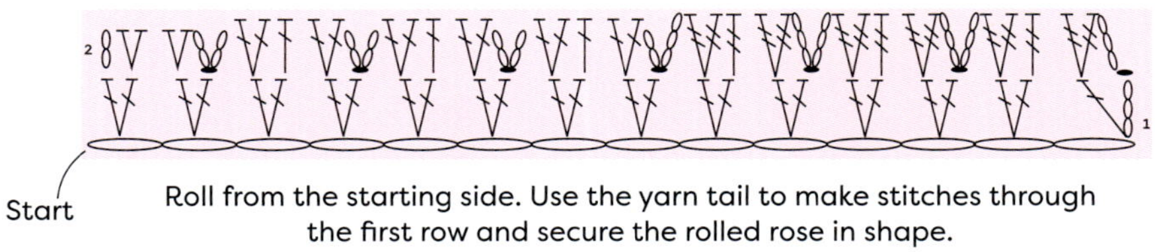


Roll from the starting side. Use the yarn tail to make stitches through the first row and secure the rolled rose in shape.

## Small Rolled Roses (make 3)

With light pink and US 7 hook, ch13.

**Row 1:** dc1 in fourth ch from hook (counts as 2dc), (dc2 in next ch) to end, turn [20]

**Row 2:** ch2 (counts as hdc), (hdc2 in next st) twice, ch2, slst in next st, ch2, (dc2 in next st, dc1 in next st, dc2 in next st, ch2, slst in next st, ch2) twice, (tr2 in next st, tr1 in next st, tr2 in next st, ch3, slst in next st, ch3) twice, omitting ch3 on last repeat.

Cut yarn and fasten off, leaving an 8" (20 cm) long tail, then roll into shape as shown in the diagram below.

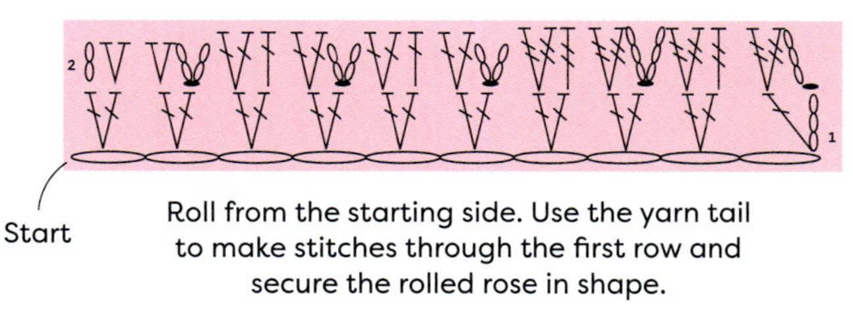


Roll from the starting side. Use the yarn tail to make stitches through the first row and secure the rolled rose in shape.

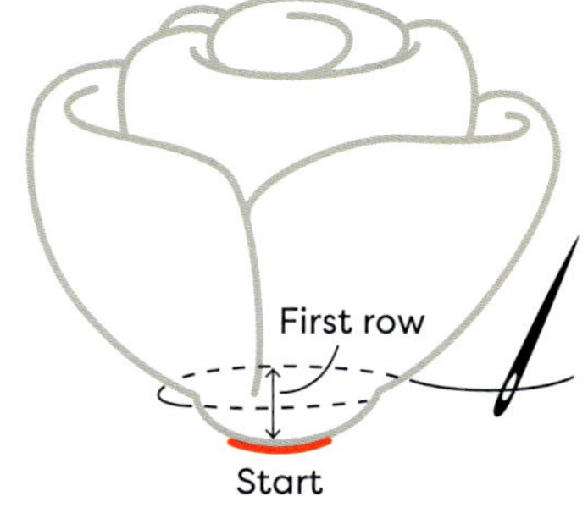


Insert the yarn tail through the base from a few different directions to secure the rolled rose in place

24

# Custard

**SHOWN ON PAGE 33**

Finished Size:
5" (13 cm) diameter x
6¼" (16 cm) tall

## TOOLS & MATERIALS

### Yarn

- 100% acrylic bulky-weight yarn
  - 99 yds (90 m) in cream
  - 20 yds (18 m) in brown
  - 14 yds (12 m) in white
  - 7 yds (6 m) in red orange

### Other Materials

- A bit of polyester stuffing

### Tools

- US 7 (4.5 mm) crochet hook
- US L-11 (8 mm) crochet hook
- Yarn needle

## CONSTRUCTION STEPS

Note: Crochet the body, caramel, and cherry using one strand of yarn with US 7 crochet hook. Crochet the whipped cream using two strands of yarn with L-11 crochet hook.

**1.** Crochet the body outside: Start with a magic ring and crochet through round 21. Cut yarn and fasten off, leaving a 20" (50 cm) long tail.

**2.** Crochet the body inside.

**3.** Insert the body inside into the body outside with wrong sides together. Use the remaining yarn tail from step 1 to whipstitch the top loops of the last round together.

**4.** Crochet the two caramel pieces and fasten off, leaving a 20" (50 cm) long tail.

**5.** Crochet the whipped cream and fasten off, leaving a 12" (30 cm) long tail. Fill with polyester stuffing and gather by pulling the yarn through the stitches indicated by the light blue dots in the diagram on page 118.

**6.** Crochet the cherry and fasten off, leaving an 8" (20 cm) long tail.

**7.** Align the two caramel pieces with wrong sides together and whipstitch together.

**8.** Sew the whipped cream to the top of the caramel. Fill the cherry with polyester stuffing and sew to the whipped cream (see **Figure A**). Bring the ending yarn up through center and out at top of the cherry. Trim the yarn, leaving ⅝" (1.5 cm) for the stalk.

***Figure A***

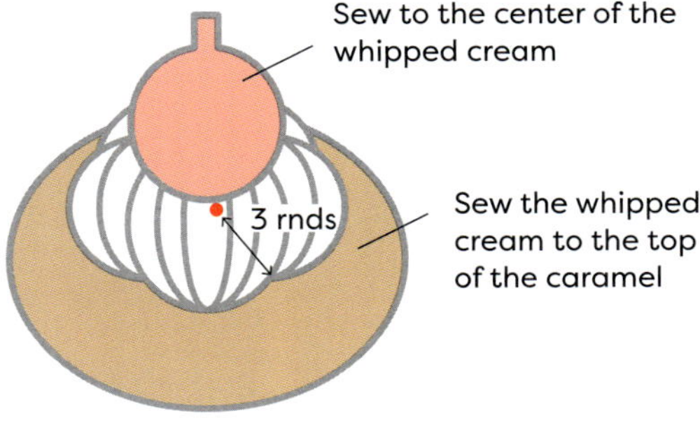


• = Starting point of caramel

## CROCHET INSTRUCTIONS

### Body Outside

With cream and US 7 hook, make a magic ring.

**Rnd 1:** ch1 (does not count as a st throughout), sc7 in magic ring, slst in beg ch1 [7]

Place stitch marker in first st of rnd 1 and move it up after each round

**Rnd 2:** ch1, (sc2 in next st) 7 times, slst in beg ch1 [14]

**Rnd 3:** ch1, (sc1, sc2 in next st) 7 times, slst in beg ch1 [21]

**Rnd 4:** ch1, (sc2 in next st, sc2) 7 times, slst in beg ch1 [28]

**Rnd 5:** ch1, sc2, (sc2 in next st, sc3) 6 times, sc2 in next st, sc1, slst in beg ch1 [35]

**Rnd 6:** ch1, (sc4, sc2 in next st) 7 times, slst in beg ch1 [42]

**Rnd 7:** ch1, sc1, (sc2 in next st, sc5) 6 times, sc2 in next st, sc4, slst in beg ch1 [49]

**Rnd 8:** ch1, sc3, (sc2 in next st, sc6) 6 times, sc2 in next st, sc3, slst in beg ch1 [56]

**Rnd 9:** ch1, sc6, (sc2 in next st, sc7) 6 times, sc2 in next st, sc1, slst in beg ch1 [63]

**Rnd 10 (BLO):** ch1, sc6blo, (sc2togblo, sc7blo) 6 times, sc2togblo, sc1blo, slst in beg ch1 [56]

**Rnds 11–13:** ch1, sc1 in each st, slst in beg ch1 (3 rnds)

**Rnd 14:** ch1, sc3, (sc2tog, sc6) 6 times, sc2tog, sc3, slst in beg ch1 [49]

**Rnds 15–16:** ch1, sc1 in each st, slst in beg ch1 (2 rnds)

**Rnd 17:** ch1, sc1, (sc2tog, sc5) 6 times, sc2tog, sc4, slst in beg ch1 [42]

**Rnds 18–19:** ch1, sc1 in each st, slst in beg ch1 (2 rnds)

**Rnd 20:** ch1, (sc5, sc2tog) 6 times, slst in beg ch1 [36]

**Rnd 21:** ch1, sc1 in each st, slst in beg ch1

Cut yarn and fasten off, leaving a 20" (50 cm) long tail.

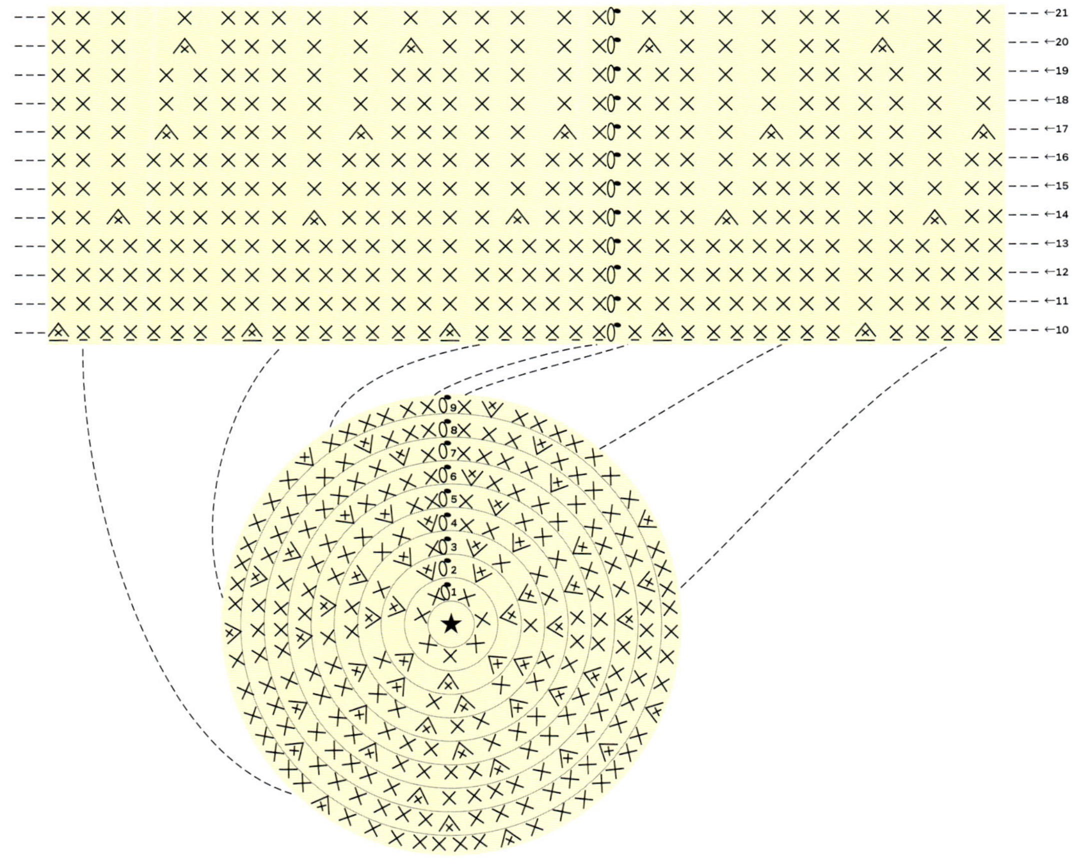

## Body Inside

Follow all instructions for Body Outside to end of Rnd 8 [56]
**Rnd 9 (BLO):** ch1, sc3blo, (sc2togblo, sc6blo) 6 times, sc2togblo, sc3blo, slst in beg ch1 [49]
**Rnds 10–12:** ch1, sc1 in each st, slst in beg ch1 (3 rnds)
**Rnd 13:** ch1, sc1, (sc2tog, sc5) 6 times, sc2tog, sc4, slst in beg ch1 [42]
**Rnds 14–15:** ch1, sc1 in each st, slst in beg ch1 (2 rnds)
**Rnd 16:** ch1, (sc5, sc2tog) 6 times, slst in beg ch1 [36]
**Rnds 17–18:** ch1, sc1 in each st, slst in beg ch1 (2 rnds)
**Rnd 19:** ch1, sc2, (sc2tog, sc4) 5 times, sc2tog, sc2, slst in beg ch1 [30]
**Rnd 20:** ch1, sc1 in each st, slst in beg ch1
Cut yarn and fasten off. Follow step 3 instructions on page 115 to join the body inside and body outside.

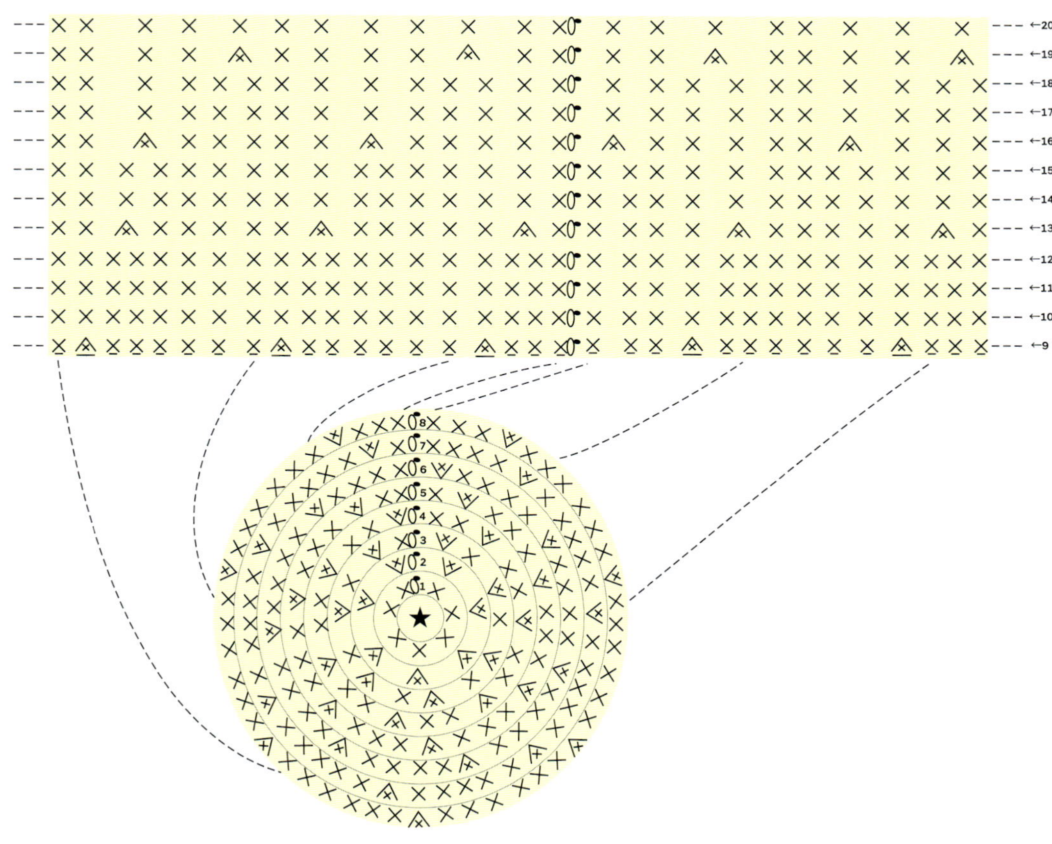


## Caramel (make 2)

With brown and US 7 hook, make a magic ring.
**Rnd 1:** ch1 (does not count as a st throughout), sc7 in magic ring, slst in beg ch1 [7]
Place stitch marker in first st of rnd 1 and move it up after each round
**Rnd 2:** ch1, (sc2 in next st) 7 times, slst in beg ch1 [14]
**Rnd 3:** ch1, (sc1, sc2 in next st) 7 times, slst in beg ch1 [21]
**Rnd 4:** ch1, (sc2 in next st, sc2) 7 times, slst in beg ch1 [28]
**Rnd 5:** ch1, sc2, (sc2 in next st, sc3) 6 times, sc2 in next st, sc1, slst in beg ch1 [35]
**Rnd 6:** ch1, (sc4, sc2 in next st) 7 times, slst in beg ch1 [42]
Cut yarn and fasten off, leaving a 20" (50 cm) long tail.
Make up following step 7 instructions on page 115.

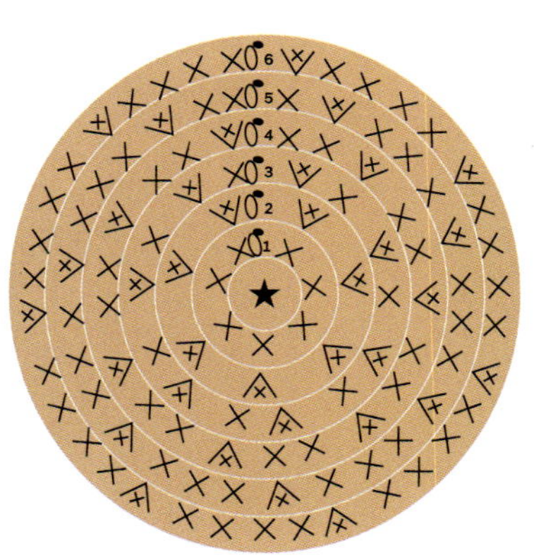

### Whipped Cream

With white and US 7 hook, make a magic ring.
**Rnd 1:** ch1 (does not count as a st throughout), sc7 in magic ring, slst in beg ch1 [7]
Place stitch marker in first st of rnd 1 and move it up after each round
**Rnd 2:** ch1, (sc2 in next st) 7 times, slst in beg ch1 [14]
**Rnd 3:** ch8 (counts as 1dc and ch5), skip first st, slst in next st, (ch2, 1dc in next st, ch5, slst in next st) 6 times, ch2, slst in third of beg ch8.
Cut yarn and fasten off, leaving a 12" (30 cm) long tail.
Make up following step 5 instructions on page 115.

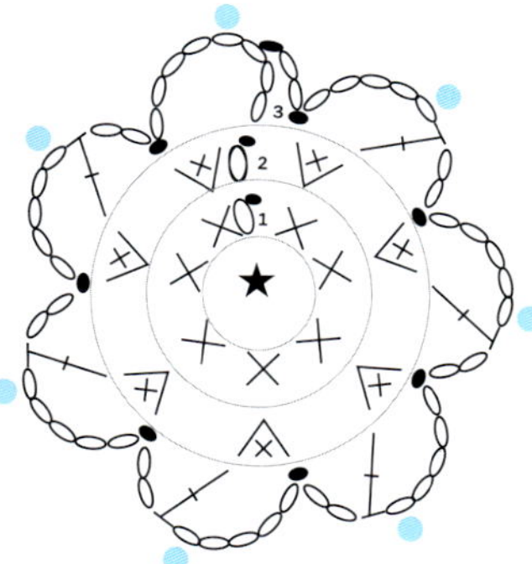

After crocheting round 3, cut the yarn, leaving an 8" (20 cm) long tail. Fill with polyester stuffing and gather by pulling the yarn through the stitches marked by ● .

### Cherry

With red orange and US L-11 hook, make a magic ring.
**Rnd 1:** ch1 (does not count as a st throughout), sc6 in magic ring, slst in beg ch1 [6]
Place stitch marker in first st of rnd 1 and move it up after each round
**Rnd 2:** ch1, (sc2 in next st) 6 times, slst in beg ch1 [12]
**Rnds 3–4:** ch1, sc1 in each st, slst in beg ch1 (2 rnds)
**Rnd 5:** ch1, (sc2tog) 6 times, slst in beg ch1 [6]
Cut yarn and fasten off, leaving an 8" (20 cm) long tail.

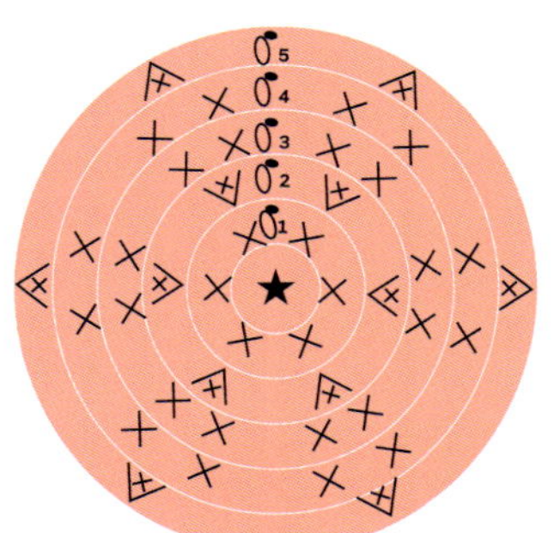

25

# Pancakes

SHOWN ON PAGE 33

Finished Size:
6" (15 cm) diameter x
3½" (9 cm) tall

## TOOLS & MATERIALS

### Yarn

- 100% acrylic bulky-weight yarn
  - 112 yds (102 m) in cream
  - 66 yds (60 m) in golden brown

### Tools

- US 7 (4.5 mm) crochet hook
- Yarn needle

## CONSTRUCTION STEPS

Note: Use one strand of yarn throughout.

**1.** Crochet body outsides: Make 7 single crochet into a magic ring and continue following diagram or written instructions through round 16. Cut the yarn, leaving a 1 yard (90 cm) long tail. Make two body outsides.

**2.** Crochet the body insides: Make two body insides following diagram or written instructions.

**3.** Crochet the butter following diagram or written instructions.

**4.** Position one body outside with the wrong side of the crochet fabric facing out. Insert one body inside so the right side of the crochet fabric is facing out. Use the remaining yarn tail from step 1 to whipstitch together along the top. Repeat process to sew the remaining body outside and body inside together.

**5.** Sew the butter to the lid (refer to **Figure A** for placement).

***Figure A***

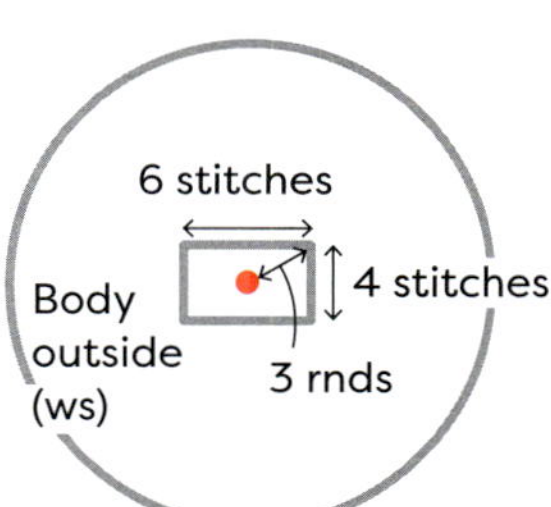


• = Starting point of body outside

## CROCHET INSTRUCTIONS

### Body Outside (make 2)

With golden brown and US 7 hook, make a magic ring.

**Rnd 1:** ch1 (does not count as a st throughout), sc7 in magic ring, slst in beg ch1 [7]

Place stitch marker in first st of rnd 1 and move it up after each round

**Rnd 2:** ch1, (sc2 in next st) 7 times, slst in beg ch1 [14]

**Rnd 3:** ch1, (sc1, sc2 in next st) 7 times, slst in beg ch1 [21]

**Rnd 4:** ch1, (sc2 in next st, sc2) 7 times, slst in beg ch1 [28]

**Rnd 5:** ch1, sc2, (sc2 in next st, sc3) 6 times, sc2 in next st, sc1, slst in beg ch1 [35]

**Rnd 6:** ch1, (sc4, sc2 in next st) 7 times, slst in beg ch1 [42]

**Rnd 7:** ch1, sc1, (sc2 in next st, sc5) 6 times, sc2 in next st, sc4, slst in beg ch1 [49]

**Rnd 8:** ch1, sc3, (sc2 in next st, sc6) 6 times, sc2 in next st, sc3, slst in beg ch1 [56]

**Rnd 9:** ch1, sc6, (sc2 in next st, sc7) 6 times, sc2 in next st, sc1, slst in beg ch1 [63]

**Rnd 10:** ch1, (sc2 in next st, sc8) 7 times, slst in beg ch1 [70]

Change to cream.

**Rnds 11–15:** ch1, sc1 in each st, slst in beg ch1 (5 rnds)

Change to golden brown.

**Rnd 16:** ch1, (sc2tog, sc8) 7 times, slst in beg ch1 [63]

Cut yarn and fasten off, leaving a 1 yard (90 cm) long tail.

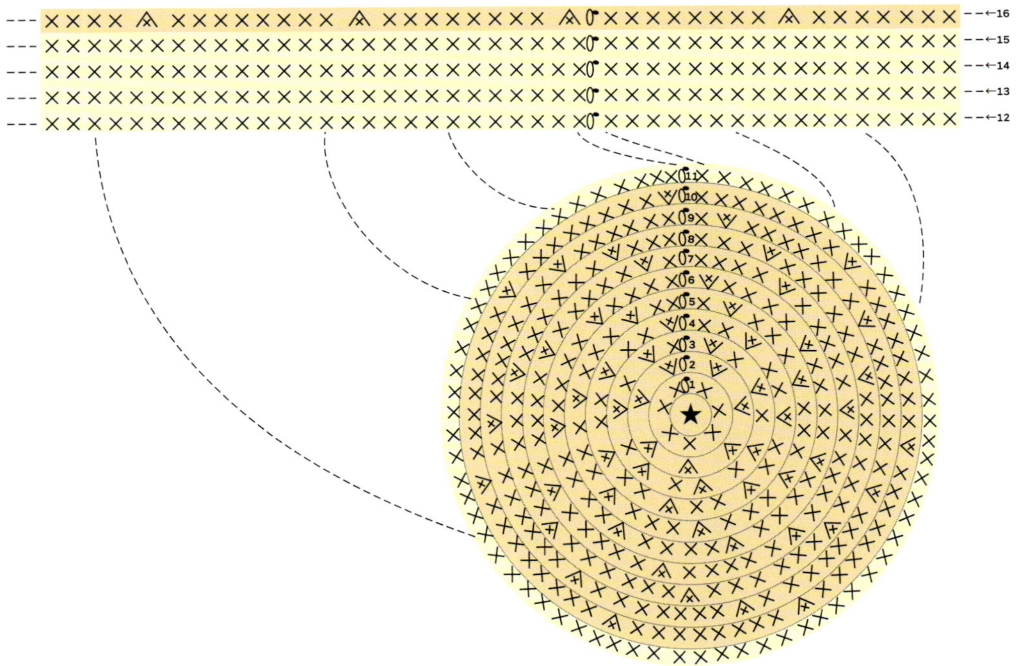

## Body Inside (make 2)

With cream and US 7 hook, make a magic ring.
Work as given for Body Outside for rnds 1–9 [63]
**Rnds 10–13:** ch1, sc1 in each st, slst in beg ch1 (4 rnds)
Change to golden brown.
**Rnd 14:** ch1, sc1 in each st, slst in beg ch1
Cut yarn and fasten off.
Follow step 4 instructions on page 119 to join the body inside and body outside.

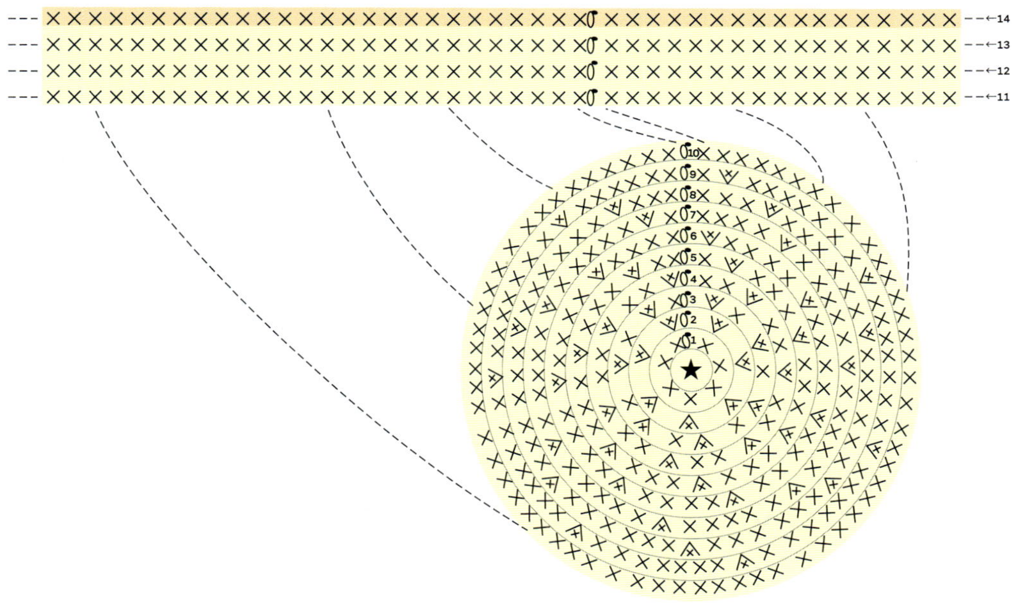

## Butter

With cream and US 7 hook, ch3.
**Rnd 1:** sc2 in second ch from hook, sc5 in end ch, turn, sc3 in next ch, slst in beg ch1 [10]
**Rnd 2:** ch1 (does not count as a st), (sc3 in next st, sc2, sc3 in next st, sc1) twice, slst in beg ch1 [18]
**Rnd 3:** ch1, sc1 BLO in each st, slst in beg ch1
**Rnd 4:** ch1, sc1 in each st, slst in beg ch1
Cut yarn and fasten off.
Make up following step 5 instructions on page 119.

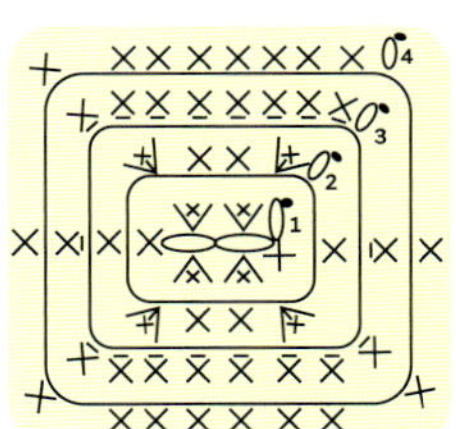

26

# Cream Soda

SHOWN ON PAGE 33

Finished Size:
4¼" (11 cm) diameter x
11" (27.5 cm) tall

## TOOLS & MATERIALS

### Yarn

- 100% acrylic bulky-weight yarn
  - 105 yds (96 m) in yellow green
  - 33 yds (30 m) in off-white
  - 27 yds (24 m) in white
  - 7 yds (6 m) in red orange

### Other Materials

- 9 g of polyester stuffing

### Tools

- US 7 (4.5 mm) crochet hook
- US L-11 (8 mm) crochet hook
- Yarn needle

## CONSTRUCTION STEPS

Note: Crochet the body outside, body inside, glass base, ice cream lid, and cherry using one strand of yarn with US 7 crochet hook. Crochet the whipped cream using two strands of yarn with US L-11 crochet hook.

**1.** Crochet the body outside: Make 6 single crochet in a magic ring and continue through round 26. Cut yarn, leaving a 20" (50 cm) long tail.

**2.** Crochet the body inside.

**3.** Insert the body inside into the body outside with wrong sides together. Use the remaining yarn tail from step 1 to whipstitch the top loops of the last round together.

**4.** Crochet the glass base. Cut the yarn, leaving a 16" (40 cm) long tail. Fill with polyester stuffing and sew to round 4 of the soda body.

**5.** Crochet ice cream lid top. Cut the yarn, leaving a 20" (50 cm) long tail.

**6.** Crochet the ice cream lid bottom. Align the ice cream lid top with the wrong side of the crochet fabric facing out and the bottom with right side out facing out, fill with polyester stuffing, and whipstitch together (see **Figure A**).

**7.** Crochet the whipped cream. Cut the yarn, leaving a 12" (30 cm) long tail.

**8.** Crochet the cherry. Cut the yarn, leaving an 8" (20 cm) long tail.

**9.** Sew the whipped cream to the ice cream lid. Fill the cherry with polyester stuffing and sew to the whipped cream (see **Figure B**). Bring the ending yarn up through center and out at top of the cherry. Trim the yarn, leaving ⅝" (1.5 cm) for the stalk.

***Figure A***

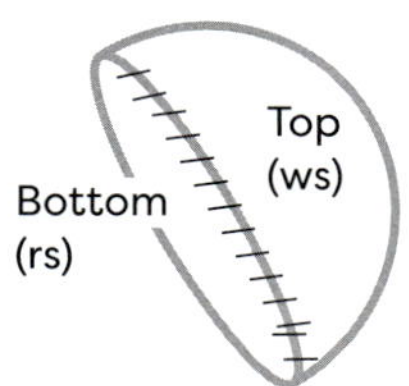


Fill polyester stuffing and whipstitch

***Figure B***

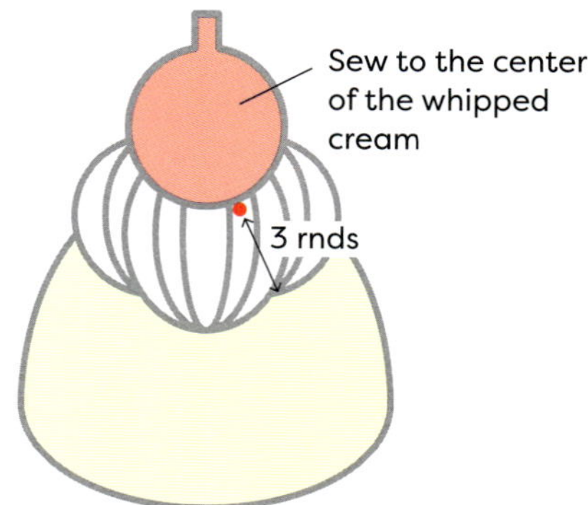

## CROCHET INSTRUCTIONS

### Body Outside

With yellow green and US 7 hook, make a magic ring.

**Rnd 1:** ch1 (does not count as a st throughout), sc6 in magic ring, slst in beg ch1 [6]

Place stitch marker in first st of rnd 1 and move it up after each round

**Rnd 2:** ch1, (sc2 in next st) 6 times, slst in beg ch1 [12]

**Rnd 3:** ch1, (sc1, sc2 in next st) 6 times, slst in beg ch1 [18]

**Rnd 4:** ch1, (sc2 in next st, sc2) 6 times, slst in beg ch1 [24]

**Rnd 5:** ch1, sc2, (sc2 in next st, sc3) 5 times, sc2 in next st, sc1, slst in beg ch1 [30]

**Rnd 6:** ch1, (sc4, sc2 in next st) 6 times, slst in beg ch1 [36]

**Rnd 7:** ch1, sc1, (sc2 in next st, sc5) 5 times, sc2 in next st, sc4, slst in beg ch1 [42]

**Rnd 8:** ch1, sc3, (sc2 in next st, sc6) 5 times, sc2 in next st, sc3, slst in beg ch1 [48]

**Rnds 9–15:** ch1, sc1 in each st, slst in beg ch1 (7 rnds)

**Rnd 16:** ch1, sc3, sc2tog, (sc6, sc2tog) 5 times, sc3, slst in beg ch1 [42]

**Rnd 17:** ch1, sc1 in each st, slst in beg ch1

**Rnd 18:** ch1, sc1, sc2tog, (sc5, sc2tog) 5 times, sc4, slst in beg ch1 [36]

**Rnds 19–24:** ch1, sc1 in each st, slst in beg ch1 (6 rnds)

**Rnd 25:** ch1, sc1, sc2 in next st, (sc5, sc2 in next st) 5 times, sc4, slst in beg ch1 [42]

Change to off-white

**Rnd 26:** ch1, sc1 in each st, slst in beg ch1

Cut yarn and fasten off, leaving a 20" (50 cm) long tail.

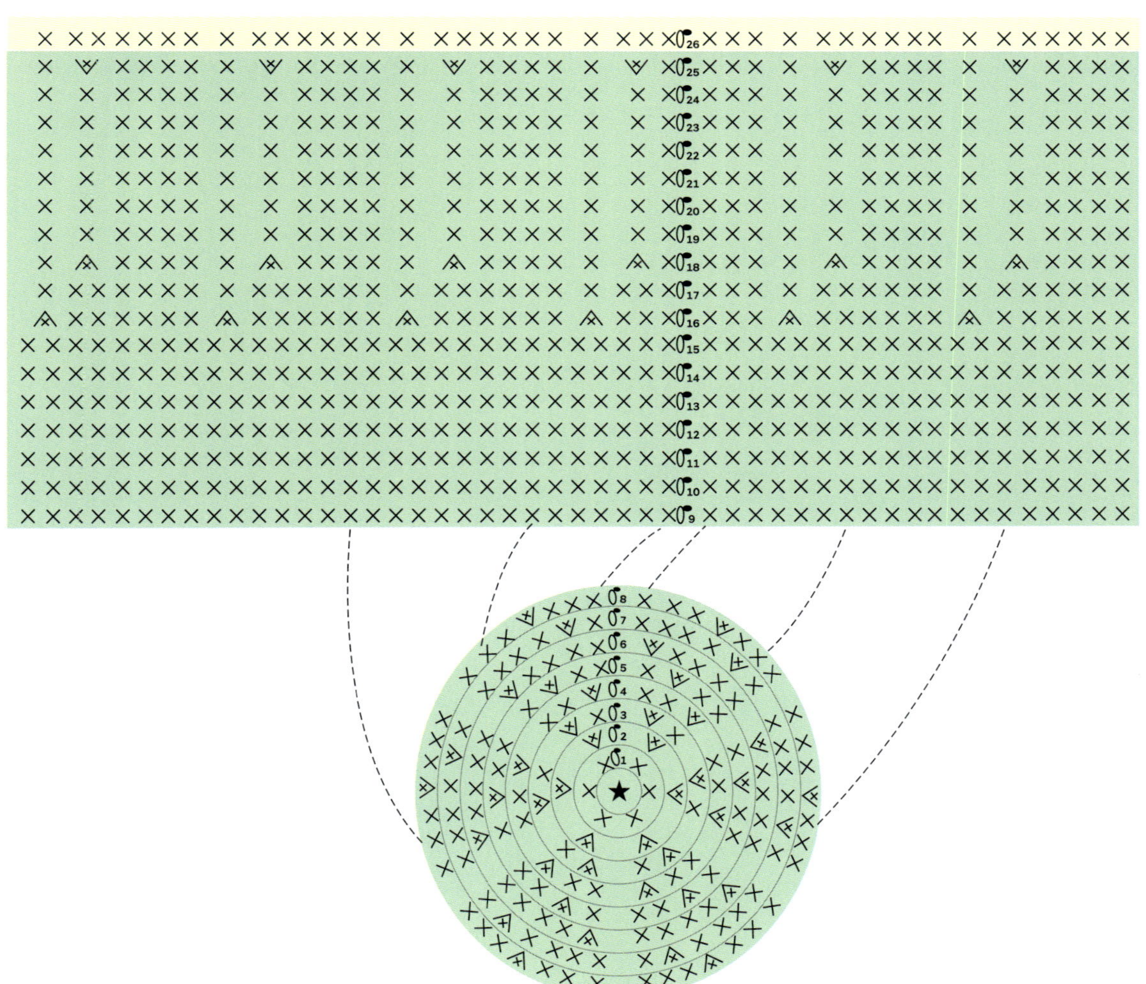

## Body Inside

With yellow green and US 7 hook, make a magic ring.
Work as given for rnds 1–7 of Body Outside [42]
**Rnds 8–14:** ch1, sc1 in each st, slst in beg ch1 (7 rnds)
**Rnd 15:** ch1, sc1, sc2tog, (sc5, sc2tog) 5 times, sc4, slst in beg ch1 [36]
**Rnd 16:** ch1, sc1 in each st, slst in beg ch1
**Rnd 17:** ch1, (sc4, sc2tog) 6 times, slst in beg ch1 [30]
**Rnds 18–23:** ch1, sc1 in each st, slst in beg ch1 (6 rnds)
**Rnd 24:** ch1, (sc4, sc2 in next st) 6 times, slst in beg ch1 [36]
Change to off-white
**Rnd 25:** ch1, sc1 in each st, slst in beg ch1
Cut yarn and fasten off.
Follow step 3 instructions on page 122 to join the body inside and body outside.

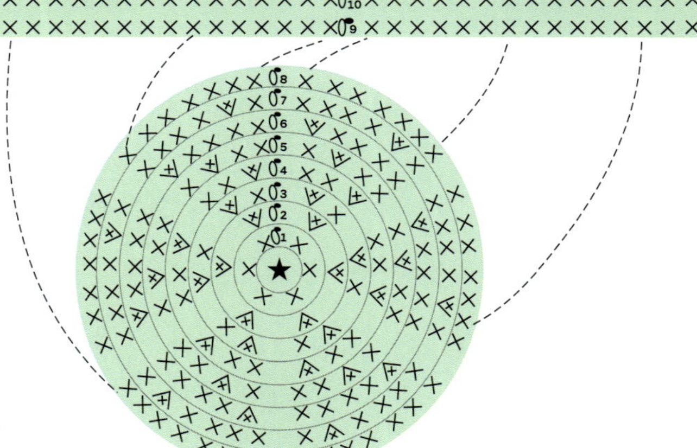

## Whipped Cream

With white and US L-11 hook, make a magic ring.
**Rnd 1:** ch1 (does not count as a st throughout), sc7 in magic ring, slst in beg ch1 [7]
Place stitch marker in first st of rnd 1 and move it up after each round
**Rnd 2:** ch1, (sc2 in next st) 7 times, slst in beg ch1 [14]
**Rnd 3:** ch8 (counts as 1dc and ch5), skip first st, slst in next st, (ch2, dc1 in next st, ch5, slst in next st) 6 times, ch2, slst in third of beg ch8.
Cut yarn and fasten off, leaving a 12" (20 cm) long tail.
Make up following step 9 instructions on page 122.

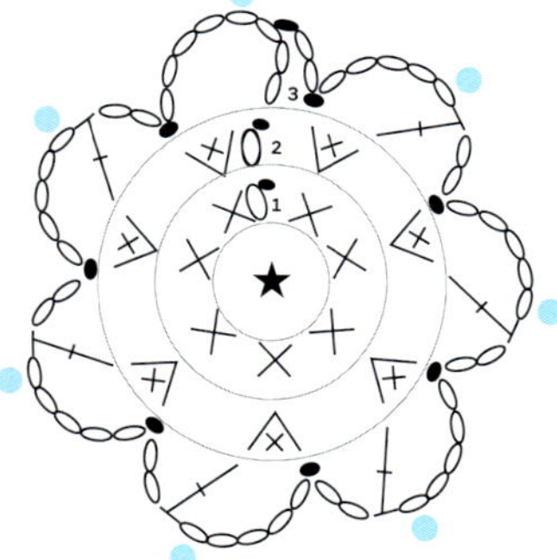

After crocheting round 3, cut the yarn, leaving an 8" (20 cm) long tail. Fill with polyester stuffing and gather by pulling the yarn through the stitches marked by ●.

## Cherry

With red orange and US 7 hook, make a magic ring.
Work as given for rnds 1–2 of Body Outside [12]
**Rnds 3–4:** ch1, sc1 in each st, slst in beg ch1 (2 rnds)
**Rnd 5:** ch1, (sc2tog) 6 times, slst in beg ch1 [6]
Cut yarn and fasten off, leaving an 8" (20 cm) long tail.
Make up following step 9 instructions on page 122.

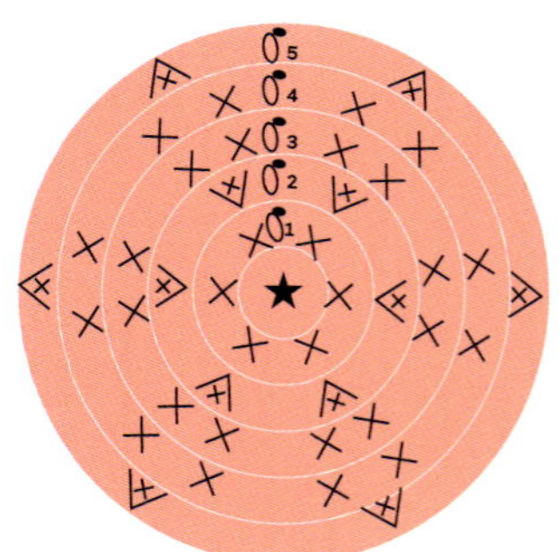

## Glass Base

With white and US 7 hook, make a magic ring.
**Rnd 1:** ch1 (does not count as a st throughout), sc7 in magic ring, slst in beg ch1 [7]
Place stitch marker in first st of rnd 1 and move it up after each round
**Rnd 2:** ch1, (sc2 in next st) 7 times, slst in beg ch1 [14]
**Rnd 3:** ch1, (sc1, sc2 in next st) 7 times, slst in beg ch1 [21]
**Rnd 4:** ch1, (sc2 in next st, sc2) 7 times, slst in beg ch1 [28]
**Rnd 5:** ch1, sc2, (sc2 in next st, sc3) 6 times, sc2 in next st, sc1, slst in beg ch1 [35]
**Rnd 6:** ch1, (sc4, sc2 in next st) 7 times, slst in beg ch1 [42]
**Rnd 7:** ch1, (sc5, sc2tog) 6 times, slst in beg ch1 [36]
**Rnd 8:** ch1, sc2, (sc2tog, sc4) 5 times, sc2tog, sc2, slst in beg ch1 [30]
**Rnd 9:** ch1, (sc2tog, sc3) 6 times, slst in beg ch1 [24]
**Rnds 10–11:** ch1, sc1 in each st, slst in beg ch1 (2 rnds)
Cut yarn and fasten off, leaving a 16" (40 cm) long tail.
Follow step 4 instructions on page 122 to sew the glass base to the soda body.

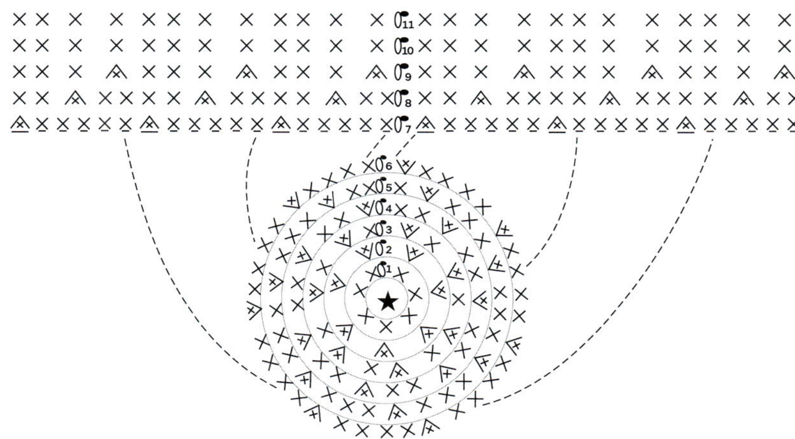

## Ice Cream Lid Top

With off-white and US 7 hook, make a magic ring.
Work as given for rnds 1–6 of Body Outside [36]
**Rnds 7–10:** ch1, sc1 in each st, slst in beg ch1 (4 rnds)
Cut yarn and fasten off, leaving a 20" (50 cm) long tail.

## Ice Cream Lid Bottom

With off-white and US 7 hook, make a magic ring.
Work as given for rnds 1–5 of Glass Base [35]
Cut yarn and fasten off. Make up following step 6 instructions on page 122.

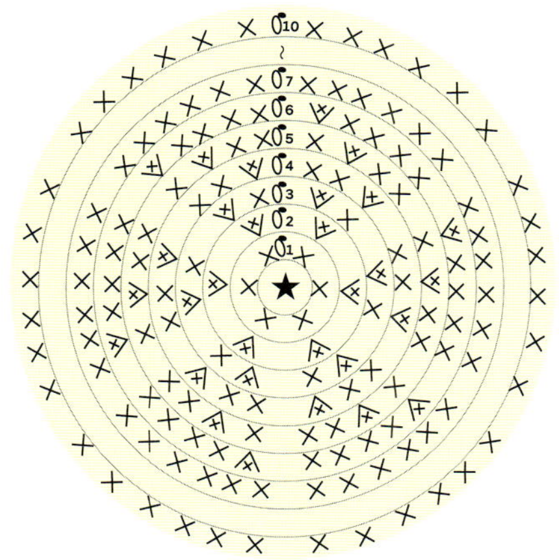

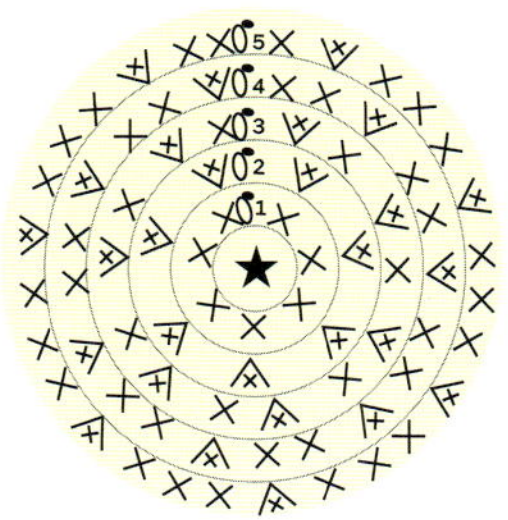

27

# Dessert Plate

**SHOWN ON PAGE 33**

Finished Size:
9" (23 cm) diameter

## TOOLS & MATERIALS

### Yarn

- 100% acrylic bulky-weight yarn
  - 40 yds (36 m) in white
  - 20 yds (18 m) in light blue

### Tools

- US 7 (4.5 mm) crochet hook
- Yarn needle

## CONSTRUCTION STEPS

Note: Use one strand of yarn throughout.

**1.** Crochet the body: Make 9 half double crochet in a magic ring and continue through round 10. Change the color of yarn from round 11 and continue through round 12. Cut yarn and fasten off. Weave in ends.

## CROCHET INSTRUCTIONS

### Body

With white and US 7 hook, make a magic ring.

**Rnd 1:** ch2 (counts as first hdc here and throughout), hdc8 in magic ring, slst in top of beg ch2 [9]

Place stitch marker in first st of rnd 1 and move it up after each round

**Rnd 2:** ch2, hdc1 in same st at base of ch2, (hdc2 in next st) 8 times, slst in top of beg ch2 [18]

**Rnd 3:** ch2, hdc2 in next st, (hdc1, hdc2 in next st) 8 times, slst in top of beg ch2 [27]

**Rnd 4:** ch2, hdc1 in same st at base of ch2, hdc2, (hdc2 in next st, hdc2) 8 times, slst in top of beg ch2 [36]

**Rnd 5:** ch2, hdc1 in next st, hdc2 in next st, (hdc3, hdc2 in next st) 8 times, hdc1, slst in top of beg ch2 [45]

**Rnd 6:** ch2, hdc3, (hdc2 in next st, hdc4) 8 times, hdc2 in next st, slst in top of beg ch2 [54]

**Rnd 7:** ch2, (hdc2 in next st, hdc5) 8 times, hdc2 in next st, hdc4, slst in top of beg ch2 [63]

**Rnd 8:** ch2, hdc3, (hdc2 in next st, hdc6) 8 times, hdc2 in next st, hdc2, slst in top of beg ch2 [72]

**Rnd 9:** ch2, hdc1 in same st at base of ch2, (hdc7, hdc2 in next st) 8 times, hdc7, slst in top of beg ch2 [81]

**Rnd 10:** ch2, hdc3, (hdc2 in next st, hdc8) 8 times, hdc2 in next st, hdc4, slst in top of beg ch2 [90]

Change to light blue.

**Rnd 11:** ch2, hdc8, (hdc2 in next st, hdc9) 8 times, hdc2 in next st, slst in top of beg ch2 [99]

**Rnd 12:** ch2, hdc2, (hdc2 in next st, hdc10) 8 times, hdc2 in next st, hdc7, slst in top of beg ch2 [108]

Cut yarn and fasten off.

28

# Nerikiri/Chrysanthemum

SHOWN ON PAGE 36

Finished Size:
4" (10 cm) diameter x
2¾" (7 cm) tall

## TOOLS & MATERIALS

### Yarn

- 100% acrylic bulky-weight yarn
  - 27 yds (24 m) in pistachio
  - 20 yds (18 m) in cream
  - 2 yds (1.2 m) in rose pink

### Other Materials

- 10 g of polyester stuffing

### Tools

- US L-11 (8 mm) crochet hook
- Yarn needle
- Tweezers

## CONSTRUCTION STEPS

Note: Use two strands of yarn throughout.

**1.** Start with a magic ring and crochet through round 7 following diagram or written instructions.

**2.** Fill with polyester stuffing, then continue round 8. Fasten off, leaving an 8" (20 cm) long tail.

**3.** Using a yarn needle, thread yarn tail through stitches of round 8 to gather. Knot to secure.

## CROCHET INSTRUCTIONS

### Body

With rose pink and US L-8 hook, make a magic ring.
**Rnd 1 (RS):** ch1 (does not count as a st throughout), sc5 in magic ring, slst in beg ch1, fasten off [5]
Place stitch marker in first st of rnd 1 and move it up after each round
**Rnd 2:** join two strands of cream in first st, ch1, (hdc-cl, ch1, hdc-cl, ch1) in each st to end, slst in first hdc-cl, slst into ch1-sp [10 hdc-cl, 10 ch1-sps]
**Rnd 3:** ch1, (hdc-cl, ch1, hdc-cl) in same ch1-sp, (ch1, hdc-cl, ch1) in next ch1-sp, *( hdc-cl, ch1, hdc-cl) in next ch1-sp, (ch1, hdc-cl, ch1) in next ch1-sp; rep from * a further 3 times, slst in first hdc-cl, slst into ch1-sp, fasten off and turn work [15 hdc-cl, 15 ch1-sps]
**Rnd 4 (WS):** join one strand of cream and one strand of pistachio in first ch1-sp, ch1, hdc-cl in same ch1-sp, ch1, (hdc-cl, ch1) in each ch1-sp around (skipping the hdc-cl stitches), slst in first hdc-cl, slst into ch1-sp, fasten off and turn work [15 hdc-cl, 15 ch1-sps]
**Rnd 5 (RS):** join two strands of pistachio in next ch1-sp, ch1, hdc-cl in same sp, ch1, (hdc-cl, ch1) in each ch1-sp around (skipping the hdc-cl stitches), slst in first hdc-cl, slst into next ch1-sp [15 hdc-cl, 15 ch1-sps]
**Rnd 6:** ch1, hdc in same ch1-sp (counts as hdc2tog), (hdc2tog over next hdc-cl and ch1-sp) 14 times, slst in first hdc2tog [15]
**Rnd 7:** ch1, (sc2tog, sc1) to end, slst in beg ch1 [10]
Fill with polyester stuffing.
**Rnd 8:** ch1, (sc2tog) to end, slst in beg ch1 [5]
Cut yarn and fasten off, leaving an 8" (20 cm) long tail. Make up following step 3 instructions above.

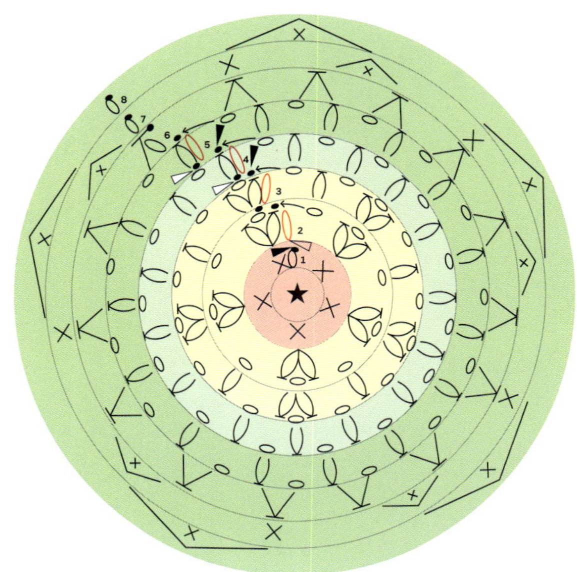

= Pistachio (2 strands)
= Cream + pistachio (1 strand each)
= Cream (2 strands)
= Rose pink (2 strands)
= Extend the yarn over the hook

29

# Nerikiri/Clematis

SHOWN ON PAGE 36

Finished Size:
4" (10 cm) diameter x 3" (7.5 cm) tall

## TOOLS & MATERIALS

### Yarn

- 100% acrylic bulky-weight yarn
  - 20 yds (18 m) in purple
  - 14 yds (12 m) in light purple
  - 14 yds (12 m) in lavender
  - 3 yds (2.4 m) in lemon

### Other Materials

- 10 g of polyester stuffing

### Tools

- US 7 (4.5 mm) crochet hook
- Yarn needle
- Tweezers

## CONSTRUCTION STEPS

Note: Use one strand of yarn throughout.

**1.** Crochet the body: Start with a magic ring and crochet through round 15 following diagram or written instructions. Fasten off, leaving a 12" (30 cm) long yarn tail.

**2.** Insert the yarn tail through every 10 stitches between rounds 14 and 15, alternating over and under. Pull gently to begin gathering (see **Figure A**).

**3.** Fill with polyester stuffing, making the bottom thicker than the top (see **Figure A**). Pull the yarn tail tightly to close and knot to secure.

**4.** Crochet the flower center. Fasten off, leaving an 8" (20 cm) long tail. Roll the flower center and sew through the foundation chain to secure (see **Figure B**). Sew to the flower center of the body.

***Figure A***

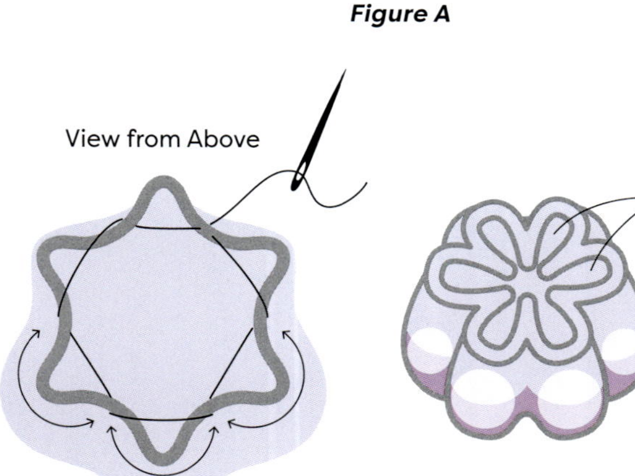


Insert needle through every 10 stitches between rounds 14 and 15, alternating over and under. Pull to gather.

Fill with polyester stuffing, making the bottom thicker than the top

***Figure B***

Roll the flower, stitch through the foundation chains, and sew to the body.

## CROCHET INSTRUCTIONS

### Body

With purple and US 7 hook, make a magic ring.

**Rnd 1:** ch1 (does not count as a st throughout), sc7 in magic ring, slst in beg ch1 [7]

Place stitch marker in first st of rnd 1 and move it up after each round

**Rnd 2:** ch1, (sc2 in next st) 7 times, slst in beg ch1 [14]

**Rnd 3:** ch1, (sc1, sc2 in next st) 7 times, slst in beg ch1 [21]

**Rnd 4:** ch1, (sc2 in next st, sc2) 7 times, slst in beg ch1 [28]

**Rnd 5:** ch1, sc2, (sc2 in next st, sc3) 6 times, sc2 in next st, sc1, slst in beg ch1 [35]

**Rnd 6:** ch1, (sc4, sc2 in next st) 7 times, slst in beg ch1 [42]

**Rnd 7:** ch1, sc2, (sc2 in next st, sc2) 13 times, sc2 in next st, slst in beg ch1 [56]

**Rnd 8:** ch1, sc1 in each st to end, change to light purple and slst in beg ch1

**Rnd 9:** with light purple, ch1, sc1 in each st, slst in beg ch1

**Rnd 10:** ch1, (sc13, sc2 in next st) 4 times, slst in beg ch1 [60]

**Rnd 11:** ch1, sc1 in each st to end, change to lavender and slst in beg ch1

**Rnds 12-14:** ch1, sc1 in each st, slst in beg ch1 (3 rnds)

**Rnd 15:** slst in each st to end.

Cut yarn and fasten off, leaving a 12" (30 cm) long tail. Make up following steps 2 and 3 on page 128.

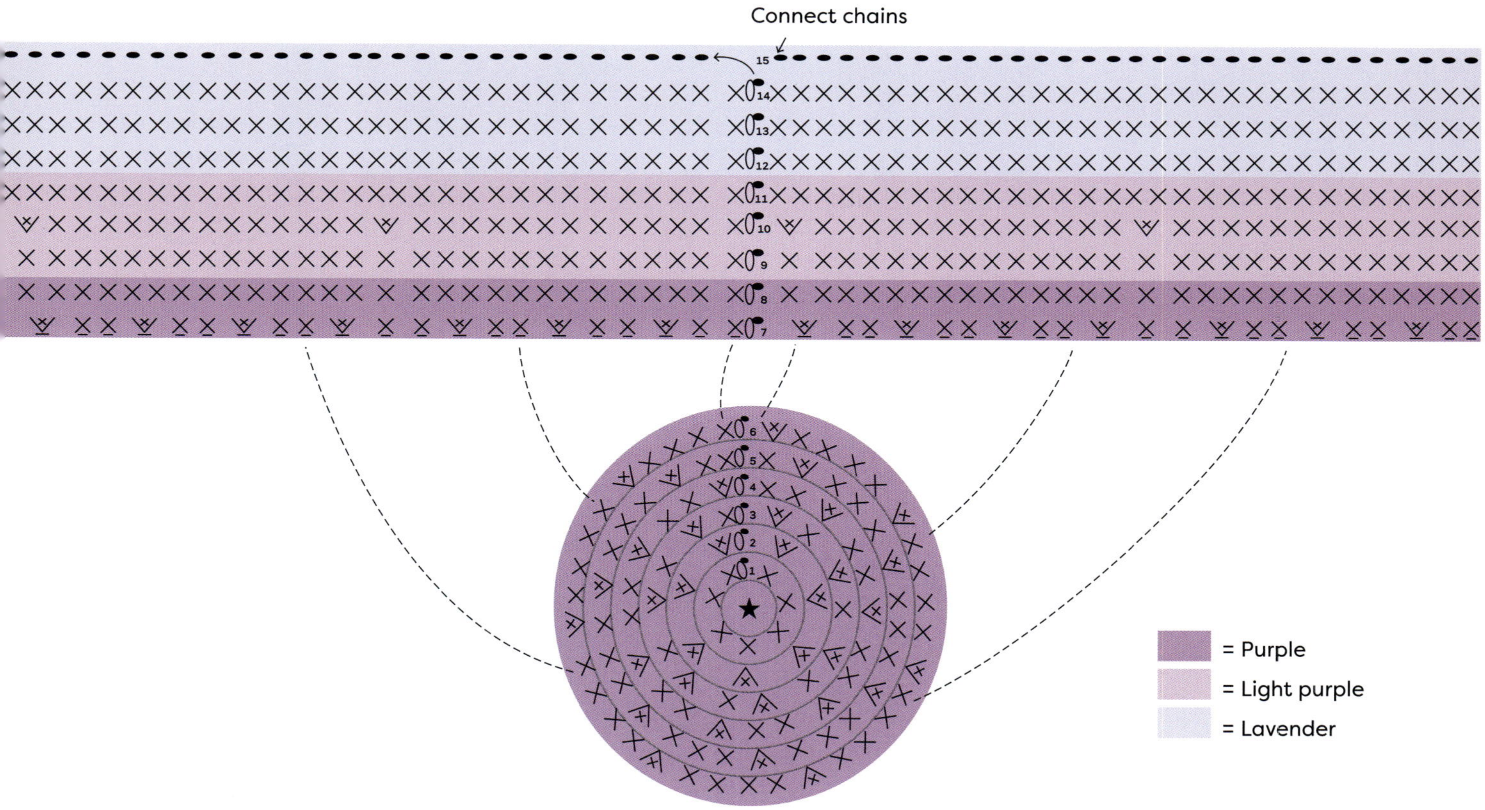

Connect chains

= Purple

= Light purple

= Lavender

### Flower Center

With lemon and US 7 hook, ch13.

**Row 1:** slst in seventh ch from hook, (ch5, slst in next ch) 6 times.

Cut yarn and fasten off, leaving an 8" (20 cm) long tail.

Make up following step 4 instructions on page 128.

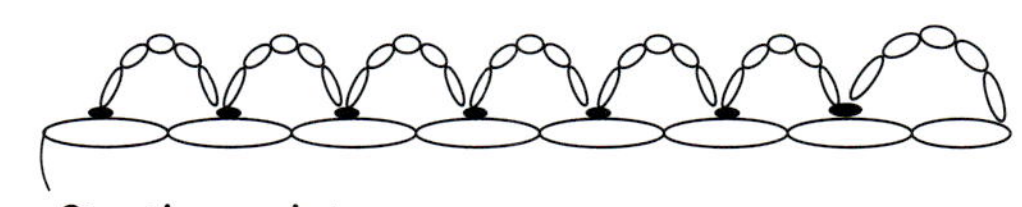

Starting point

30

# Sakura Mochi

**SHOWN ON PAGE 37**

Finished Size:
4½" (11.5 cm) wide x
3½" (9 cm) tall x
2½" (6.5 cm) thick

## TOOLS & MATERIALS

### Yarn

- 100% acrylic bulky-weight yarn
  - 40 yds (36 m) in light pink
  - 27 yds (24 m) in matcha
  - 3 yds (2.4 m) in pistachio

### Other Materials

- 10 g of polyester stuffing

### Tools

- US 7 (4.5 mm) crochet hook
- Yarn needle
- Felting needle
- Tweezers

## CONSTRUCTION STEPS

Note: Use two strands of yarn for the mochi and one strand of yarn for the cherry leaf.

**1.** Crochet the mochi: Start with a magic ring and crochet through round 9. Turn the crochet fabric inside out, fill with polyester stuffing, then crochet round 10. Cut the remaining yarn, leaving an 8" (20 cm) long tail. Weave through stitches of round 10 and gather.

**2.** Crochet the cherry leaf: Start with a magic ring and crochet to round 19.

**3.** Embroider the leaf of veins with pistachio yarn. Use a felting needle to secure the embroidered stitches in place.

**4.** Wrap the cherry leaf around the mochi and and sew in place on underside of leaf (see **Figure A**).

***Figure A***

Sew through the underside of the leaf stitches to attach to the mochi

3 rounds

4 rounds

• = Starting point of mochi

## CROCHET INSTRUCTIONS

### Mochi

With light pink and US 7 hook, make a magic ring.

**Rnd 1:** ch1 (does not count as a st throughout), sc6 in magic ring, slst in beg ch1 [6]

Place stitch marker in first st of rnd 1 and move it up after each round

**Rnd 2:** ch1, (sc2 in next st) 6 times, slst in beg ch1 [12]

**Rnd 3:** ch1, sc1, (sc2 in next st) 4 times, sc2, (sc2 in next st) 4 times, sc1, slst in beg ch1 [20]

**Rnd 4:** ch1, sc2, *sc2 in next st, sc1, (sc2 in next st) twice, sc1, sc2 in next st*, sc4, rep from * to * once, sc2, slst in beg ch1 [28]

**Rnds 5-7:** ch1, sc1 in each st, slst in beg ch1 (3 rnds)

**Rnd 8:** ch1, sc2, *sc2tog, sc1, (sc2tog) twice, sc1, sc2tog*, sc4, rep from * to * once, sc2, slst in beg ch1 [20]

**Rnd 9:** ch1, sc1, (sc2tog) 4 times, sc2, (sc2tog) 4 times, sc1, slst in beg ch1 [12]

Fill with polyester stuffing.

**Rnd 10:** ch1, (sc2tog) 6 times, slst in beg ch1 [6]

Cut yarn and fasten off, leaving an 8" (20 cm) long tail.

Make up following step 1 instructions on page 130.

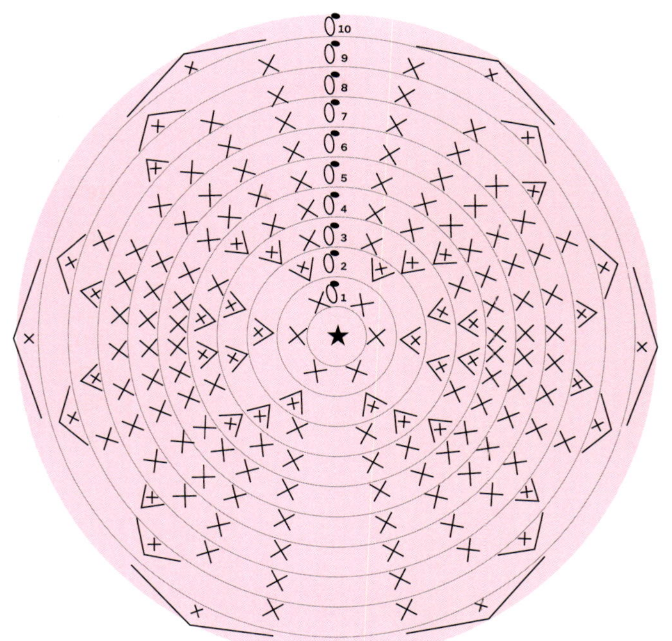

### Cherry Leaf

With matcha and US 7 hook, ch12.

**Row 1:** sc1 in second ch from hook, sc1 in each ch to last ch, sc3 in last ch, rotate and work along the opposite side of ch, sc9, turn, leaving remaining ch unworked [22]

**Row 2:** ch1 (does not count as a st throughout), sc10, sc3 in next st, place stitch marker in second of these 3 stitches to mark center st, sc10, leave last st unworked, turn [23]

**Row 3:** ch1, sc1 in each st to center marked st, sc3 in marked st, move st marker to second of these 3 sts, sc1 in each st to last 2 sts, turn [23]

**Rows 4-14:** Rep row 3 (10 rows)

**Row 15:** ch1, sc9, sc2 in next st, sc3, sc2 in next st, sc7, turn [23]

**Row 16:** ch1, sc7, sc2 in next st, sc5, sc2 in next st, scs7, turn [23]

**Row 17:** ch1, sc6, sc2 in next st, sc9, sc2 in next st, sc4, turn [23]

**Row 18:** ch1, sc5, sc2 in next st, sc9, sc2 in next st, sc5, turn [23]

**Row 19:** ch1, sc8, sc2 in next st, sc5, sc2 in next st, sc6, turn [23]

Cut yarn and fasten off.

Make up following steps 3 and 4 on page 130.

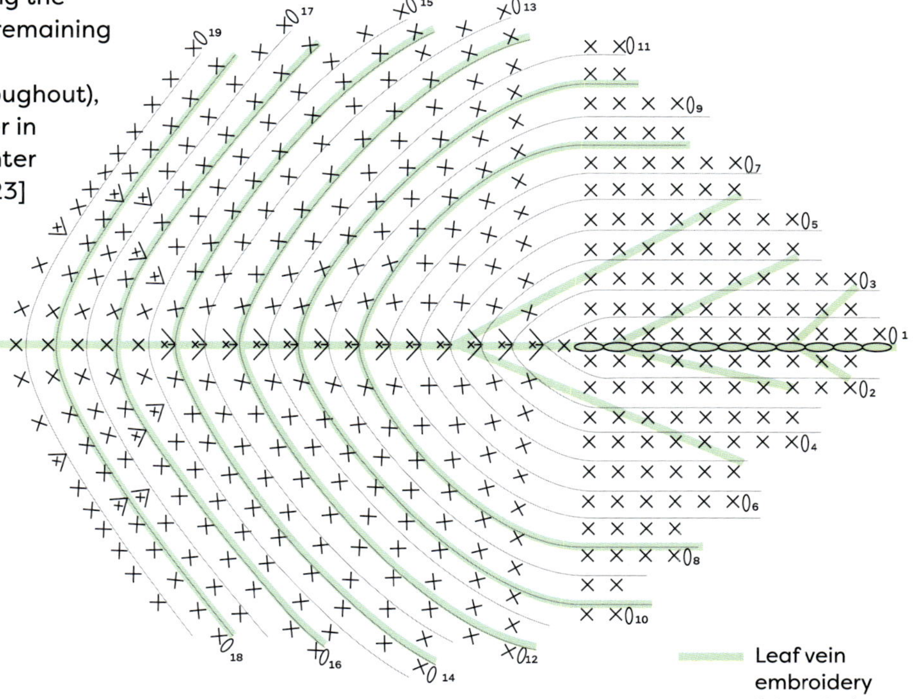

31

# Taiyaki

SHOWN ON PAGE 37

Finished Size:
7½" (19 cm) wide x
5" (12.5 cm) tall x 2½"
2" (5.5 cm) thick

## TOOLS & MATERIALS

### Yarn

- 100% acrylic bulky-weight yarn
  - 60 yds (54 m) in dark beige

### Other Materials

- 15 g of polyester stuffing

### Tools

- US 7 (4.5 mm) crochet hook
- Yarn needle
- Felting needle
- Tweezers

## CONSTRUCTION STEPS

Note: Use one strand of yarn throughout.

**1.** Crochet the body: Make 5 single crochet in a magic ring and continue through round 17 following the written instructions or diagram. Cut yarn, leaving a 12" (30 cm) long tail. Fill with polyester stuffing and close the facing stitches on round 17 using whipstitch.

**2.** Crochet the top and bottom fins. Cut yarn, leaving a 20" (50 cm) long tail. Fold in half and close the facing stitches using whipstitch (see **Figure A**).

**3.** Sew the top and bottom fins to the body.

**4.** Crochet the side fins. Cut the remaining yarn, leaving an 8" (20 cm) long tail. Sew a fin to each side of the body, positioning one fin with the right side facing out and the other fin with the wrong side facing out.

**5.** Embroider the eyes and mouth with dark beige yarn. Use a felting needle to secure the embroidered stitches in place (see **Figure B**).

***Figure A***

**Top Fin**

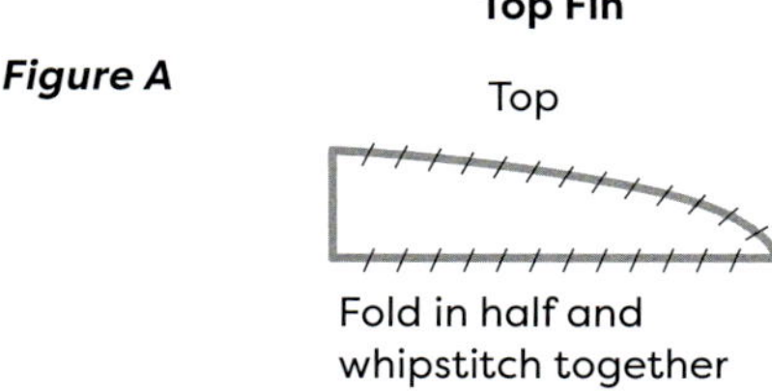


Fold in half and whipstitch together

**Bottom Fin**

Fold in half and whipstitch together

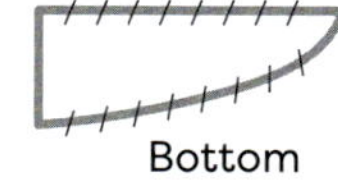


***Figure B***

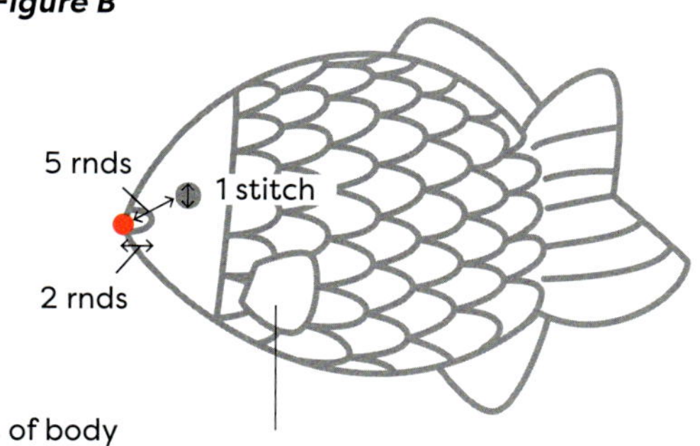


● = Starting point of body

Side fin (right side)
Attach other fin to other side of body so the wrong side faces out

## CROCHET INSTRUCTIONS

### Body

With dark beige and US 7 hook, make a magic ring.

**Rnd 1:** ch1 (does not count as a st throughout), sc5 in magic ring, slst in beg ch1 [5]

Place stitch marker in first st of rnd 1 and move it up after each round

**Rnd 2:** ch1, (sc2 in next st) 5 times, slst in beg ch1 [10]

**Rnd 3:** ch1, (sc1, sc2 in next st) twice, sc3, sc2 in next st, sc1, sc2 in next st, slst in beg ch1 [14]

**Rnd 4:** ch1, sc1, (sc2 in next st, sc4, sc2 in next st) twice, sc1, slst in beg ch1 [18]

**Rnd 5:** ch1, sc1, (sc2 in next st, sc6, sc2 in next st) twice, sc1, slst in beg ch1 [22]

**Rnd 6:** ch1, sc1, (sc2 in next st, sc8, sc2 in next st) twice, sc1, slst in beg ch1 [26]

**Rnd 7:** ch1, sc1, (sc2 in next st, sc10, sc2 in next st) twice, sc1, slst in beg ch1 [30]

**Rnd 8:** ch3 and dc2tog in same st at base of ch3 (counts as first 3dc-cluster), ch1, skip 1 st, (3dc-cluster in next st, ch1, skip 1 st) to end, slst in first 3dc-cluster, slst in next ch1-sp [30]

**Rnds 9-10:** ch3 and dc2tog in same sp at base of ch3 (counts as first 3dc-cluster), ch1, skip 1 st, (3dc-cluster in next ch1-sp, ch1, skip 1 st) to end, slst in first 3dc-cluster, slst in next ch1-sp [30]

**Rnd 11:** ch3 and dc2tog in same sp at base of ch3 (counts as first 3dc-cluster), ch1, skip 1 st, (3dc-cluster in next ch1-sp, ch1, skip 1 st) 5 times, 6dc-cluster over next two ch1-sps, ch1, skip next st, (3dc-cluster in next ch1-sp, ch1, skip 1 st) 7 times, slst in first 3dc-cluster, slst in next ch1-sp [28]

**Rnd 12:** ch3 and dc2tog in same sp at base of ch3 (counts as first 3dc-cluster), ch1, skip 1 st, (3dc-cluster in next ch1-sp, ch1, skip 1 st) to end, slst in first 3dc-cluster, slst in next ch1-sp [28]

**Rnd 13:** ch3 and dc2tog in same sp at base of ch3 (counts as first 3dc-cluster), ch1, skip 1 st, (3dc-cluster in next ch1-sp, ch1, skip 1 st) 3 times, 6dc-cluster over next two ch1-sps, ch1, skip next st, (3dc-cluster in next ch1-sp, ch1, skip 1 st) 5 times, 6dc-cluster over next two ch1-sps, ch1, skip next st, 3dc-cluster in next ch1-sp, ch1, skip last st, slst in first 3dc-cluster, slst in next ch1-sp [24]

**Rnd 14:** ch3 and dc2tog in same sp at base of ch3 (counts as first 3dc-cluster), skip 1 st, (3dc-cluster in next ch1-sp, skip 1 st) twice, 6dc-cluster over next two ch1-sps, skip next st, (3dc-cluster in next ch1-sp, skip 1 st) 7 times, slst in first 3dc-cluster [11]

**Rnd 15:** ch4 and 1tr in same st at base of ch4, dc2 in next st, hdc3 in next st, (dc4 in next st) twice, hdc3 in next st, dc2 in next st, (tr2 in next st, tr1 in next st) twice, slst in top of beg ch4 [26]

**Rnd 16:** ch4 (counts as first st), FPtr1, dc1, FPdc1, hdc1, FPhdc1, hdc1, (FPdc1, dc1) 4 times, FPhdc1, hdc1, FPhdc1, dc1, FPdc1, (tr1, FPtr1) 3 times, slst in top of beg ch4 [26]

**Rnd 17:** ch4 (counts as first st), FPtr1, dc1, FPdc1, hdc1, FPhdc1, hdc1, (FPdc1, dc1) twice, FPdc around same st as dc just worked, (dc1, FPdc1) in next st, dc1, FPdc1, dc1, FPhdc1, hdc1, FPhdc1, dc1, FPdc1, (tr1, FPtr1) 3 times, slst in top of beg ch4 [28]

Cut yarn and fasten off, leaving a 12" (30 cm) long tail. Make up following step 1 instructions on page 132.

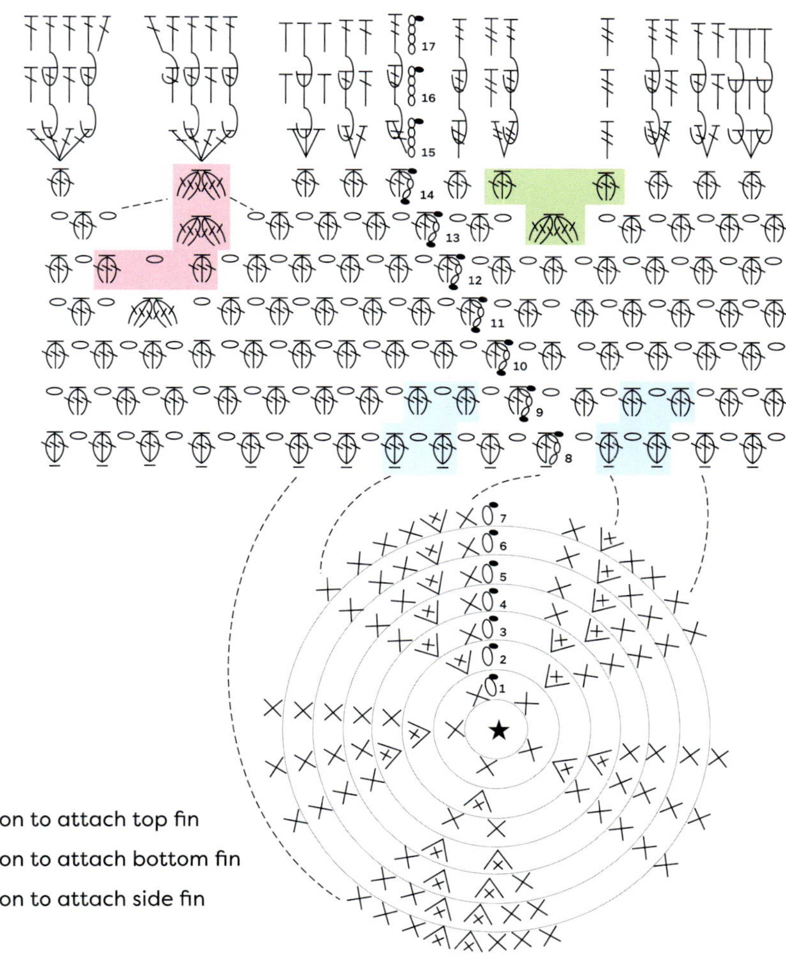

## Top Fin

With dark beige and US 7 hook, ch15.

**Row 1 (RS):** sc1 in second ch from hook, sc1, hdc1 in next 2 ch, dc1 in next 6 ch, hdc1 in next 2 ch, sc1 in last 2 ch [14]

Cut yarn and fasten off, leaving a 20" (50 cm) long tail. Make up following steps 2 and 3 on page 132.

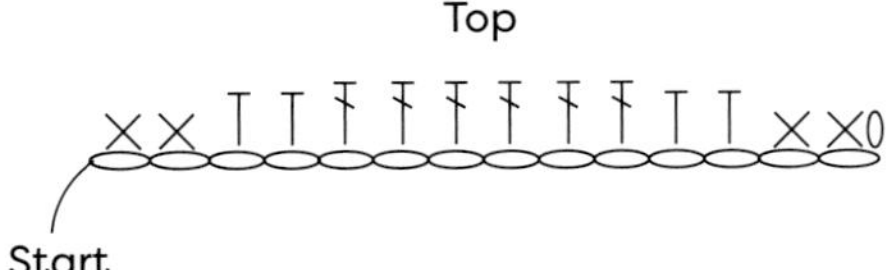


## Bottom Fin

With dark beige and US 7 hook, ch11.

**Row 1 (RS):** sc1 in second ch from hook, hdc1, dc1 in next 6 ch, hdc1, sc1 [10]

Cut yarn and fasten off, leaving a 20" (50 cm) long tail. Make up following steps 2 and 3 on page 132.

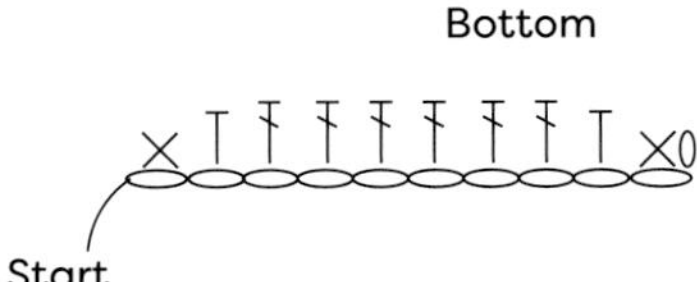


## Side Fins (make 2)

With dark beige and US 7 hook, ch4.

**Row 1 (RS):** dc1 in third ch from hook, tr2 in next ch, ch5 and slst in same ch.

Cut yarn and fasten off, leaving an 8" (20 cm) long tail. Make up following step 4 instructions on page 132.

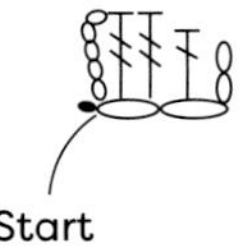

# Crochet Stitch Symbol Guide

**Slip stitch (slst):** Insert the hook into the previous row, yarn over, and pull the yarn through.

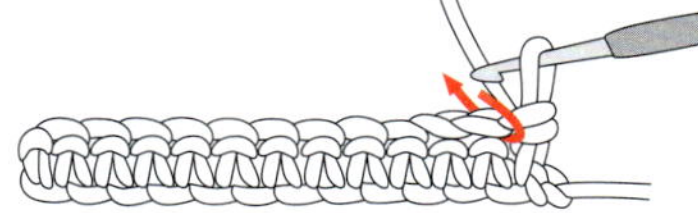
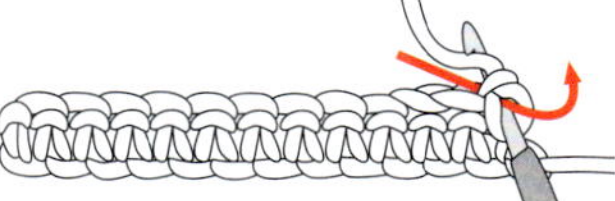
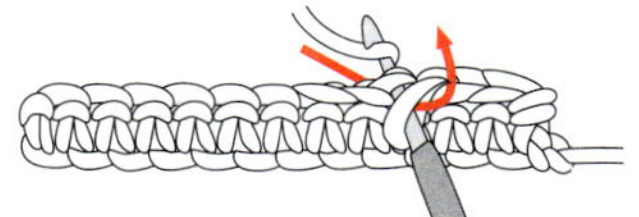

**Chain stitch (ch):** Wrap the yarn around the hook and pull the yarn through.

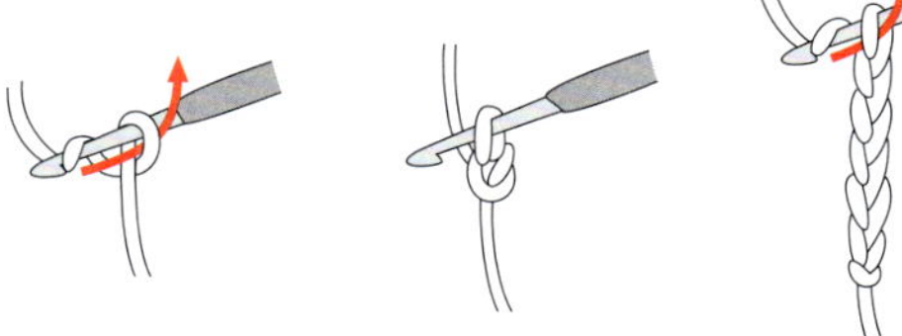

**Single crochet (sc):** Do not count the first chain stitch. Insert the hook through the top loop and pull the yarn through, yarn over and pull the yarn through two loops.

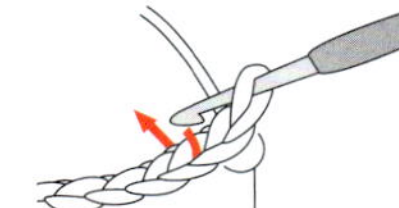
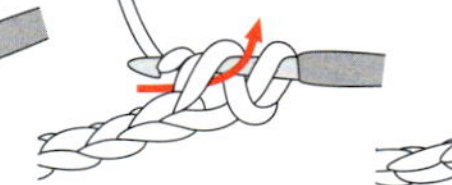
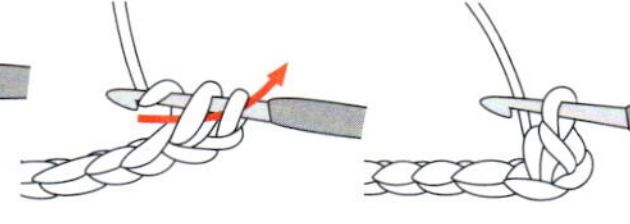


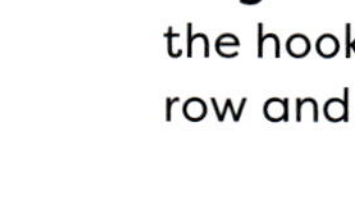

**Single crochet back loop only (sc blo):** Insert the hook through back loop of the previous row and make single crochet.

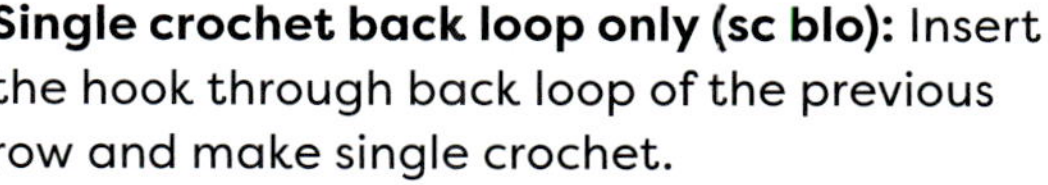

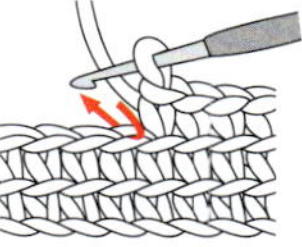

**Reverse single crochet (rsc):** Keep the direction of the crochet fabric the same and single crochet from left to right.

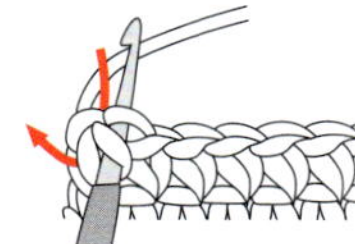
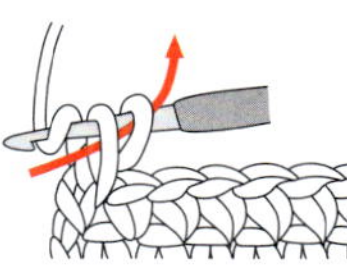
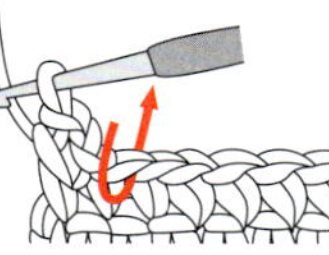
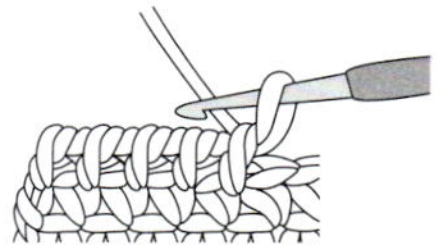

**Half double crochet (hdc):** Yarn over the hook and pull through, further yarn over and pull three loops through at once.

**Half double crochet back loop only (hdc blo):** Insert the hook through back loop of the previous row and make half double crochet.

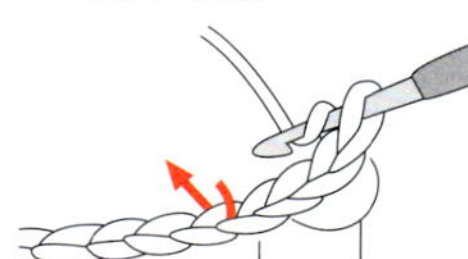

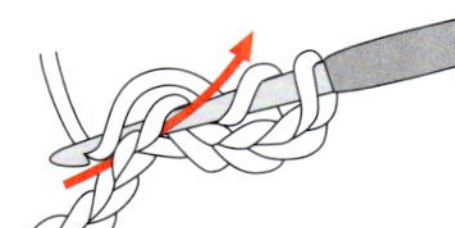
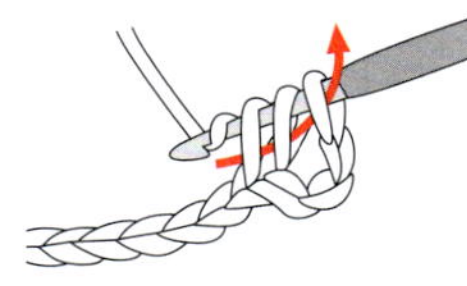
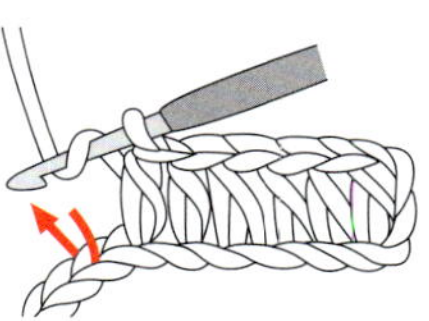

**Double crochet (dc):** Yarn over the hook and pull through, further yarn over and pull two loops through, and repeat again.

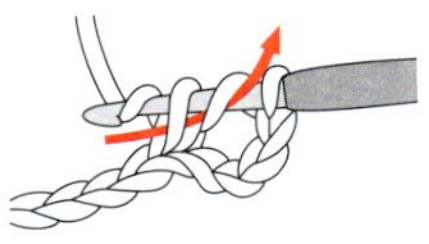
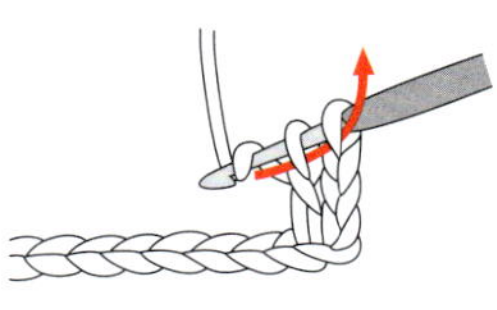
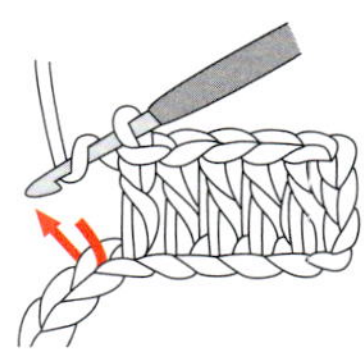

**Triple crochet (tc):** Wrap the yarn over the hook twice and pull through, further yarn over once and pull two loops through, and repeat two more times.

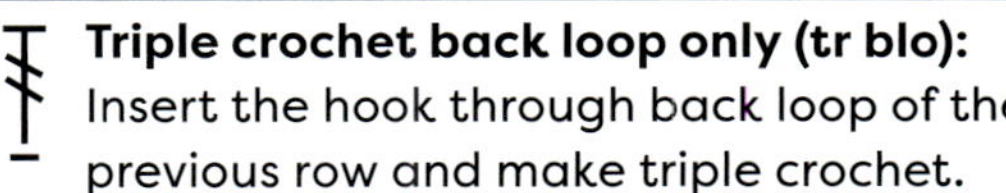

**Triple crochet back loop only (tr blo):** Insert the hook through back loop of the previous row and make triple crochet.

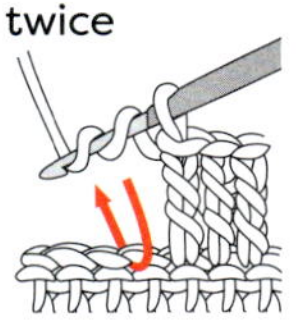

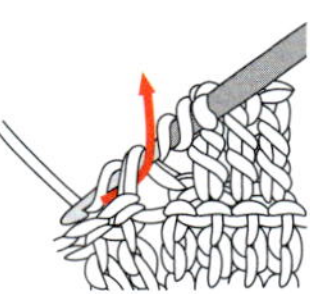
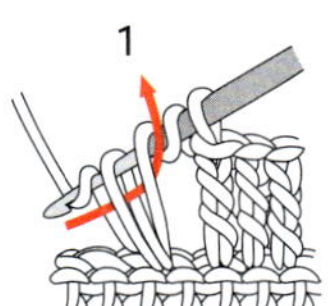

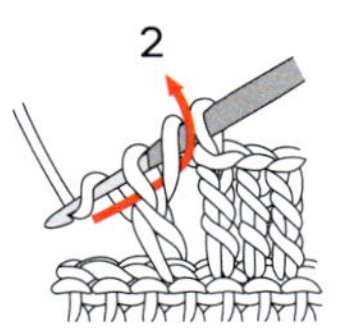

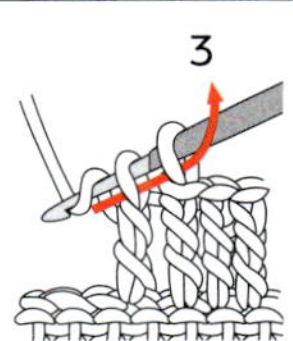

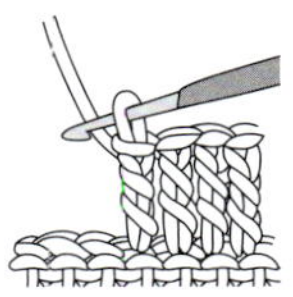

**Front post double crochet (fpdc):** Scoop the base of previous row from front and make double crochet.

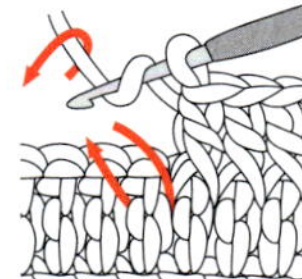

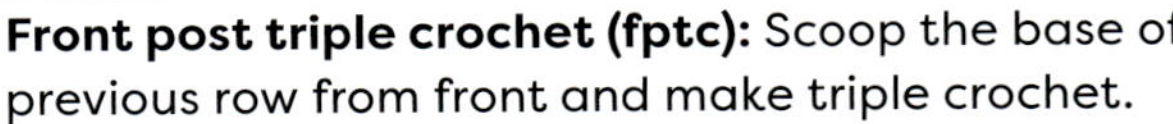

**Front post triple crochet (fptc):** Scoop the base of previous row from front and make triple crochet.

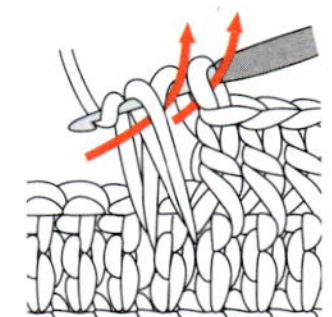

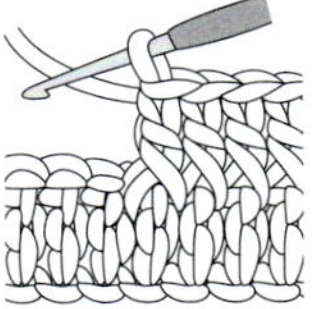

**2 single crochet increase:** Make two single crochet in the same stitch.

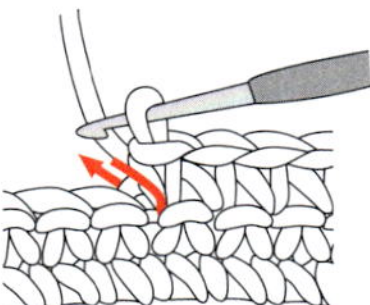

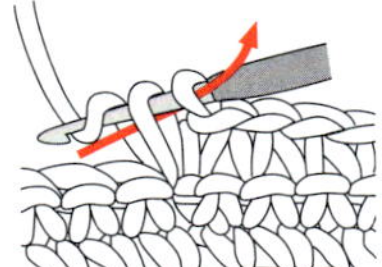

**3 single crochet increase:** Make three single crochet in the same stitch.

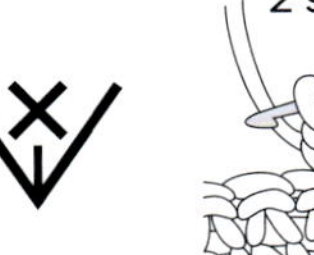

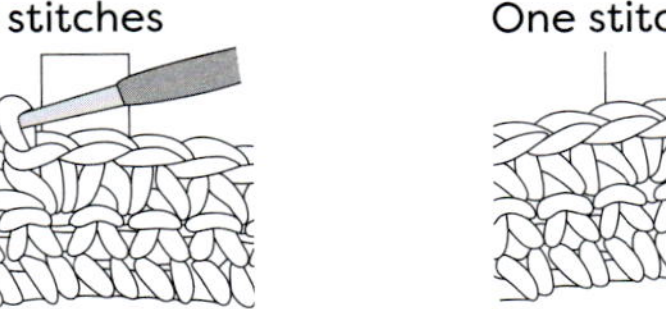


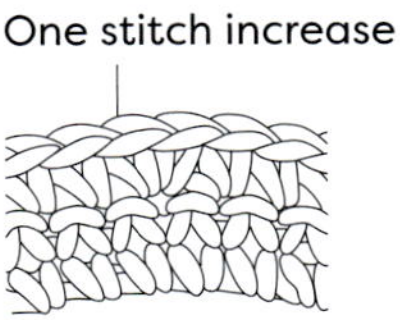


**Single crochet 2 together (sc2tog):** Insert the hook at first stitch and yarn over and pull through, pull the next stitch through, and pull 3 loops through at once.

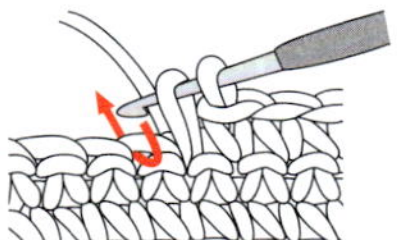

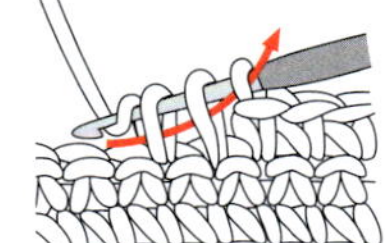

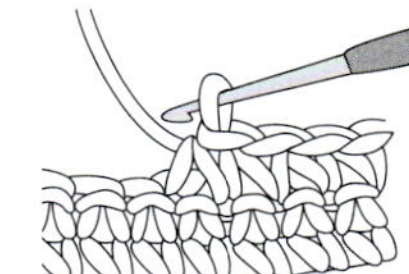

One stitch decrease

**Half double crochet 2 together (hdc2tog):** Make unfinished half double crochet at first stitch and the second stitch, and pull 5 loops through at once.

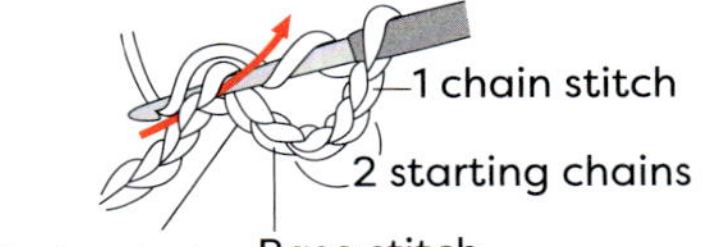


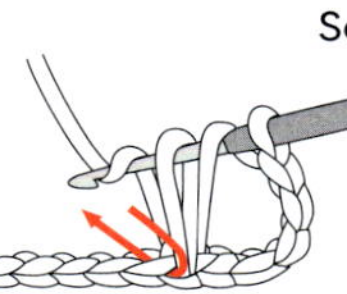

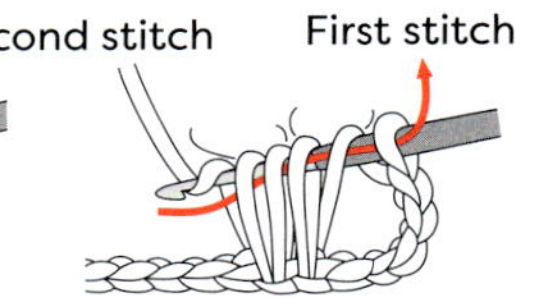


**3dc in one stitch:** Make 3 double crochet in the same stitch.

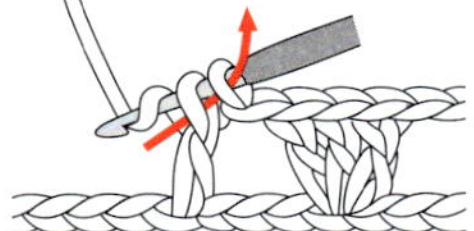

**2hdc in one stitch:** Make 2 half double crochet in the same stitch.

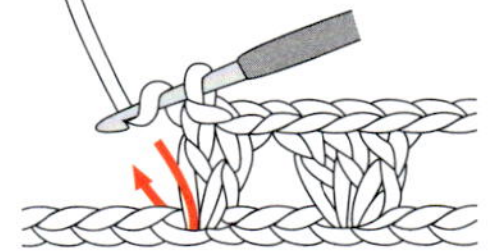

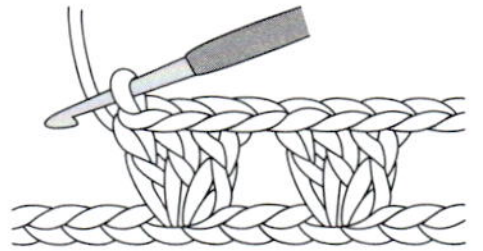

**3 double crochet cluster:** Make 3 unfinished double crochet in the same stitch, yarn over, and pull 5 loops through at once.

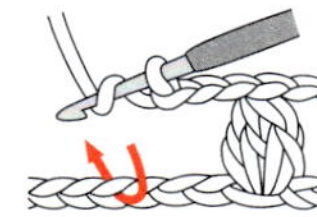

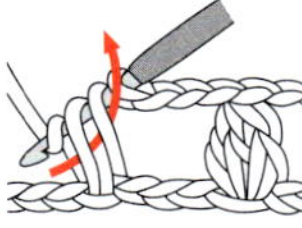

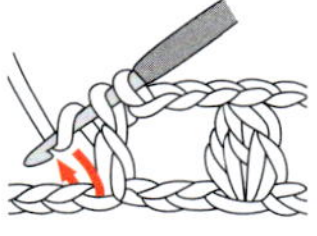

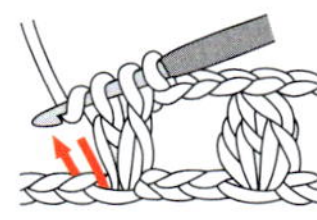

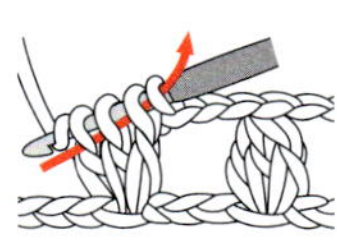

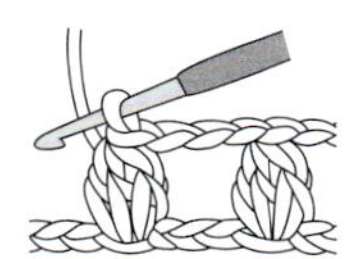

**3 half double crochet cluster:** Make 3 unfinished half double crochet in the same stitch, yarn over, and pull through at once.

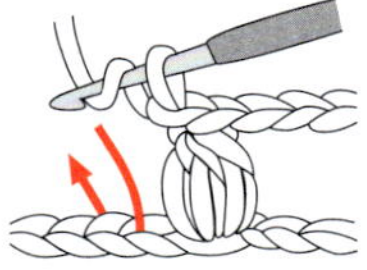

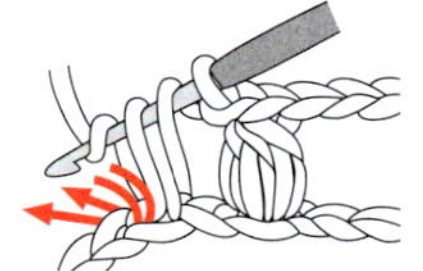

**2 half double crochet cluster:** Make 2 unfinished half double crochet in the same stitch, yarn over, and pull through at once.

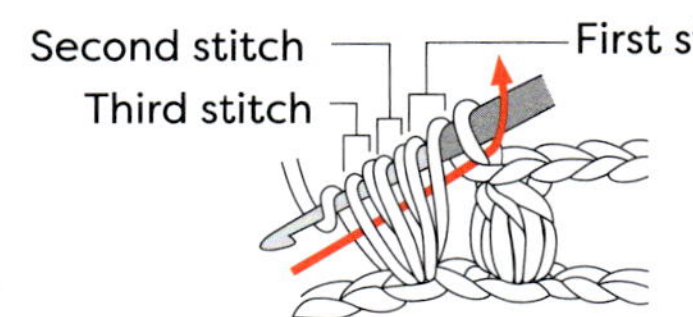


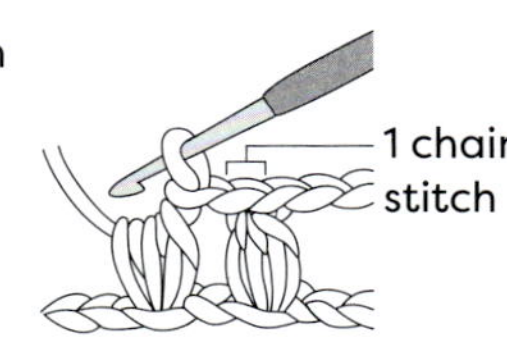


**Connect chains:** Bring the ending yarn through, and put through the first stitch. Bring back to the last stitch and finish at wrong side.

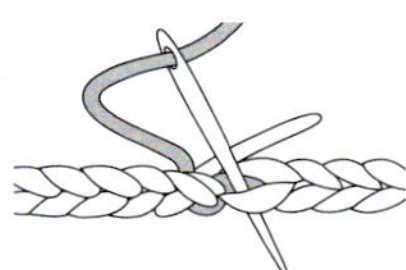